I0759466

LEAP YEAR

THE PHILADELPHIA EAGLES' ASCENT
TO SUPER BOWL CHAMPIONS

Zach Berman

Library of Congress Cataloging-in-Publication Data available upon request.

This book is available in quantity at special discounts for your group or organization. For further information, contact:

Triumph Books LLC
814 North Franklin Street
Chicago, Illinois 60610
(312) 337-0747
www.triumphbooks.com

Printed in U.S.A.
ISBN: 978-1-63727-945-8
Design by Nord Compo

For Emily,
who brought me a love beyond covering football.

And Reid and Sloane,
who make us feel like we've won two Super Bowls since 2017.

CONTENTS

FOREWORD

WHAT A SEASON IT WAS—defined by toughness, resilience, and a connection between team and city that felt deeper than ever. From the first snap to the final play, this group played with heart, and the fans matched it every step of the way. There's nothing like the passion of this fan base—loud, loyal, and always present. They made every home game electric and every road game feel like a fight worth showing up for.

Zach Berman has always told the story of this team with heart and accuracy. He understands what made that season special, and he captures it in a way that brings it all back.

If you're holding this book, you're in for something real.

Brandon Graham *played 15 seasons for the Eagles before announcing his retirement in March 2025. A 2010 first-round pick, Graham set franchise records by playing 206 regular season and 20 postseason games. His 76.5 sacks rank No. 3 in franchise history. Graham was named second team All Pro in 2016 and earned a Pro Bowl invitation in 2020. Most notably, he won two Super Bowls with the Eagles and recorded the game-clinching strip sack on Tom Brady in Super Bowl LII that remains one of the most iconic plays in Philadelphia sports. Graham was a two-time nominee for the Walter*

Payton Man of the Year and won the 2025 Good Guy Award from the Pro Football Writers of America. He collaborated on the 2025 children's book BG's ABC: Tackling Football & Life.

INTRODUCTION

SOMEWHERE BETWEEN JALEN HURTS lighting a cigar in the back corner of the locker room and a dance circle around entertainer Gillie Da Kid, an Eagles executive spotted me minutes after the Philadelphia Eagles won the NFC Championship Game to clinch a spot in Super Bowl LIX.

If the Eagles could win one more game, he told me, I would have another book to write. And it would be an incredible story to tell, he added, before rejoining the celebration.

They won one more game. Here's another book. And the executive was correct—this was a fun story to share. By the final page, you should see why.

The "another book" referenced two previous books about the Eagles. In 2018, I wrote *Underdogs: The Philadelphia Eagles' Emotional Road to Super Bowl Victory.* That chronicled the Eagles' first Super Bowl, an improbable story about a team that few outside the locker room believed would win the Lombardi Trophy—especially after mounting injuries to key players. The second book, *The Franchise: Philadelphia Eagles*, was published in 2024 and was a curated history of the 25-year run from the start of the Andy Reid era to present day. As I wrote in the introduction of that book, it was *supposed* to be a story about the Eagles' 2022 Super Bowl run. That was the original conceit of the book offer in the days before the Eagles' dramatic loss to Reid and the Kansas City

Chiefs in Super Bowl LVII. The book project pivoted. The story, though, only became richer.

For the first 51 years of the Super Bowl era, the Eagles never won a Super Bowl and only reached the final game twice. In the eight seasons since, the Eagles have had two unforgettable parades up Broad Street and made three appearances in the final game. So if you walked by the bookshelf or searched on the bookseller's website and saw two titles in my name in two years, the explanation is that you cannot necessarily plan for a team winning the Super Bowl. It could have been 52 years waiting for another one. As the expression goes, opportunity is not a lengthy visitor. When the Eagles rebounded from a devastating 2023 collapse to become the NFL's best team in 2024—and did it with compelling characters and a dramatic arc—it was a story I was eager to share.

That's what makes this story unique. Every Super Bowl winner is shaped by the original path that led to a title. Nobody wins by accident. For the 2024 Eagles, it was about a team that came so close two years earlier and seemed so far by the end of the previous season. It was about the moves that were made to close the gap—and the moves *not made* that could have altered the club's history. It was no longer about satisfying a starving fan base. As Howie Roseman explained, the first Super Bowl came with a sense of relief. The second one did not have the same baggage. It was about *this* team more than carrying the history—the burden, even—of the franchise and the fan base.

The first book was also more of a surprise. They were the underdogs, after all. Although it's true that the Eagles did not enter the 2024 season as Super Bowl favorites and there was a time in September when it seemed likelier that there would be a coaching change than a championship parade, they were nobody's underdog. There were legitimate Super Bowl ambitions. Jeffrey Lurie said in March 2024 that the Eagles had "all the ingredients."

When Terry Bradshaw presented Lurie the George Halas Trophy for winning the NFC, the FOX analyst asked Lurie how "unexpected" it was for the Eagles to reach the Super Bowl.

"It's kind of expected," Lurie answered.

He was correct. Somebody asked recently when I first became convinced about the Super Bowl possibility. I answered that I thought they were Super Bowl caliber entering the season, but it was the drive back from Baltimore after a Week 13 physical domination of a team that is usually physically dominant when I recognized the force the Eagles had become. There were still contenders in the NFC that posed a threat, and the prospect of the top teams in the AFC always loomed as a Super Bowl challenge, but you could not have a conversation about realistic champions in January without discussing the Eagles. They peaked at the right time, reaching a crescendo in the Super Bowl and punctuating the unforgettable season. "I'd almost like to say that has there been a better NFL team than the 2024 Eagles?" Lurie asked in March. It's not a far-fetched question. In the following pages, you will learn why.

This book is a compilation of reporting accumulated throughout the season and contextualized by reporting from my 13 years covering the franchise every day. One of the enduring lessons from the first Super Bowl book was that in-the-moment accounts of a season were often far more reliable than recollections. It can be convenient to suggest that there was a sentiment that the season would always end on the Art Museum steps. If you were in that muggy locker room in Tampa Bay on September 29, the story might be different. The fan base was behind Nick Sirianni when he accepted the Lombardi Trophy in New Orleans on February 9. What was the sentiment about Sirianni when the Eagles were in New Orleans on September 22? Saquon Barkley and Zack Baun became Offensive Player of the Year and Defensive Player of the

Year candidates, respectively. What did they expect—and what was expected of them?—when they walked into the NovaCare Complex to sign contracts on March 14, 2024? Hurts' satisfaction puffing the cigar next to a well-earned Lombardi Trophy is better understood if you saw him walking through the stadium in Glendale, Arizona, two years earlier.

The benefit of covering the team every day for 13 seasons is that you're not only in the locker room for the best moments or the worst moments, but all the moments in between. There's a casual conversation with Jordan Mailata on a Friday in October that can help better understand the team. There's a small nugget from Lane Johnson on an otherwise forgettable Thursday in November that explains what happens months later. There's a small Post-It note sitting next to Darius Slay's locker stall that reveals the winding clock on his Eagles tenure. This book is told through that daily reporting—the stonecutter hammering away at the rock. This time and context should also help make the characters in the story three-dimensional. I've sat in Sirianni's childhood living room, ate lunch at the restaurant across from Barkley's childhood home, and experienced a pep rally at Hurts' high school. I was in New York City the night Johnson was drafted in 2013, chatting with him about how his life was about to change. I heard Brandon Graham's perspective in the days before he feared he might be released in 2014, when the notion that he would become a franchise icon seemed far-fetched.

Of course, it's easier to understand a story when you know the ending. It's like watching a film for the second time—those Easter eggs make more sense. When you see Vic Fangio draped in an Italian flag, leaving a winning Super Bowl locker room after a sterling defensive performance against Patrick Mahomes in the Super Bowl, you better understand the significance of his hire. When you witness Cooper DeJean returning an interception for a touchdown in the Super Bowl, that trade on the second night of the draft in April seems even more important. When you realize Nakobe Dean made the game-clinching interception when he properly defended a wheel route against Jacksonville, you remember he was outpaced on the same route back during a training camp practice in August. And when Saquon Barkley makes an unforgettable backward leap that same night in an iconic image that graces the cover of this book, you think back to the afternoon you spent at Whitehall High School hearing about his exploits as a teenager. It's always easier to connect the dots when you have the answer key.

It's important to note that this is the Eagles' story. I'm the messenger—an observer and inquirer, but not a character in their story. After this preface, you won't read first-person accounts in this book. I was present, and that should be realized through the reporting, but the players, coaches, and executives are the reason this book could be written. There's no parade on Broad Street because I write a sharp article or record an entertaining podcast. My role is to be the eyes and the ears (and, in some cases, the nose) for those reading.

The quotes you read were all told directly to me or in group interviews and press conferences. If it was said exclusively to somebody else, the source is identified within the text. The one major exception is on-field and in-meeting dialogue. Those came directly from videos distributed by Eagles Entertainment and NFL Films. They're identified upon first reference in each chapter and are used often to convey the authenticity of the moments. In some cases, retelling from players and coaches is sufficient—when I asked Sirianni about pulling Barkley short of setting a single-game rushing record in his first game against the Giants, Sirianni's account turned out to be verbatim—but the on-field and in-meeting microphones and videos became an invaluable primary-source resource that enhanced the reporting on the team. No matter how thorough I yearn to be, there's nothing that replicates hearing authentic conversations and speeches.

In the preface of *Underdogs*, I wrote how deeply personal sharing the Super Bowl story had been, considering I grew up reading Eagles coverage in the very pages where fans were learning about the team. Even while becoming desensitized to the fanaticism that pulses through those reading the book, I've tried to ensure I've never become dehumanized. I know how much the franchise means to those who read my stories and watch my shows. For 13 years, I've taken more than 100 flights to and from Eagles games and events. There's seldom an empty seat, and there are always passengers in green. From São Paulo to New Orleans, there are fans who spend hard-earned money to attend games I'm compensated to cover. That's a privilege—a responsibility, even—that is never lost on me. When I walk into the stadium's entrance for home games and realize those parking lots have been full for hours by those who make this the highlight of the week, I recognize why this story is so important. The billows of smoke from those tailgate grills are just as much a part of this story as the cigar smoke by Hurts' locker. The executive was correct about this being an incredible story to tell. That would have been true had it been a story in any of 30 NFL markets. But it would not have been as meaningful—both to the readers and to this writer. It was my joy to share it.

CHAPTER 1

CELEBRATING THE LEAP YEAR

FOLLOW THE SCAVENGERS OF GREEN CONFETTI through the double doors of Room No. 1000 at the Superdome for an immediate sensory experience. "Good luck in there," an Eagles executive says with a dry smile. That was about the only thing dry for the next hour. (Or two. Or three. Or perhaps for the next week?) You could smell the thick waft of cigar smoke, a plume from celebratory Plasencias clouding the locker room. You could hear "Yes Indeed" by Lil Baby, part of the rotating mix of party music that provided the beat for dozens of players, coaches, and executives dancing in the middle of the room. Try to avoid it, but you might even taste the champagne being sprayed on anyone in sight from gold bottles of Armand de Brignac "Ace of Spades." Players also clutched cans of OPEN Beer, chugging and shotgunning the beverages as if final exams had just finished in college. If the Eagles' first Super Bowl seven years earlier offered any lesson, the postgame locker room is the home to the best Super Bowl celebration. Broad Street is enticing. Same with Bourbon Street in 2025. But if you want to see (or smell or hear) the satisfaction of a Super Bowl victory, simply observe this locker room party that had started minutes earlier.

It was 10:21 PM local time, and the Eagles had been Super Bowl champions for an hour. They knew they would be champions well before a 40–22 domination that dethroned the defending champion Kansas City Chiefs and offered redemption from Philadelphia's heartbreaking defeat two years earlier. If they're being honest, they might have known even before they arrived at the stadium. This was a confident Eagles team that simply believed it was better. On the eve of the game, Saquon Barkley told his teammates during a riveting series of speeches captured by team footage, "These guys can't fuck with us." The result of the game was affirmation. By this point, they had already participated in the formal trophy presentation on the field. They had posed for photos with each other, hugged family and friends. There were tears of the type of joy coach Nick Sirianni demanded during training camp, smiles that could seemingly stretch to Baton Rouge. Even when they walked off the field wearing gray T-shirts that read Super Bowl Champions LIX, the gravity and reality of the moment was still settling. "Best in the motherfucking world!" defensive lineman Milton Williams shouted to everyone and no one at the same time when he walked into the tunnel. "Y'all thought I was crazy?" safety C.J. Gardner-Johnson exclaimed, referencing his confidence that the Eagles were the team to beat back when it seemed as if Sirianni was on the hot seat. Howie Roseman, the architect of the team, held his arms in the air like Rocky. But this would need to be *Rocky II*, because the Eagles won this time. There was no celebrating valiance anymore.

And inside that locker room, there was no room for modesty. The party was not for wallflowers. That's where the music blasted—any moment of silence in a song punctuated with an "aye" from the dancing crowd, with a spray of whatever liquid was in hand for good measure. From stars to starters, reserves to practice squad players, it did not matter. You could join the celebration. There is star defensive tackle Jalen Carter feet away from long snapper Rick Lovato. Look up and there's offensive guard Mekhi Becton.

Swivel your head, and you see executive Julian Lurie, the son of Eagles owner Jeffrey Lurie, standing in a locker stall bopping his head to the music with a cigar in hand.

At one point, Jeffrey Lurie entered the middle of the circle while All-Pro wide receiver A.J. Brown and defensive tackle Moro Ojomo cheered him on. He danced with the Lombardi Trophy as a well-earned companion. Ojomo held his cell phone upright to capture the video. "When you love your team and you achieve the ultimate—world championship—it's incredible," Lurie said minutes later while holding a bottle of water outside the party.

Second-year pass-rusher Nolan Smith had torn his triceps earlier in the game, although one arm worked well enough (or perhaps the alcohol worked well enough) for Smith to dance with a beer can held high in the air and raining throughout the room. Safety Reed Blankenship was not as interested in spraying the beer on others; he poured it on himself in a moment of ecstasy. Pro Bowl offensive guard Landon Dickerson chugged a beer with one hand and rolled an IV pump with the other.

Barkley, who had perhaps the best season by a running back in NFL history and who team leaders said was the Eagles' missing piece, arrived late to the party and made up for lost time. The shirtless Barkley tucked his cell phone into his game pants, grabbed a can of beer, sliced it in the middle, and put the beer up to his face in a move that would have been familiar to his former classmates at Penn State. He grabbed a bottle of champagne and poured it into the mouths of teammates.

"I definitely allowed myself to enjoy the locker room—I think it's all over video," Barkley later recalled with a laugh. "Those are the moments."

Howie Roseman frequented the middle of the circle, dancing as if it were his wedding night in clips that went viral—the unbridled joy of an executive who could point to two Lombardi Trophies for any validation anyone needed about his career. "The first time, there was a sense of joy—but also relief, that we had done it for the first time," Roseman later explained. "I think this time, it was easier to let go a little bit and understand how unique and special it was and kind of have fun with it."

When Sirianni walked into the locker room after fulfilling an assembly line of postgame media obligations, the party was already in full swing. Somebody handed him a bottle of champagne. He shook it, was ready to pop it, but handed it back. Sirianni then went around the room embracing the players. He had been a punchline one year earlier. He was a champion now. When former Eagles coach Doug Pederson was in that same spot seven years earlier, he gathered the team together for a memorable postgame speech. Sirianni often has postgame speeches with messages he wants to convey. There was no speech this time. What else needed to be said? "They were having so much fun," Sirianni later said. "Know when to talk, know when not to talk, know when to have somebody else talk." Two weeks earlier, he took in the scene of the victory party after the NFC Championship Game, and all he could think about was the next game, the unfinished business ahead. His thoughts at this moment in New Orleans? "It wasn't about the next one," he said with a smile the next morning. "Just gratitude. Thankfulness for the moment. Thankful for the guys we have on this football team.... It's awesome to be able to embrace guys at that moment. Those are things you'll remember.... You'll remember the games and the confetti falling, no doubt. We'll have pictures of that. But the celebration. We've embraced that celebration so much."

No Super Bowl team might have embraced celebration more. The Lombardi Trophy was handed around, and players lined up for pictures and videos. That was not the only prop. Dom DiSandro, the head of team security and a cult figure in Philadelphia, carried an Italian flag around the room that was popular in photos—including those with defensive coordinator Vic Fangio, who oversaw the NFL's top defense and a superb game plan against Chiefs superstar Patrick Mahomes that gave him his first Super Bowl in four decades of coaching.

Brandon Graham, the 15-year veteran and all-time Eagle who raced back from a purported season-ending injury to play his final game in the Super Bowl (and re-injured his triceps while playing), savored the party. At one point, while Graham spoke to a television camera, Roseman tried pulling him away so as not to miss out on the fun. Graham explained how two years earlier, the Eagles felt like they let the Super Bowl slip away. That fueled them throughout the week—for two years, really. Graham FaceTimed former teammate Jason Peters, who carried the Lombardi Trophy out of the locker room after the Eagles' last Super Bowl party. Graham stood up to hold the phone to the room, showing Peters the scene. Graham was like the Peters of this team.

A few minutes of celebration was enough for some players, who retreated to the locker room to take in the moment. Brown was one of them, reclining with his phone in hand, watching all that unfolded as if he was capturing a snapshot of the moment. "This is what I came for," Brown said. "Moments like this."

Players came in and out, but you knew when Jalen Hurts entered the room. The franchise quarterback and Super Bowl MVP said on the sideline during the game that the loss two years earlier "changed my soul." He was now on top of the sport. Hurts, ever purposeful, strutted to his locker. Wearing his Super Bowl cap backward, he collected a victory cigar, spent a few moments working to light it, and then took a big puff. With a dance beat in his stance, he rummaged through his locker to find goggles.

At one point, Roseman came up to him for a hug. Hurts took his cap off, wrapped his head in goggles, and made his way around the locker room. Three minutes later, he found Brown by the star receiver's locker and the two shared an embrace.

On the field, teammates asked Hurts if he would finally smile. This has been an ongoing question for the stoic quarterback. Two years earlier, when Hurts seemed unsatisfied even with an undefeated record, he was asked if there was ever a win that would leave him satisfied. "The last game," he said. So on the night the Eagles won the Super Bowl, when the locker room started to clear, Hurts sat on the floor with his back against the wall and cradled the Lombardi Trophy in front of him like a toddler. If the Michael Jordan "Jumpman" logo on his goggles and cleats did not give it away, this was his Jordan moment—like Jordan in June 1992 crying into the NBA Finals trophy after his first title. At last, Hurts was satisfied. "When you come into that moment, you don't have any expectations for how you're going to feel or how you're going to respond to it. Is it what you imagined?" Hurts said a few days later. "All I think about, truly, is the effort that was put in…to hopefully be the last man standing. And we were indeed the last man standing."

From there, the party went to the Hilton Riverside, where the team had spent the past week. The first-floor ballroom was home to an invitation-only celebration. Celebrity guests mingled with players, coaches, executives, organization staffers, and their family and friends. Hours passed and Sunday became Monday, and players retreated upstairs or elsewhere in New Orleans. Hurts walked through wearing a Prince-like purple suit, surrounded by his fiancée and family. Sirianni remained. He had been on stage at one point, singing along to Bobby Brown's "My Prerogative":

Everybody's talking all this stuff about me
Why don't they just let me live?
I don't need permission, make my own decisions
That's, that's my prerogative

This might have been Sirianni's way of saying, "I told you so."

The lights came on just past 3:00 AM. Sirianni was not ready to leave. He accepted congratulations. He offered appreciation. He took photos with everyone who asked, the cigar not leaving his mouth. He was a man fulfilled, and he was not the only one. Graham came back down going through a similar car wash of fans and admirers. Wearing an open overshirt revealing his bare chest and a Super Bowl cap on his head, Graham spotted his coach and they embraced, the last men standing tall until the end.

Five hours later, Sirianni and Hurts were shuttled to the convention center for the day-after press conference and photo opportunity reserved for the Super Bowl–winning coach and the Super Bowl MVP. Hurts, wearing a "Breed of One" shirt, took a photo with the MVP trophy. "Thank you," a league official said, ushering the program along. Hurts was not finished. The Lombardi Trophy sat on the table. "This is the one I care about here," he said. He wanted a photo with *that* trophy. "When it's all said and done for me, I won't measure my success off any numbers or statistics or passing yards or touchdowns," Hurts said. "I measure it off of rings and championships."

Sirianni, who had spent four years focused on his connection with his players, wore Brown's high school jersey. On this date two years earlier, Sirianni oversaw the final practice before the painful loss to Kansas City. On this date one year earlier, Sirianni had finalized a new coaching staff and tried to recreate a culture that fractured during a collapse that almost cost Sirianni his job. He was now a Super Bowl champion, and even while bleary-eyed and trying to find cogent thoughts on little sleep, it would have been his prerogative to forget all that had happened before the Leap Year. Instead, he realized the celebrations from the past 24 hours would not have happened had it not been for the past 24 months.

"As crazy as it sounds, I'm grateful for how last year ended," Sirianni said. "Because it shaped us to who we are today and where we're standing today."

CHAPTER 2

THE SCARS AND THE COLLAPSE

REWIND TO START WITH THE CONFETTI, because that is also where this story finished. It was February 12, 2023, and the Eagles saw the Super Bowl slip away on a slippery field. Jalen Hurts played perhaps the finest game of his NFL career, pushing to the verge of winning the Super Bowl—and Super Bowl MVP—against the vaunted Kansas City Chiefs. The Eagles could not maintain a 10-point halftime lead. A polarizing penalty flag on James Bradberry in the waning minutes of the game allowed the Chiefs to chew away the clock and keep the Eagles from an earnest effort at a game-winning drive. When the final seconds ticked away in 38–35 a loss to former Eagles coach Andy Reid and face-of-the-league quarterback Patrick Mahomes, the red and yellow confetti rained down on the State Farm Stadium field. There was Hurts, walking through the confetti to the losing team's locker room. It pained him—it even changed his soul, as he would later say—and he wanted that moment seared in his mind

Apparently, he also wanted it seared on his cell phone. Hurts kept the image as his wallpaper—it was not intended to be made public, but a candid photo of Hurts with his phone circulated on social media—and it became a frequent reminder of the quest to experience the green, black, and white confetti fall from above.

"You either win or you learn, that's how I feel," Hurts said after that loss.

"It always hurts, right?" coach Nick Sirianni said. "We'll use this pain, we'll use this failure for motivation for us moving forward."

That devastation provided the subtext for the 2023 season and all that came after. Reach within three points of the Super Bowl, and you cannot forget it. ("We've probably internally talked about the frustration of not winning that game. Maybe you could even call it, to use maybe a stronger word, bitterness or whatever… toward some of the things that played out in the fourth quarter in that game," owner Jeffrey Lurie recalled two years later. "So we held onto a lot of that. Probably played to our benefit [in 2024], but there was all of us feeling that that was an incredible missed opportunity and a feeling that there was a Super Bowl there to be taken.") When the 2023 offseason program started, Sirianni showed an image of the red and yellow confetti on the big screen in the team's auditorium. It becomes easy for players to suggest they simply turn the page, that each season is different. There were invariably questions about how long it took them to get over the Super Bowl loss. The false premise of that question, though, suggests they were able to move past it.

"That was the toughest loss I've ever had in my career, and the only thing I wanted to do from that time on is get back, start this season so we could go out there and prove [it]," tight end Dallas Goedert said. "If anything, it puts a chip on the entire team's shoulder."

Sirianni works long hours in his South Philadelphia office. There were times during the summer of 2023 when there would be a random expletive heard down the hallways. "Is everything all right?" an assistant would ask. It was Sirianni rewatching the Super Bowl. There was a time when he sat with his son for dinner and NFL Network replayed the game. Sirianni must be a glutton for punishment to endure the footage on repeat.

"To me, it's very healthy to do that," he said. "It's healthy to—as [former NFL coach] Frank Reich used to say to me—drag yourself through the mud.... This is the accountability piece of our program. It's healthy to drag yourself through the mud. To get real dirty, and to [be] like, 'Oh, I messed that up.' But then there's got to come a time where you get yourself out of the mud and you realize you're here for a reason and you're confident in your abilities and to move on. But there is a healthy portion of dragging yourself through the mud because that's how you get better. 'What did I screw up? What are the things I didn't like about what we did?'.... So, of course, I've had those with that game. I've probably watched that game an obsessive [number] of times."

He took walks in his south New Jersey neighborhood that summer, planning messages for the team. The pain of the Super Bowl was among the themes—but not the only one. When he showed the image of the confetti falling in Arizona, he also included an accompanying message: *You can't admire the results and desire the reward if you don't embrace the routine that produces the reward.*

"Our goal every day isn't to come in here to chase the Super Bowl," Sirianni said in 2023. "You hope it gets to that, but it's to look at the daily increments, right? And how we get better, how we get better, how we get better.... You got to be really good to win. You got to be really good to get to the playoffs even, right? Then you're gonna have some luck involved in it. So are we doing the things that we can control every single day to put ourselves in position to go win another?"

Here's the rub: it was a different team in 2023. The 2022 group was a special blend of talent and timing, with an offseason of star-studded acquisitions (wide receiver A.J. Brown and pass-rusher Haason Reddick among them) blending in with an ascending roster of young talent (including Jalen Hurts), established veteran leaders (such as Jason Kelce, Lane Johnson, and Fletcher Cox), and year two of a coaching staff for one of the most prolific offenses in franchise history and the most sacks by any defense to play in Philadelphia. They also benefited from good health and untimely injuries by opponents to cruise to the Super Bowl. An example: the Eagles had 22 of 22 starters healthy for the Super Bowl and were third in the NFL in adjusted games lost, as ranked by Football Outsiders. "I think for us to expect the same results as last year would be naïve at a minimum," Howie Roseman said. They knew it would be different in 2023—especially the hardened veterans. Kelce had acknowledged it would be more difficult because opponents had spent the offseason studying how the Eagles excelled.

"I go back to [2023] on the Tuesday after we lost the Super Bowl and Nick walked into my office, and he said, 'How you doing,' and I said to him, 'I think the thing that I'm most upset about is how many good people we're going to lose on and off the field,'" Roseman said. "So I knew what was coming. I knew the schedule was going to be harder. I knew that it was probably easier to get the offense to a place quicker than it was the defense."

There is a price of success in the NFL, as the Eagles have learned the hard way. The price is often paid by other franchises, who are inclined to raid your roster and coaching staff in an effort to tap into whatever magic leads to a Super Bowl. That was especially felt following the Chiefs loss with the exits of both offensive coordinator Shane Steichen and defensive coordinator Jonathan Gannon to head coaching jobs elsewhere. The Eagles knew Steichen was set to depart—the Indianapolis Colts hired him, coincidentally making him the second consecutive Eagles offensive coordinator to go from Super Bowl appearance to the Colts—and there was more of a defined internal pipeline to replace him. Brian Johnson was next in line. He was a well-regarded quarterbacks coach who had played for Hurts' father in high school and knew Hurts since the Eagles quarterback was a child fetching balls at practice in the Houston sun. Even though he had not been an NFL offensive coordinator or a primary play-caller, Johnson would have earned an offensive coordinator job elsewhere had the Eagles not promoted him.

The defensive coordinator change was more complicated. Gannon was known to be a hot candidate on the coaching circuit, and the Eagles' preferred replacement was Vic Fangio. A veteran coordinator who had been a head coach in Denver, Fangio had even worked with the Eagles as a consultant in January 2023 leading up to the Super Bowl. The hope was to hire him to lead the defense if Gannon received a job as a head coach. When the Houston Texans did not hire Gannon in January 2023, he was expected to return to Philadelphia for year three. Fangio accepted the defensive coordinator job in Miami. Unbeknownst to the Eagles at the time, the Arizona Cardinals were interested in Gannon for the head coaching vacancy. They reached out to Gannon leading up to the Super Bowl. The contact came outside of the formal NFL protocols. The Eagles did not learn about the interest until later in the process. Gannon was officially hired quickly after the loss. The Eagles were left scrambling.

Had the Eagles known the defensive coordinator role would be vacant, would Fangio have kept his availability for Philadelphia? "I think that's a fair assumption," he said when he was hired one year later.

"It was very frustrating we didn't get him [in 2023] because he was all set," Lurie would later say.

Instead of hiring the originator of the Fangio defense, the Eagles hired protégé Sean Desai. He was a former Fangio assistant who had one year as defensive coordinator at Chicago, but he did not come with the résumé nor gravitas of Fangio. Plus, the Eagles needed to refill their defensive coaching staff that included the exits of two respected position coaches. Because Desai was not hired until late February, the Eagles were hiring staff members into March. That is well beyond the typical calendar for coaching changes in the NFL, and it limits the pool of candidates. The Eagles hired a linebackers coach and defensive backs coach who had never filled those roles in the NFL. Everybody requires a first chance, of course, but combined with a young coordinator, the Eagles were left with an inexperienced defensive coaching staff for the 2023 campaign. In an effort to mitigate this, the Eagles hired former Detroit Lions head coach Matt Patricia as a senior defensive assistant. A longtime Bill Belichick assistant in New England, Patricia did not have the schematic overlap with Sean Desai. His presence was, in theory, meant to add an experienced coach to lend insight and expertise to the staff. It was hard to ignore him as a looming successor if the defense underachieved.

It might seem skeptical to suggest the defense would underachieve, but this was the other price of the success. Key starters from that 2022 defense were set to hit the open market—and they were in demand. Pro Bowl defensive tackle Javon Hargrave signed a lucrative contract with San Francisco, one of the Eagles' chief contenders in the NFC. Both starting linebackers, T.J. Edwards and Kyzir White, found greener pastures elsewhere (greener in dollars, at least). Safety C.J. Gardner-Johnson, a key playmaker in the secondary who also brought an identifiable competitive zeal to the defense, wanted a bigger contract than what the Eagles offered. The protracted dispute led the Eagles to reroute their initial off-season plans—including re-signing cornerback James Bradberry, who was a second-team All-Pro but was initially thought to be too expensive for the Eagles to keep. Gardner-Johnson departed for a one-year contract in Detroit. Fellow starting safety Marcus Epps exited for Las Vegas. The Eagles were down five starters from the middle of their defense, plus their coordinator and two key position coaches. Add in the reality that Reddick's contract was an under-the-radar issue, and there were warning signs about the Eagles defense entering 2023.

The offense lost running back Miles Sanders and right guard Isaac Seumalo, although the top players remained. And even with the loss of Steichen, there was a degree of continuity with Johnson taking on an elevated role and the remaining offensive staff in place. Plus, Sirianni was a major part of the offense—he considered his offensive acumen part of the reason why he was hired—and he could even take on a larger presence in the offense. With the way the offense excelled in 2022, Sirianni did not seek to change much about the scheme or the operation. "It's not always about coming up with new plays and new wrinkles and new things like that," Sirianni told the *Philadelphia Inquirer* podcast *unCovering the Birds* before the 2023 season. "Sometimes it's just getting better, and a lot of times it's just getting better at your base stuff. And how do you coach it better? And how do you do it better? And, off of that, what are some wrinkles off of that? Not necessarily new things. But things that are wrinkles.... That's the same way I thought about year three: I don't think it's anything new, it's about how do we get better at what we're already doing?"

The problem: they did not get better at what they were doing. It might have seemed that way early in the season, when the Eagles had the best record in the NFL. But they were not the best team in the NFL. This might not have been blatant at the moment; in fact, there were high-water marks that made you think a return trip to the Super Bowl was possible. They won their first five games. They stymied a high-powered Miami offense—and scored 31 points against Fangio's defense. The Eagles went to Kansas City and avenged the Super Bowl loss with a 21–17 win, after which Sirianni hollered while walking into the tunnel, "I don't hear shit anymore, Chiefs fans!" and joked with a reporter who suggested the Chiefs had the better coach and quarterback combination in the game. When the Eagles followed that up with a come-from-behind, overtime victory against Buffalo, an Eagles fan's mind could reasonably wander toward a Lombardi Trophy. They were 10–1. They had topped bona fide Super Bowl contenders. There were nitpicks, sure, but was that not always the case? Except inside the locker room, it did not feel like a 10–1 team. Perhaps it could have been rationalized as a competitive group with Super Bowl aspirations unimpressed by an October victory. But the joy from the year before seemed to be missing. And the victories obscured problems hiding in plain sight. They were outlasting opponents in close games, not pummeling teams the way they did one year earlier. If you find point differential to be an indicator of a team's brawn, then you would have been less impressed with the Eagles than their record suggested. The Bills game was followed by back-to-back losses by a combined 43 points to San Francisco and Dallas—two NFC heavyweights—and the alarms were beginning to sound with actions as much as volume. Sirianni made the bold decision to demote Desai in December after the Cowboys loss, effectively removing Desai from his defensive coordinator duties and inserting Patricia. This backfired. Patricia was coordinating a scheme on the fly he did not introduce, and it went as well as one would expect. Similarly concerning was the regression of the offense. It appeared unimaginative. Hurts changed the play at the line of scrimmage before a brutal interception to seal a loss in Seattle. When the Eagles lost to the lowly Arizona Cardinals in Week 17—a team coached by Gannon—the term "collapse" was beginning to enter the lexicon of Eagles fans. The offense tried to solve problems with simplification. The defense tried fixing problems by becoming more complex. Neither solution worked. They closed the regular season with five losses in six games, and they were listless entering the postgame against Tampa Bay. By then, there was little confidence the Eagles would win. They bottomed out with a 32–9 loss in the opening round of the playoffs, their sixth loss in seven weeks.

"Obviously we were in a big slide," Sirianni said. "Any time that's the case, I always look at myself first. And I didn't do a good enough job. Obviously, we lost five in the last six and lost today. And it was almost like you couldn't get out of the rut.... And that's all of us. We'll have to look ourselves in the mirror and accept that and find answers, find solutions. But obviously, when you start 10–1 and you get into what will happen for us and obviously that the expectations were high. Expectations were even higher when we started off 10–1 [and] we fell into a skid. So I'll look at everything. I'll obviously look at the play-calling, I'll look at the scheme, I'll look at practices. I'll look at everything."

Roseman greeted Kelce and Cox with emotional embraces in the tunnel after the game, expecting that to be their final games in their storied careers. But the focus that day was less on whether Kelce and Cox would return and more on whether Sirianni would be back. Such a question seemed unthinkable seven weeks before. An unprecedented tailspin would do that.

"I'm not thinking about that," Sirianni said. "As the head coach, [I'm] trying to be there for our guys and our staff right now."

"I didn't know he was going anywhere," Hurts said. "I have a ton of confidence in everyone in this building."

Lane Johnson, one of the best (and most honest) players in franchise history, did not mince words on the devastating late-season slide. He recognized how unthinkable the collapse had been and that in a "wild business," "nobody's safe."

"Probably the first fucking team to end like this after starting the season the way you did," Johnson said. "It's frustrating. We offered plenty of explanations, but at the end of day, we never did get the result we wanted to. So shit's got to change."

What would change? That was how the Eagles entered the 2024 offseason.

CHAPTER 3

KEEPING SIRIANNI

IT IS STANDARD OPERATING PROCEDURE for a returning head coach to hold an end-of-season press conference in the days after the final game of the season. More than one week passed before the franchise sent Sirianni onto the stage—seemingly because a decision needed to be made about his future. There were internal deliberations and discussions. The Eagles never made a formal announcement or issued a press release that Sirianni would return for his fourth season. Rather, word leaked that Brian Johnson would not return as offensive coordinator. Sean Desai, who had already been stripped of his responsibilities, was not being brought back as defensive coordinator. That was a signal that the changes would be at the coordinator level—not the head-coaching level.

And when Jeffrey Lurie explained what went into keeping Sirianni, there were two factors: a vision for a revamped, innovative coaching staff, plus the equity Sirianni had built in his three years as head coach. Of course, Lurie has dismissed accomplished coaches before. So what Sirianni articulated mattered more than what Sirianni achieved.

"Nick's conscious desire to have top-notch coordinators under him really drove a lot of the strategy and he was hellbent on making sure we had the best," Lurie explained in March 2024 in his first public comments after retaining Sirianni. "Highly encouraged by both his analysis of where we're at, no excuses, a fundamental understanding of what needs to be better than the last five or six weeks of the season, and not only a return to our championship-caliber performance and execution, but improve on that, too."

The new coordinators were Kellen Moore on offense and Vic Fangio on defense. The Fangio hire might have happened in a quicker period than a ride from Philadelphia to his native Dunmore, Pennsylvania, if it were permitted. He was the target one year earlier, and when he left Miami after one year, the Eagles were the ideal fit. There was a longer interview period to land Moore, who, even at age 35 at the time of the hire, had spent four years as offensive coordinator in Dallas and one year leading the Los Angeles Chargers offense. The two hires brought 25 combined years as NFL coordinators—a departure from the inexperience of one year earlier.

Sirianni insisted the decision was not foisted upon him. Lurie framed it as Sirianni recognizing the Eagles needed a change—what Sirianni termed "fresh ideas," which also included taking a step back from the offense.

"We got a little bit stale on offense by the end of the year, and these ideas and this new person coming in is meant to take away the staleness and add the value of what they're adding to the offense," Sirianni said.

The use of the word "stale" and insistence on "fresh ideas" was the clearest signal that there would be change in the scheme. It would be somebody from the outside—not an internal hire. Sirianni said that it "would be crazy" not to mesh new concepts with what worked for the Eagles offense during the previous three seasons, although he made clear that "I'm hiring [a coordinator] to do a job and to be in charge of the offense." This was a big step for Sirianni. Even if he had not called plays since the middle of the 2021 season, he still viewed it as his offense. He remained a part of every offensive meeting and helped create every offensive game plan.

"The things with Nick were really impressive were wanting to truly improve the ingredients of the offense, truly improve who was going to lead the offense and the direction it would go, [wanting] to be much more innovative, much more dynamic," Lurie said.

Lurie pushed back on the idea that Sirianni ceding either play-calling or offensive oversight reflected on the head coach. The owner had long advocated for offensive innovation, which led to curiosity about why he would keep Sirianni if he were unhappy with the offense. That goes into the other elements of Sirianni's leadership ability and coaching acumen. Plus, as Lurie framed it, "It's the head coach's responsibility to get the plays called really well—it doesn't matter who's calling the plays."

But the change led to a question in a press conference that came to define the perception of Sirianni entering 2024: *If the offensive coordinator is going to be in charge of the offense and the defensive coordinator is going to be in charge of the defense, what is your role going to be?*

"The head coach of the football team," Sirianni answered.

And what would that entail?

"I guess it would be very similar to what's going on right now," Sirianni said. "Does that mean I'll sit more into defensive meetings at times? Maybe. Instead of always being in an offensive meeting, maybe I go to a defensive meeting here and there. But my job is to be the head coach of the team, not the head coach of the offense, not the head coach of the defense, not the head coach of the special teams, but be the head coach of the football team. So that's building the culture. That's making sure the culture is working with our five core values.... That's diving into that, building the culture, having a relationship with the guys on the football team because I know when I have that connection with the guys on the football team, that's when the culture is working and working at a high level, and that's where our connection with the players and their connection with each other works well, too."

The framing of all of this made it sound like the meme-inducing line from *Office Space*: "What would you say you do here?" But "head coach of the football team" was a reasonable and accurate answer, because Sirianni's job was to lead the team—not simply to have a top offense. Although head coaches that call offensive plays had grown in popularity and was also the norm in Philadelphia with Andy Reid, Chip Kelly, and Doug Pederson, the "CEO coach"—as it had come to be labeled—was also an effective model. Look at John Harbaugh and Mike Tomlin. Look at Sean McDermott and Pete Carroll. Look at Jim Harbaugh and Dan Campbell. Best of all? Look at Bill Belichick.

In fact, part of the intrigue about Sirianni's status had been the availability of Belichick for the first time since winning six Super Bowls in New England. A longtime Eagles adversary who competed against the Eagles in two Super Bowls, Belichick was a coaching free agent and there was mutual respect between the coach, Lurie, and Roseman. In fact, ESPN reported that while Lurie and Roseman still "strongly believed" in Sirianni, Lurie "thought it was worth asking a confidant of his about Belichick." Belichick was reportedly interested in the job. Roseman even had a conversation with Belichick, per ESPN, although it was described as a "check-in" after Belichick's departure rather than a discussion about the Eagles' vacancy. The Eagles elected to keep Sirianni, of course, which also meant they were not pursuing Belichick. The ESPN report suggested the Eagles did not want to "start over again" and that if Belichick changed "everything and every person," the Eagles would need to start from scratch.

When Sirianni was asked if he needed to sell his vision of the team, he called the end-of-season meetings "business as usual," although he added, "You'd better believe that I'm thinking after that 1–6 finish after starting the way we started and doing the things that we've done in the past that I'm thinking I'm going to prove them right again, and we're going to prove them right. We've got to re-prove ourselves. We've got to go prove it again."

Implicit in that statement is the fact that Sirianni had already proven himself. That was also part of Lurie's evaluation and decision to keep Sirianni. Lurie had dismissed Pederson three seasons after winning the Super Bowl—two of which resulted in postseason appearances—and he moved on from Andy Reid when the future Hall of Fame coach had amassed more wins than any coach in franchise history. Chip Kelly reached double-digit wins in his first two seasons and was fired in the middle of his third. Difficult decisions were not foreign to Lurie. At that point, Sirianni had made the postseason in all three seasons as head coach, reached double-digit wins twice, and came close to winning a Super Bowl. That needed to be taken into account.

"I do know until we were hitting that streak of not playing well at the end of the year, we were 31–7 in the previous 38 regular season games," Lurie said. "To say the least, that's exceptional. And that's starting with taking a team that had a four-win season in our final year with Doug [Pederson] and taking it to a playoff team right away, and then to the Super Bowl, and then to a 10–1 beginning.

"Very disappointing ending, but I don't take [lightly] 31–7 in the [NFL]. That's extraordinary. The ingredients I've always seen with Nick are very obvious—the ability to connect, the ability to be authentic, incredible work ethic, high football IQ. All the reasons he was hired in the first place have been almost magnified in the first three years."

This was not said to absolve Sirianni from the 2023 collapse—"I don't mean to diminish that in the slightest, because I lived that," Lurie said—and Lurie was especially disheartened that the team lacked the resilience and resolve to rebound from rough results. The best teams have those qualities; the Eagles were not one of the best teams. But Lurie also thought Sirianni, with a revitalized staff, could improve the team's prospects.

"There's no recency bias, there's no latency bias—there's no bias," Lurie said. "Take a very hard look at exactly what the entire season looked [like, what the] entire history has been for the few years, for our organization, for our team. And listen…. It doesn't matter how the season ends. It's the same exact, very rigid—very sort of analytic process—where you try to assess your strengths, your weaknesses, and what can we do a lot better, what can we look forward to, what's the plan. That's for players, that's for personnel, that's for culture."

There was also an acknowledgment of Sirianni's sideline demeanor. Sirianni does not hide his emotions. He had long leaned into being himself, which is part of his authenticity with his players. When the Eagles win, it can be charming—grating for the opponents, perhaps, but charming for his own fans. When the Eagles lose, Sirianni can be charged with going overboard. Reid had become the standard-bearer for head coaches under Lurie, and his equanimity had become iconic. That is not Sirianni. It does not have to be. But there also needed to be improvement.

"One of the aspects that makes Nick really good is he's authentic. He doesn't hold back. That can also be a negative at times," said Lurie, who is especially cognizant of how the demeanor could affect officiating. "…I love his passion. I think he recognizes that it [can] be a little bit counterproductive if he overdoes his own passion, but you don't want to stop where that passion is coming from. You got to find a sweet spot. I think he wants to find a sweet spot of what that's like. But I love his passion."

The sideline decorum would be under scrutiny in 2024. Then again, everything would be scrutinized. Sirianni earned a fourth year. He was not promised a fifth year. He needed to win—and perhaps win big—to keep his job.

The "ingredients" were important to note, because this was not a rebuild. With Jalen Hurts signed to a five-year, $255 million contract, the team was set with a franchise quarterback. General manager Howie Roseman always prioritizes the line of scrimmage, and the Eagles' offensive line included Lane Johnson at right tackle, Jordan Mailata at left tackle, Landon Dickerson at left guard, and Cam Jurgens ready to take over at center for Jason Kelce. At wide receiver, A.J. Brown and DeVonta Smith combined to form perhaps the best wide receiver combination in the NFL and certainly the best in Eagles history. Combined with Dallas Goedert, there was continuity and high-level play in the passing offense. On the defensive line, Jalen Carter was a former top-10 pick entering his second season as a cornerstone player, and defensive tackle Jordan Davis and edge rusher Nolan Smith were fellow first-round picks expected to be part of a core on the defensive front. They also had steady contributor Milton Williams entering his fourth season. The futures of Josh Sweat and Haason Reddick were both unknown entering the acquisition period, although both had been Pro Bowl players. Darius Slay was set to return as a high-profile cornerback. Roseman had work to do, but the expectation was that Sirianni would coach a Super Bowl–caliber roster.

Lurie maintained confidence in the roster Roseman would assemble during the 2024 offseason. There was optimism in Hurts' standing in the organization. The chair would not be pulled on them if the Eagles failed to meet expectations. The team was ready to make a leap, and the pressure was on Sirianni to show them how high to jump.

"Every coach is in a high-pressure situation," Lurie said. "Nick has had a pretty spectacular first three seasons, and he's shown all the ingredients to have outstanding success. I'm just looking forward. There's no coach that's not feeling pressure to perform. That's the way it is in the [NFL]. But I think Nick has all the ingredients."

Time Out: Jeffrey Lurie

Two months had not yet passed when Jeffrey Lurie walked around the luxurious resort grounds of the Breakers Palm Beach in the spring of 2025 as the envy of the other NFL owners. They all gather at the annual league meetings—not to mention the general managers and coaches—and it's a group that often has access to whatever they desire. The Lombardi Trophy is an exception. They all want it. Lurie was the only one who held it this year, allowing for well-earned—and once-elusive—pride when meeting with his peers.

"You did some things right, let's put it that way," Lurie said. "I know our effort is always there. There's no shortage of wanting to win on any of our part at all. But yeah, you walk through, and you know how hard it is, and everyone's congratulating you. It is a good feeling."

Lurie purchased the franchise in 1994 for a then-record $185 million—and he will never forget that the *Wall Street Journal* was critical of the investment.

During the 2024 season, Lurie sold an eight percent stake in the franchise at a then record valuation of $8.3 billion.

It is fair to say the investment paid off. The growth of the NFL during this period has helped the league's economics explode, but the Eagles have transformed into one of the league's premier franchises during his ownership. This period included the construction of the franchise's own practice facility and stadium early in his tenure, helping to change the reputation within the league. But more than anything, the Eagles won at an unprecedented rate. The Eagles made one conference championship from 1970 to 2000. In the 25 seasons since, the Eagles have been to the NFC Championship Game eight times, the Super Bowl four times, and twice put the Lombardi Trophy in the trophy case of that new facility.

"I'd just rather focus on getting that third, honestly," Lurie said when asked about his legacy in April 2025. "I don't think that way. I'm proud of the culture we have more than anything. I'm proud of everything we've accomplished. It's so hard."

He knows from experience. The Eagles were on the doorstep early in the 2000s, making the NFC Championship Game in four consecutive seasons, but they never ever won the Super Bowl. Lurie figured if they could be competitive every season, they would eventually win one. It did not happen during Andy Reid's tenure—Reid, Lurie's second hire, has the most wins of any coach in franchise history—and Lurie needed to wait until 2018 before he finally experienced a parade in Philadelphia. It took him only seven years to win one again, and he thought it came two years belated.

"It was more relaxing in the fourth quarter for one. A lot more relaxing," Lurie said. "It's hard to compare. The first one is the first one. It's incomparable, your first one. But the second one was sort of incredibly gratifying because you feel you have the team you have, and you were able to hit on all cylinders in a way in which it was just incredibly gratifying. So they're both extraordinary experiences in one's life when you devote your life to this existence in the NFL and football. Incredible. But now, I've got to say, an interesting sort of look at oneself. I feel like I'm just as hungry, if not more now, for a third. Ever since the parade, I don't know that there's been one day where we're not discussing something in terms of the planning process to try to get a third. It's nonstop. Now maybe June, July, there's less one could do. But I find myself, it's a burning desire to get that third, and we'll go from there.... It's an obsession. Maybe it's not healthy, but I think it's worthwhile."

Lurie has been the constant during this run. Every coach he's hired has had double-digit wins and a postseason appearance within two seasons. Three of the five coaches he hired reached the Super Bowl. Jason Kelce once credited the culture and environment for the franchise's relatively sustained success, and he said it starts from the top down. Lurie, who looked up to executives like Red Auerbach and Bill Walsh, pointed to the "stability of culture and a stability of special people." He noted how the 49ers needed to change from Joe Montana to Steve Young, but the culture endured. Lurie credited Reid for establishing the foundation. Lurie has been the one who has overseen it.

"The league always evolves. You never want to be part of the consensus," Lurie said. "You want to think on your own and be genuine to yourself. If you do what everyone else does, you'll be 8–8.... You got to try to do what's exceptional and avoid risk [aversion]. But at the same time, make calculated decisions. And sometimes they're not going to work. And in my opinion, don't try to be popular. Never try to make the popular choices. Do what you think is right. Sometimes it's going to work, sometimes it's not. But if you're true to yourself and your own culture, focus on what is most meaningful to winning."

And not just winning, but as Lurie said, "winning big."

"Go for it," Lurie said. "That's always been a core principle."

In a quiet moment outside the coach's office when the locker room started to clear after the Super Bowl, the gravity of what the franchise had accomplished during the past seven years was not lost on the owner. They beat Tom Brady and Patrick Mahomes. They beat Bill Belichick and Andy Reid. The night in New Orleans changed the way Lurie's franchise is viewed around the NFL—and maybe even at the posh resorts with every NFL owner each spring, too.

"You got to be resilient, you got to have the core values, you got to build the rosters right, and you got to have the culture. So I'm very proud of what we're able to do," Lurie said. "I thought we were going to be able to do it two years ago. And here we are able to do it, two years later.... We've got to remain humble. I just believe being humble is a part of our culture. Once you think you're better than you are or better than you should be, you'll lose that edge. I want everyone to remain [humble] from the top down, and that starts with me. There's a lot of smart franchises in this league. I'm grateful that we're able to be world champs in a league with a lot of smart franchises."

CHAPTER 4

FREE AGENCY

HOWIE ROSEMAN HAS AN EXPRESSION he repeats often: when he has his best seasons, the Eagles have their best seasons. As Nick Sirianni likes to say, what makes good coaches? Good players. Roseman is tasked with finding and acquiring those players. He has done it for two decades during a run as general manager that will put him in consideration for the Hall of Fame. Roseman entered the 2024 offseason understanding what was at stake. The Eagles regressed in 2023. The defense required an overhaul. The offense needed to evolve.

Roseman had identified the 2024 free agency period as one in which they would be active adding to the team. It was a class they targeted, and they were armed with cap space and cash reserves with which they could be creative.

"Every year we're going into the offseason trying to compete for a championship, but I felt like we had enough core players to do it, enough resources at our disposal to do it," Roseman said. "We, as a front office, had to kind of set the tone in the offseason."

In Philadelphia, this has come to be known as "Howie SZN"—a reference to the acquisition period when Roseman is in charge. Roseman realized the responsibility and motivation from the moment he stood in the corridor of Tampa Bay's Raymond James

Stadium after the Eagles' postseason loss in January 2023 and he shared an emotional embrace with Jason Kelce and Fletcher Cox. "I felt like I let those guys down," Roseman said, expecting that to be the final game of their storied careers. Before the Eagles added players for 2024, they felt the retirements of the franchise icons. Kelce announced his decision on March 4, 2024, with a 41-minute speech that put a bow on 13 storied seasons. (Within the emotional speech, Kelce was also bullish on what was ahead for the Eagles during a segment about Nick Sirianni: "Although last season truly sucked, I wouldn't trade any of my time with you or those teams for the world. Everything happens for a reason. And I've truly enjoyed my time with you, Coach. Sometimes the flowers get knocked back a bit, but the roots remain. And I can't wait to watch what reblossoms this next season.") Cox retired on March 10, with a press conference one month later when his entire family could travel from Yazoo City, Mississippi. Kelce and Cox played 25 combined seasons and made 13 combined Pro Bowls. They earned gravitas within the locker room and organization. Their retirements reaffirmed a reality of 2024: it was bound to be a year of change, from the coaching staff to the scheme to the roster. The roster would be reimagined.

One day after Cox's retirement, the NFL's legal tampering period opened. This three-day window allows for teams to negotiate with the agent of a player—even if informal discussions of potential interest often occur two weeks earlier at the scouting combine. Most of the big-name players are committed to sign somewhere by the time free agency commences on Wednesday afternoon.

A few minutes into the tampering window, the Eagles lost starting running back D'Andre Swift to the Chicago Bears. This was notable because the Eagles had different plans for the position in free agency—and the Bears, a team flush with cap money to spend, were not going to sign the running back that interested the Eagles.

The Eagles are not known to be big spenders at running back. They had not signed a veteran running back to a multi-year deal in a decade. Roseman had not made a running back one of the highest-paid players at his position since LeSean McCoy in 2012. The Eagles had cycled through running backs on rookie contracts or bargain-bin free agents. That was about to change in 2024.

It's rare that a player like Saquon Barkley hits the open market. Barkley, a former Penn State star who was the No. 2 overall pick by the New York Giants in 2018, had proven to be one of the most talented running backs when healthy. The Giants had used the franchise tag on him one year earlier—a sign that he's among the best valued runners in the NFL. But he was not valued enough by the franchise that drafted him and for whom he had declared he wanted to spend his entire career. Barkley and the Giants went through two years of contract disputes. Going into free agency, the Giants were ready to let Barkley hit the open market to see if he could find a team willing to meet his asking price, because Giants general manager Joe Schoen was not prepared to meet it. He had signed quarterback Daniel Jones to a lucrative contract and wanted to redirect resources to the offensive line. The negotiations later played out on HBO's *Hard Knocks,* which offered an inside look at how the Giants allowed one of their most popular players to sign with a division rival. It was a potential result that made Giants owner John Mara shudder.

"I might have a tough time sleeping if Saquon goes to Philadelphia, I'll tell you that, as I've told you. Just being honest," Mara said to Schoen, as documented by *Hard Knocks*. "I have been around enough players…but he's the most popular player we have by far."

There were other teams interested—the Houston Texans among them—but the Eagles made clear they wanted Barkley and offered an appealing situation. Barkley had never won a game in Philadelphia, a sign of the Eagles' superiority to the Giants during his time in the NFL. They featured the best collection of offensive talent that Barkley would play with in his career, and running behind the Eagles' offensive line offered the potential to bring Barkley to a different level. Philadelphia was a short ride from his childhood home of Coplay, in Pennsylvania's Lehigh Valley, where his family still lived. And of course, there was the three-year, $37 million offer with $26 million guaranteed and an average annual value that exceeded the franchise tag value at the position.

"For us, it's hard to find special players at any position," Roseman said. "We think Saquon is a special player. We think he's a special person. And so when you're trying to find those guys, they're hard to find—especially on the open market. And then you put into the dynamic of has the pendulum swung so far at this position—I mean, the guy touches the ball 300 times a year, hopefully. There's not a lot of other players, skill-position players, that are touching the ball that many times and have that effect."

Internally, the Eagles pushed back on the idea that this was a departure for them. They had been willing to pay elite running backs before—they just had not paid middle-of-the-road running backs near top-of-the-league money. Eagles assistant general manager Alec Halaby on the spectrum of running backs, Barkley must be considered "special"—the word that kept emerging. Even more, there was a thought that running backs had become *undervalued.* The market for the position became too depressed because of their fungibility. It was not difficult to find a good running back. It was hard to find an elite one. And the elite ones drew comparable contracts on the open markets to No. 3 wide receivers or solid starting guards. This inefficiency in the marketplace was one the Eagles were ready to seize.

"We've always actually valued the running back position going way back to Ricky Watters and LeSean McCoy and Brian Westbrook," Jeffrey Lurie said. "When you can find one that's outstanding, we always thought to pair it with a great offensive line and a triple-threat quarterback to accentuate the ability of that running back to have lots of open space. That was something we always wanted to do and Saquon, it was just something where you had a player that we always recognized was a world-class talent, historical talent. And what would happen if you were ever able to get Saquon with this offensive line and this triple-threat quarterback and the skill position players we had? And really, to understand the allocation of resources [it] was similar to [signing] a good reserve guard or a tight end or whatever. And as we internally discussed it, it was a no-brainer because [of] where we were at as a franchise. If we didn't have that offensive line or that triple-threat quarterback, I don't know that we would have projected it the way we did, but it was like huge upside there. We're not risk averse. The downside was it wasn't going to work out quite that great, and we could deal with that."

The risk was injury or Barkley falling prey to an age curve that affects running backs more than other positions. They were less worried about the latter because, as Roseman stated, Barkley is a "freak" with his testing numbers and body. They viewed an exceptional player as the exception. Yet even the most optimistic projections could not have foretold Barkley having one of the best seasons in NFL history and joining Hall of Famers like Reggie White on the short list of the best free-agent signings in NFL history.

"Not a hard trigger to pull," Roseman said before the Super Bowl. "I think I'm being consistent with what I said in March. Was extremely confident in the player and the person. I'd like to say he's exceeded expectations, but he's always been one of the best players I've ever seen whenever I've watched him, and I've always known about what kind of person he is, because it's not hard to find that out, so I'm really not surprised by any of this. And I don't say that in an arrogant way. It's based on who he is."

It was at least within the realm of the imagination that Barkley could win Offensive Player of the Year. What could never have been expected was that Zack Baun, who also agreed to a contract on March 11, would become a Defensive Player of the Year candidate. The Eagles targeted him at the start of free agency, although not to play a key role on defense. When Fangio coached in Miami, Andrew Van Ginkel developed into one of the NFL's most versatile linebackers—somebody who could rush the passer and drop into coverage. Van Ginkel might have been the ideal fit for the defense, except he signed a bigger contract with Minnesota than the Eagles wanted to spend. They instead sought a player with a similar skill set and a less accomplished profile. That was Baun, Van Ginkel's teammate at Wisconsin, who spent four years mostly as a reserve and special teams player in New Orleans and signed a one-year, $3.5-million contract.

"You saw that guy in Vic's defense, has the ability to play off the ball, has the ability to play on the edge, has these tools in his body, really ascended under Vic," Roseman said when Baun signed, referencing Van Ginkel. "We think Zack's a versatile player who can rush from the edge, can play off the ball, tremendous special teams player. We were excited—he was a targeted guy for us."

Baun wanted to rush the quarterback. That was part of the Eagles' pitch to his agent. And with Haason Reddick on the trade block, Baun figured to be part of the rotation at edge rusher while contributing to special teams coordinator Michael Clay's unit. Roseman figured that was the floor. Fangio had different plans. When the defensive coordinator watched Baun, he saw an off-ball linebacker. "I thought he could do it," Fangio said. "Was I going to bet my life savings on it? No. But I had a good feeling he could do it."

At safety, the Eagles and C.J. Gardner-Johnson acted like they were at the end of a romantic comedy. An ideal pairing in 2022 experienced a bitter split in 2023, then both sides realized what they were missing. They let bygones be bygones. Gardner-Johnson is a playmaking safety who had more interceptions in 2022 than all the Eagles safeties combined in 2023. Plus, he brings a swagger to the defense that the Eagles missed without him. Gardner-Johnson had a forgettable year in Detroit spoiled by a torn pectoral injury that sidelined him throughout most of his one-year deal. The Eagles wanted him to return. Gardner-Johnson wanted to return. They reached a three-year, $27 million contract with $10 million guaranteed.

"We were looking to gain our swagger and mentality back," Roseman said. "Obviously what happened at the end of the year didn't feel good, wasn't acceptable for any of us. You get players who can bring that and have that motivation and that mentality."

When Gardner-Johnson arrived for his opening press conference, he started singing lyrics by Eminem: *Guess who's back... Back again. Shady's back...*

"Like I never left!" he said.

Gardner-Johnson said he was ready to "turn the lights on in the building." That's one way to put it. He had thought about returning before he returned, although he also needed to make amends for the messy departure.

"Take your feelings out of it and just be willing to be a man about certain things and accept certain things as a man," Gardner-Johnson said. "I think right now coming back was like a relief because I'm familiar with the people here, with the place, and I'm comfortable, if that makes sense. The difference from last year to this year is we both saw eye-to-eye."

Gardner-Johnson even apologized to Eagles fans. He had called them "obnoxious" in a live stream upon exiting. Gardner-Johnson reasoned that he's obnoxious, too.

"I thought it was a compliment to be obnoxious, to be honest with you!" Gardner-Johnson said. "All jokes aside, I was just in my feelings. You want to be somewhere so bad, to the point where you can't control certain things. So certain things was said but there was no meaning to it. I'm back. So I guess we all happy. Family reunion, huh?"

On the field, the upgrade was clear. The Eagles had cycled through safeties next to Reed Blankenship. They traded for Kevin Byard. Those patchwork solutions did not work. Gardner-Johnson gave the Eagles a ballhawk in the middle of the field with the versatility to pair with Blankenship. And he was not afraid to share his standing in the NFL. "I think it's my time to be cocky.... I'm still one of the best young safeties in the league," he said.

"It didn't go great when he left, but anytime people leave, it's hard to go well," Roseman said. "But we felt like it was a good fit coming back here this year and adding some things to this team on and off the field that we needed."

The Eagles found a favorable return on the under-the-radar signing of Oren Burks, who was billed internally as one of the best third linebackers in the league and someone who could contribute on special teams. Burks started in the Super Bowl next to Baun. Roseman also made a swap of draft picks to acquire former first-round pick Kenny Pickett from Pittsburgh as the backup quarterback, bringing home the Ocean Township, New Jersey, player who grew up idolizing Eagles quarterbacks as a cost-controlled backup quarterback behind Jalen Hurts.

Even in his best offseason, Roseman does not hit on every signing—even the high-profile moves. Barkley might have been the most notable splash, but he was not the most expensive one. At the start of free agency, the player the Eagles targeted and were most eager to sign was Bryce Huff—an ascending edge rusher who commanded a three-year, $51 million deal to enhance the Eagles' pass rush. He had been a situational player with the Jets who reached double-digit sacks, and the Eagles hoped more playing time and a bigger role could turn Huff into more of a force.

As it proved during the year, that was not the case. He was slow adjusting to the scheme during the summer. He was hindered by an injury during the season. He was inactive in the Super Bowl. The Huff signing might have become a footnote considering the other moves that turned to gold, but it cannot be forgotten that Huff was the big-ticket item of the offseason.

The Huff signing was even more critical because the Eagles traded Haason Reddick to the New York Jets on April 1, marking April Fool's Day by sending away one of the most important players on the defense. Reddick desired a new deal—he would later hold out in New York—and the Eagles were not meeting his contract demands. The Eagles also floated Josh Sweat's name on the trade market, but they reached an amended one-year contract with Sweat that would allow him to rebuild his value after a disappointing end to his 2023 season. Combined with a one-year pact for Brandon Graham—seemingly a formality, considering Graham had said he was ready for a "farewell tour" in Year 15—the Eagles were turning the edge rusher spot to Huff, Sweat, Graham, and 2023 first-round pick Nolan Smith.

The Eagles also missed on former first-round pick Devin White at linebacker, who drew bigger headlines than Baun during the free agency period. White offered more name appeal than football fit in Fangio's defense, and he did not even finish the season with the team. There were other low-profile signs that did not hit—DeVante Parker at wide receiver, Matt Hennessy on the offensive line—and there were smaller moves that were not as consequential. But a general manager is playing the odds. He does not need every move to hit. If he hits enough—especially the big ones—he'll keep his job so he has a sample size to know which offseasons are his best ones. This might have been Roseman's best.

While acquiring talent, Roseman was also aggressive in keeping talent. During a two-month period in the spring of 2024,

Roseman reached contract extensions with Landon Dickerson, Jordan Mailata, A.J. Brown, and DeVonta Smith. These four players were all foundational pieces for the Eagles, and what was notable was how quick the Eagles acted in ensuring they remained in Philadelphia and did not have the type of contract disputes that lingered for Barkley in New York. (And could have affected Reddick in Philadelphia.) Mailata and Dickerson gave the Eagles continuity on their left side of the offensive line, which was undergoing a major change with Kelce's decision to retire. They were homegrown talents who had developed into key locker room leaders—and Mailata's story as an Australian rugby player who had never played organized football before becoming one of the best players in the NFL under the Eagles' watch (and, most specifically, under offensive line coach Jeff Stoutland's watch) is ever an example of out-of-the-box thinking and a focus on player development.

The Brown and Smith deals were critical because they were among a group of top-of-the-league wide receivers in line for new contracts. The Eagles benefit from the "first-mover advantage"—they set the market rather than reacting to the market. Had they waited on re-signing Smith and Brown, the contracts would have cost the Eagles more than $10 million per season combined. They locked up both players to contracts that satisfied the player and also would give the team future flexibility, utilizing a strategy that had worked for the franchise for three decades dating back to Joe Banner's time as team president. These contract extensions tend to be overshadowed when remembering Roseman's 2024 offseason, but they were pivotal in the construction of the roster.

Of course, free agency, re-signings, and trades are levers to pull in roster construction. The one that might matter the most is the NFL draft. A big part of what might have been Roseman's best offseason came in April, when the Eagles found the rookies who would join the Super Bowl roster.

CHAPTER 5

NFL DRAFT

AT THE START OF THE 2024 OFFSEASON, one of Howie Roseman's takeaways was that the Eagles must give their young players a chance to play. Free agency, when executed correctly, can elevate a roster. Trades can be an effective tool in building a roster. But the most time-tested way to acquire talented young players who fit in the locker room is to draft and develop. The Eagles try to "draft-proof" their roster so they do not need to push to fill needs in the draft, but cornerback and right guard stood out as two spots where the Eagles could find young players to contribute.

Cornerback was a popular position for the Eagles in mock drafts. It was also frequently noted that the Eagles had not selected a cornerback in the first round since 2002, although that had less to do with organizational priorities than how the board had fallen in certain years. There were years when the Eagles were pushing to draft a cornerback, but the prospect was selected just before the Eagles. Their spending had indicated that they consider cornerback a premium position. Of course, when it comes to Roseman, picking a player along the line of scrimmage is often a safe bet. It all depends how the board falls. It's easier to be selective in the top 10 than when 21 players are off the board at No. 22 overall, which was the Eagles' first-round pick in 2024.

It was a rich draft for offensive linemen and quarterbacks. The Eagles were not going to take a quarterback in the first round, but an offensive lineman seemed like a strong possibility. The class was not considered as robust on the defensive side of the ball. At cornerback, their top players were Quinyon Mitchell and Cooper DeJean. Mitchell, a standout at Toledo who ran a 4.33-second 40-yard dash at the scouting combine, was not expected to fall to the Eagles in the 20s. A slight trade up seemed possible—the Eagles had not drafted in their original spot since 2020—but it would have been ambitious to think they could stand still and have their top cornerback fall to them.

Then the draft started and there was an early run on quarterbacks. Six went in the first 12 picks. And the other six picks were all offensive players. In fact, the first defensive player was not selected until No. 15. The Eagles thought any chance of Mitchell falling into their range would require six quarterbacks going early in the draft, and that was all part of the scenarios they simulated. They did not expect the dearth of defensive players early in the draft. The run on offensive linemen hurt the Eagles' interest in that position—six linemen went in the top 20—but it also meant cornerbacks were pushed down the board. No cornerback had been selected when the Eagles were on the clock. It was the first time a cornerback did not go in the top 20 since 2019. Somehow, Mitchell was available for the Eagles at No. 22.

"It's a beautiful thing," Roseman said in the draft room, as captured by team footage. "Who knew being patient would pay off? Definitely not me!"

Roseman called Mitchell, who was in the green room in Detroit for the draft.

"What do you think of coming to Philly?" Roseman asked Mitchell.

"I'm fucking ready, man!" Mitchell answered.

"I know it. I love it!" Roseman said. "We can't wait to get you here, brother. Congratulations. We're going to pick you with this pick. You're an Eagle."

Nick Sirianni, whose former college teammate (and housemate) at Mount Union was Toledo coach Jason Candle, used his relationships with the Mid-American Conference program to conduct his own research on Mitchell. There can be a risk in going for a player who faces inferior competition, which was why any advanced intelligence is helpful.

"I've been hearing about you for about three years from all my guys over there," Sirianni told Mitchell. "They've been lobbying for that for a long time, so congratulations. We can't wait."

"We never thought we'd actually have a chance to get you at 22," Jeffrey Lurie said to Mitchell. "We're just thrilled."

Even before he came to Philadelphia, Mitchell had identified Darius Slay as a cornerback to emulate. The Eagles have had success in recent years with apprenticeships for early draft picks. Jalen Carter was Fletcher Cox's understudy at defensive tackle. Cam Jurgens soaked up knowledge from Jason Kelce on the offensive line. After Mitchell went through the car wash at the draft, he spoke again to the draft room via a video call. Roseman made clear the Eagles wanted Mitchell to learn from Slay.

"I want you to live next door to Slay! I want you to sleep next to Slay. That's your guy," Roseman said.

"I might move in with him, real talk," Mitchell said. "I'm finna text him now."

Going into the draft, the Eagles likely thought that coming out of the first round with Mitchell would have required them packaging an additional pick. Because Mitchell fell to them, Roseman had more draft picks with which to be aggressive.

"I think the most important thing was we didn't jump the board," Roseman said after the draft. "This guy was standing out on our board. He was the highest-ranked guy. It just seemed like a pretty easy pick."

If Roseman made history by the Eagles taking a cornerback in the first round for the first time since 2002, then he was prepared to recreate history on the next day. The Eagles took a cornerback in the first and second rounds 22 years earlier, and Lito Sheppard and Sheldon Brown were linked thereafter and developed into one of the NFL's top cornerback combinations. Even though the Eagles drafted Mitchell No. 22, he was not the only cornerback on their radar. Had Mitchell gone off the board when the Eagles expected, their first-round pick might have been DeJean.

"We never thought Quinyon Mitchell would be a possibility where we were drafting," Lurie said during the week of the Super Bowl. "And the irony with all that is we had another player have an equal grade, which has almost never happened in my history, where it's literally a tie. So when we chose Quinyon, we made a commitment to do everything possible to get Cooper. We never thought it would be possible."

This was not after-the-fact credit claiming. It appeared to be the case at the moment. The Eagles always simulate different scenarios in the days leading up to the draft to prepare them for decisions in real time. They start with the worst-case scenarios and work from there. In their simulations, there were times they came away with DeJean as the first-round pick—and were pleased with the outcome.

DeJean, a standout third-year player at Iowa, fractured his fibula in November 2023 at Iowa. This sidelined him for part of the pre-draft process, clouding his evaluation. There were also questions about what position he would play in the NFL—cornerback, slot cornerback, safety? But there was little question about his talent. The Eagles' draft grade said as much. They marked 24 prospects with grades for the first round of the draft. Draft boards are often spread horizontally and vertically—vertical by position, horizontal by grade. This allows teams to be mindful of tiers. When there is an outlier, the Eagles could pounce. DeJean was the outlier.

"We didn't have 32 first-round guys, so when you get that opportunity to get two first-round guys, especially picking where we were, we felt like it was an opportunity," Roseman said.

That compelled the Eagles to try to trade up in the second round. They had two second-round picks—Nos. 50 and 53—at their disposal. Roseman benefited from patience on Day 1. He knew patience would not work on Day 2. He spent Friday trying to move up in the draft. Ten minutes before the second night of the draft, Roseman updated the draft room on his progress.

"Washington is the first one where I have a chance at," Roseman said, as seen on the footage the team released. The Commanders had picks No. 36 and 40.

"They have two picks," Lurie responded. "How about Carolina?"

Roseman had negotiated a potential trade with the Panthers that would move the Eagles up 11 spots in the second round, although the Panthers were also in talks with other teams. Roseman engaged with the Los Angeles Chargers and the Tennessee Titans for early second-round selection ahead of the picks in play with Carolina and Washington, but neither conversation gained traction.

The Commanders emerged as the best trade partner. At 7:13 PM, the Eagles and their NFC East rival agreed to the framework of a deal that would move the Eagles up 10 spots in the second round *if* the player they wanted was available. That player was DeJean.

The negotiations were almost for naught. One spot before the Commanders, the Panthers traded their pick to the Rams. The air was let out of the draft room.

"That's it," Roseman said.

"That is it, unfortunately," Lurie said.

Then the Rams, who needed help in the secondary, traded up to select defensive lineman Braden Fiske.

There was an ovation in the draft room. DeJean was still available. (And he did not expect to go to the Rams, it was later learned. "I didn't talk to them much pre-draft," DeJean said. "But I'm glad they didn't [pick me].") It would not be the last time a close call with the Rams set up an opportunity with the Commanders.

Roseman connected with Commanders general manager Adam Peterson to consummate the trade.

"Fifty, 53, 161 for 40, 78, and 150," Roseman said on the phone. "Call it in. Appreciate it!"

Except there was a wrinkle that the Eagles omitted from their video that the Commanders' entertainment department released on their behind-the-scenes footage. Roseman tried to send an inferior fifth-round pick at the last minute.

"Just keep saying no, they're gonna do it," said Commanders owner Josh Harris, who also owns the NBA's Philadelphia 76ers (and who did not endear himself to Philadelphia fans by purchasing the Eagles' division rival).

"You're a pain in the ass," Peters joked with Roseman.

In the Eagles' draft room, there was applause and fist bumps. They landed their target.

In Washington's draft room, they surveyed their trade chart. They did well in the deal.

"Howie, he drives a hard bargain, but he's a good man," Peters told his draft room.

"Probably didn't win on any of those charts going on the internet, for sure," Roseman said hours after the deal, "but felt like it was the right thing to do for us and our team."

Roseman phoned DeJean, who watched the draft back in Iowa. This time, the call was real. DeJean had been pranked one day earlier when a caller identified himself as being from the Green Bay Packers.

"Cooper, it's Howie Roseman, brother. You're a fucking Eagle!" Roseman said. "Let's go! You sat way too long. We're excited to have you. Can't wait to get you here. Last night, [I] went to bed trying to get you."

"I didn't immediately sleep last night because this is what I wanted to have happen," Lurie told DeJean. "We were obsessed with getting you today."

"I'm going to Philly," DeJean told his party before crying in his mother's arms.

This was the result they craved. "I told you you'd be back!" security chief Dom DiSandro told DeJean when he visited the Eagles facility the next day.

Brandon Graham, who was in his native Detroit for the draft, announced the pick to a live audience while inserting a "Dallas sucks!" sentiment. Watching from the draft room on the second floor of the NovaCare Complex, Eagles officials chuckled.

Then they went back to work. Because of the trade, they no longer had two second-round picks. Roseman, who is as aggressive as any NFL general manager ever on draft weekend, made a series of trades in the third round to move back and acquire more picks. When they finally added a third player, it was one who few watching the draft had ever seen. The Eagles are always looking for high-upside pass rushers, and that was the plan with selecting an outside linebacker from Houston Christian who started his college career as a safety at Cornell: Jalyx Hunt. That's far from the SEC pedigree from previous drafts, but it's hard to find a 6'4", 252-pound frame with 34⅜-inch arms, a 4.64-second 40-yard dash, and a 95th-percentile 40-yard dash. The scouting staff had earmarked Hunt during the previous summer and Vic Fangio was drawn to him during the pre-draft process. The Eagles could have tried to wait until Day 3, but Hunt might not have lasted. In fact, when NFL Network analyst and former Eagles scout Daniel Jeremiah included Hunt among the best available players in the third round, Roseman wanted to text his former colleague to urge him to delete it. An Eagles scout posted a simple question in the draft room: "Where can this guy be in two years?"

"He's got freaky tools in his body. He's an explosive guy," Roseman said. "If you watch his best plays, he's doing things that are unique. He can bend. He can close. He can finish. He's long. He's an extremely smart kid obviously coming from Cornell.

"You can say, 'Well, that's the third round and you're a good team, why are you doing that?' Because these guys are hard to find. We believe in edge rushers, and we just felt like there was a tremendous buy-in from our staff about this player. Obviously from the coaching staff, from the front office, we thought this guy had tremendous tools. When you get guys like that, it's exciting to see what they can become."

Hunt has a colorful personality that also allowed him to quickly immerse himself in the locker room and the city. That was evident from his draft-night phone call. Players can often be at a loss for words, reserved, or nervous when speaking to the general manager on draft night. Not Hunt.

"What up, big pimpin'?" he said to Roseman.

"Hey coach, I need the playbook ASAP!" he said to Sirianni.

Before the final day of the draft, Roseman holds a meeting with the entire scouting staff and coaching staff. He has called it the "passion meeting"—a chance for the scouts to put their names on the players they're passionate about. He does not want to hear about what should have been after the fact.

"Draft starts today, we know that," Lurie said, as seen on the team footage.

"This is, as we talk about, one of our favorite meetings," Roseman told them. "When you talk about the first day, the second day, there's a lot of constituents on those picks. But everyone we take on Day 3 starts with you guys and the work that you do. I'm very appreciative of that, so if there's a guy you feel strongly about, speak up."

Two days before the draft, the Eagles held a meeting called the "Red Star meeting" when they identified the players who were designated with red stars—what they consider characteristics that embody the Eagles with performance and mentality. In that meeting, Michigan offensive lineman Trevor Keegan, Clemson linebacker Jeremiah Trotter Jr., and Clemson running back Will Shipley were among the players discussed. Each was on the board at the start of Day 3. So were Florida State wide receiver Johnny Wilson and Texas A&M wide receiver Ainias Smith. Roseman again made multiple trades and landed all five of those players, along with North Carolina State center Dylan McMahon. Overall, they drafted five "Red Star" players. The Eagles also added an extra third-round pick, fourth-round pick, and fifth-round pick in the 2025 draft in the process.

The most emotional call was the one the Eagles made to Trotter, whose father is a franchise Hall of Famer. Roseman insisted there was no sentimentality in the draft selection—"As much as you like those stories...we just started that story, but it's got to be skill set, and he has a skill set, and that's why we drafted him," Roseman said—but Lurie was brought to tears on his phone call with Trotter, whose mother, Tammi, had passed away from breast cancer in 2023.

"Jeremiah, how old were you when I first met you—two, three, four?" Lurie said, as captured by the team's cameras. "Congrats, man. Just really huge congrats. Congrats to your dad. And I loved your mother. Congrats. Can't wait to see you."

Entering draft weekend, Roseman would have been surprised if the Eagles went through the first two days without addressing the offensive line. But the team also has contingencies in place. On the day after the draft, the Eagles reached an agreement on a one-year deal with offensive lineman Mekhi Becton. A former No. 11 overall pick who was 6'7" and 363 pounds but had fallen out of favor with the New York Jets, Becton was in the market for a fresh start and was selective about where he would play. Only 25 years old, Becton saw the chance to learn under offensive line Jeff Stoutland as a way to help rebuild his career. For the Eagles, Becton was the latest attendee of "Stoutland University" and offered rare traits—"critical factors," as Stoutland called them—to provide depth on the offensive line. At the time of the signing, it might have been ambitious to expect him to develop into a starting right guard. That would come during the next few months. This was also part of the sliding doors scenario in the draft. Had the Eagles taken an offensive lineman in the first round, they likely would not have signed Becton. Mitchell's fall in the draft did not just address cornerback, but it also inadvertently addressed the Eagles' offensive line.

In an offseason of change, the Eagles added a deep draft class with rookies who were in position to contribute early in their careers. Roseman had said in February the Eagles needed to play younger players. Cornerback was one spot to look.

"History's yet to be written," Roseman said.

The Eagles intended to write it.

Time Out: Howie Roseman

Howie! Howie! Howie!

Howie Roseman walked to the microphone at his second Super Bowl parade to chants of his name. If you hear the first name in Philadelphia, you'll know who it is—like LeBron or Oprah. There is no need to add the Roseman as an identifier. The general manager has become an icon in the city, drawing lines that stretch through a shopping mall for autograph signings (yes, the general manager in Philadelphia has autograph signings) and a nickname for his offseason work: "Howie SZN."

Roseman's forehead was bloodied when he spoke at the parade after a beer can hit him in the head. Maybe there was some symbolism at work. Roseman has been beat up in this town before—metaphorically speaking—but he gets the final word.

And after building two Super Bowl champions with different quarterbacks, different coaches, and different cores, his record speaks for itself. The first Super Bowl might have been vindication for Roseman, who was once the youngest general manager in the NFL at age 34 and had his decision-making duties stripped in 2015, before regaining them and maintaining them since. The second Super Bowl could be seen as validation. Fans who might have once wanted Roseman packing might pack to see him in Canton, Ohio, one day.

"If I look at anything in the big picture that I'm really proud of, it's that we've been in the playoffs seven of the last eight years and been in three Super Bowls," Roseman said. "And I think that to me—that's the validation that we've been doing it well for a long period of time. You can take any one year and say, this was a terrible year, and that means you're a terrible GM, or you had a great year and you're a great GM.... But when you have consistency, I think that's really the validation that what you're doing has had some success."

Roseman, as most introductory biographies would tell you, did not play football in high school or college. He wanted to be a general manager from a young age in New Jersey and went to the University of Florida because they had the best football program at the time. He enrolled in law school to differentiate himself, sent handwritten notes to every NFL team, and latched onto the Eagles as an intern for former team president Joe Banner. The Eagles are the only organization for which he's ever worked. He ascended from intern to the most powerful general manager in the NFL, bypassing those thought to have more traditional backgrounds along the way. Earlier in his career, his bona fides were questioned. Now that he's been in this role since 2010, Roseman is viewed as a standard bearer in the NFL.

"I've known for years he's the best GM in football," Jeffrey Lurie said. "He's always thinking what could improve the team, 365 days of the year. He's not risk-averse. He's aggressive—that's what I want. We've collaborated for 20-something years. He's incredibly good. A future Hall of Fame GM."

Lurie's confidence in Roseman has been pointed to as a factor in Roseman's success because he is afforded job security that other general managers might lack. But Lurie would not have confidence in Roseman if he operated differently—if he did not view his move with an extended time horizon, if he was afraid to take a swing because the move could backfire. Plus, Roseman effectively lost his job once before when Chip Kelly banished him to the other side of the building—literally—while Lurie pushed the chips in on his head coach and kept Roseman under employ for insurance. (Roseman took the "gap year" to meet with different executives in other leagues to build his perspective on roster building.)

"I'm not concerned about my job security—not because I'm on scholarship—just because I think at the end of the day, if you start worrying about that and not about what's best for the team, it changes your focus," Roseman said. "I'm not going to stop taking risks, and at some point, if it gets me fired, I'd rather that than have any regrets. I don't want to leave this job with regrets. I feel like I did the first time I did that, and I feel like since I've been back for better or worse, I've done the things that I thought were the right things to do."

Spend 14 years building rosters, and there will be regrettable picks and signings. Roseman still hears about taking Jalen Reagor over Justin Jefferson. But there are enough hits—and an aggressive, forward-thinking approach—that the expectation is the postseason every year since Roseman returned to power.

"The three best years we probably had as a front office have led to three Super Bowls," Roseman said. "When you can see that…there's some sort of correlation between how well we do our job, and the opportunity it allows everyone in the organization to do their job well throughout it, it's inspiring."

When the clock ticked near zero in the fourth quarter of the Super Bowl, Roseman shared an emotional embrace with Saquon Barkley. Barkley thanked Roseman for believing in him. Roseman thanked Barkley for believing in *him*—Roseman told him they would put a Super Bowl roster together.

"I know it's about players making plays," A.J. Brown said, "but I think Howie Roseman is the reason why we're here."

Lurie mentioned "Hall of Fame," and it is an association that's increasingly being made with Roseman. He is one of five general managers who have won the Super Bowl with two different quarterbacks. The other four are already in the

Pro Football Hall of Fame: Bobby Beathard, Al Davis, Ozzie Newsome, and George Young. Roseman dismissed the talk early in 2025 by noting that he's 49 years old and is "in the middle of my career." He does not want to lose focus on trying to build his next Super Bowl team—"I love picking the team. I love being around the players. I get tremendous energy about doing this job. I love the draft. I love free agency. I love the all-star games. I love every single part of this," he said—and his wife wondered what he was doing when he watched Senior Bowl film three nights before departing for New Orleans for the Super Bowl.

When Roseman was asked what the 49-year-old Roseman would think of the 34-year-old Roseman, he said that his younger self would be more excited.

"When you become a GM, you say, 'Can I be a GM and win a world championship?' And then you win a world championship, you say, "Can I win a second world championship?'" Roseman said. "I think I have a lot of ways to continue to get better, and that excites me. I don't feel like I'm at my best yet."

Still, he admitted he allowed himself to enjoy the moment more the second time. He was not looking to settle scores. As he explained, the first one was a relief. By the second time, he realized how special it was and let loose dancing in the middle of the locker room. The blood on his forehead healed, and he could not wait to try to get bloodied again.

"Sometimes I try to wake up and remind myself, 'Hey we did these kinds of things,'" Roseman said. "But because we're in it and it's so competitive and everyone's gunning for you, if I get that mindset that I'm too much focused on the accomplishments as opposed to the opportunities, then that's when you start getting your ass kicked."

CHAPTER 6

OTAs/TRAINING CAMP

IT WAS NOT JUST THE COACHING STAFF and roster that represented noticeable changes for the Eagles during the offseason. Their practice schedule changed, too. And it included more practice.

Nick Sirianni's offseason program included seven organized team activities (OTAs) and three days of mandatory minicamp. It was the first time in Sirianni's four seasons that the Eagles held the mandatory minicamp. Overall, there were four more practice sessions during the offseason than the previous year. This was a pattern that continued into the season, when the Eagles eschewed "Victory Mondays"—giving the player the day off after games—and adjusted their practice regimen.

"Every year you go through it and you think to yourself, 'What can we do better this year?'" Sirianni said of the offseason changes. "And I think…one of the things that we did—there's many things—we wanted to get some extra practices in."

One reason for that was the new coaching staff. They were introducing new schemes on both sides of the ball. The offseason period was important for installation. It was also a look at how Sirianni would operate in his "new" role—he was still the head coach, of course, but the popular phrase during the summer was "CEO coach." Sirianni said the big difference was that it allowed him to take the "30,000-foot view" of the operation instead of focusing mostly on the offense. That was not easy for him to surrender, but it was what he felt was necessary for change to occur—just like what he did during his first season when he yielded play-calling duties to Shane Steichen.

"You have to do what you think is best for the team, right? And I think that's selflessness, right?" Sirianni said. "Regardless of how much I love something, it's what's best for the team and in this case, what was best for the team is that. I brought Kellen [Moore] in, I let him run with the offense. We share some thoughts, and he goes with it and so that's what I felt was best for the team. I felt like Shane calling plays in 2021 was best for the team, right? I felt that switching [defensive] coordinators last year was best for the team and I felt like there's a lot of decisions that I have to make, and I have to listen [to] a lot of different input.

"At the end of the day, I have to do what's best for the team and sometimes it is hard, right? And I won't lie to you: That was hard, but I knew in my gut what was best for the team, and I see a lot of positives from it. I'm able to see things from a 30,000-foot view. That doesn't mean I don't have opinions on what this should look like.... Me being able to step out of all rooms together and have a conversation with a player who needs me at that certain time to be his head coach is critical, and so you do what you need to do. You do what's best for the team because you love the team—not because you love your selfish reasons of what you want."

His obsession became the team's culture, which eroded in 2023. He spent time with former Villanova men's basketball coach Jay Wright and South Carolina women's basketball coach Dawn Staley. He conferred with Larry Kehres, his coach at Mount Union. The focus was not scheme, but on leadership—the essence of why he became a coach in the first place. Sirianni remembered the track athletes who his father coached coming to his family's home for dinner in Jamestown, New York, when Sirianni was a kid, and they always returned to their home even after graduation. There was something to this. It's the connection Sirianni preaches, one of his core values. Focus on the player as much as the plays. When the offense struggled at the end of 2023, Sirianni trapped himself in his office trying to find answers. He did not allocate the time he felt he should have to players who needed him. During the offseason, Sirianni would roam from one position group to another during practice. He sat in assistant coach Jeremiah Washburn's meetings with edge rushers. Sometimes, young players would straighten their backs when Sirianni came into the room. It quickly became the norm. Sirianni said there was not "a playbook" for how he could become a CEO coach, but he saw that he could spend time with his entire team during the offseason.

"I felt like a mistake that I made was [not having time for players] and that's not what's best for the team, and what's needed for the team is me to be the head coach not the offensive coordinator," Sirianni said. "For multiple reasons."

Of course, the relationship that mattered most was the one he had with his quarterback. And Jalen Hurts was not doing his part in helping quell curiosity about the coach-quarterback dynamics. On the last day of mandatory minicamp, Hurts was asked a rather innocuous question about what it says about Sirianni that he was open-minded about changes with the offense.

"That's a great question," Hurts said. "I don't know that I know the answer to it."

There was a follow-up question about what Hurts had seen from Sirianni during the spring.

"I think he's been great in the messages he's delivering to the team," Hurts said. "Trying to be very intentional in what he's saying. Yeah."

The comments were benign. But that was the point. They could have been a lay-up, and instead they created a month of controversy and curiosity about the coach-quarterback dynamic. When the team returned from the summer break, it was the biggest story to open training camp. Sirianni and Hurts were left putting out unnecessary fires—especially amid reports about a disconnect between the two during the 2023 season.

"Jalen and I's relationship is good," Sirianni said.

"I think we're in a great place," Hurts said.

Hurts implied the two were not always in sync the year prior. Losing did not help. There were efforts to reconnect for 2024.

"Any time you have any frustration, any time you have any adversity that you have to overcome, it's supposed to test you. It's a matter of being on the same page," Hurts said. "If we're on the same page, maybe we would have accomplished the things we would have. And we didn't. It's a learning experience. It's as simple as, if I made it happen, I can make it happen."

Hurts' focus during this period was learning a new offense—and his newfound responsibility of making calls at the line of scrimmage. Those had mostly been Jason Kelce's duties. "Over the years, it's something I wanted to do," Hurts said. He deferred to Kelce. During the summer, Hurts said the increased duties allowed him to build a relationship with Cam Jurgens, who was trusted with the burdensome task of replacing Kelce.

Moore became Hurts' eighth different play-caller in eight seasons. Other than former Eagles offensive coordinator Shane Steichen returning as the play-caller in 2022, Hurts needed to spend every offseason since he left high school adjusting to a different offensive coordinator. It has almost become an annual rite of spring. Even though Moore worked with Eagles assistant Kevin Patullo to blend his offense with what the Eagles had done during the previous three seasons, Hurts estimated that 95 percent of the offense was new to him. There might have been carryover concepts that required different reads from the quarterback, so it was not as if it was a radically different system. But there were staples that Moore had run in the past, such as pre-snap motion, that was expected to be integrated into the Eagles offense. And Hurts wanted to take some ownership of the offense, too, articulating to Moore the concepts that he thought fit him best.

"Everyone has a different opinion on that statement [of 95 percent being new], but everyone's not the quarterback. For me and my job and what I'm asked to do, I can see those differences from my vantage point," Hurts said early in training camp. "And I've spent a lot of time with that.... Just really trying to make it my own. That's been a process. It's been a really good process."

Hurts said when there is no continuity, it becomes "tough" to learn how to best communicate with the coordinator and find the "same page"—a phrase you will come to see Hurts utters often—and the spring and summer was his chance to do that with Moore. Hurts had an uneven performance in the spring before a stellar performance in the summer. As important as the on-field progress was his work behind the scenes with the new coaching staff.

Moore had been on the Eagles' radar long before they hired him as offensive coordinator. He was an undersized quarterback at Boise State who turned into a Heisman Trophy candidate and one of the most prolific players in the country. He was an undrafted rookie who squeezed out six NFL seasons with the Detroit Lions and Dallas Cowboys before immediately going into coaching. By age 32, he became an offensive coordinator. By 34, he was in Jeffrey Lurie's living room interviewing to become the head coach with the Eagles. Sirianni beat him out for the job in 2021, but the front office held Moore in high regard ever since.

"Nick really brought Kellen into the picture of who we should hire. It was his first choice," Lurie said. "[We] had the fortune of getting to know Kellen quite a bit in the head coach interviewing process. We all did and spent five, six, seven hours with Kellen. We were able to fully evaluate where we thought he was at that point. I rely on Nick's judgment on this. And on the other hand, I think internally he's one of the most dynamic offensive coordinators in football. We had to play against him every single year. And he's worked with outstanding young quarterbacks. And he's always had a very sort of difficult-to-defend multiple attack."

Similar to Sirianni (and Hurts), Moore is a coach's son who grew up around the game. Moore and Sirianni had sons that played young sports together in South Jersey. Sirianni made an external hire with Moore, but he was quick to take Moore's input in filling the coaching staff. Moore even brought in Doug Nussmeier as quarterbacks coach after working with him in Los Angeles and Dallas. Nobody would confuse Moore with an in-your-face style like Dan Campbell, but his NFL career resonated with players in the locker room and gave him credibility as a coordinator. They also saw his intelligence—players described him as a "wizard" and "genius" toward the end of the season—and he proved his ability to adapt as the season progressed.

"I think Kellen is very detailed in everything that he does. Very smart. Played at a very high level and has done this at a very high level, so he can relate to the players in that aspect," Sirianni said. "Puts the guys in good positions to succeed. Can lead men. Is a good leader of men. You know, as I get to sit here and watch him install the offense, you can see that and you can say, 'Man, he'd be great in front of the team.' He's in front of the offense right now but man, he'd be great in front of the entire team, inspiring the team, getting his message across to the team, coaching football to the team. Coaching the ins and outs of football. Just can't say enough good things about what he's done here as our coordinator, how much I think of him as a play-caller and offensive coordinator. I think of him very highly as a person."

The scheme aside, it helped to have as much talent as Moore had at his disposal. He was tasked with maximizing an offense brimming with high-end skill players, one of the best offensive lines in the NFL, and a quarterback who had already led his team to the Super Bowl. Saquon Barkley noticed it from his first moment in the huddle during OTAs. It was his "Welcome to Philly" moment.

"You see A.J. Brown, DeVonta Smith, Dallas Goedert, and Jalen Hurts," Barkley said. "That's not a bad group to be out there with. And that's not even including the offensive linemen."

The Eagles also experimented with Mekhi Becton at guard during the offseason program. He had never played it before, but offseason absences and curiosity from the coaching staff compelled the Eagles to try a player who had once been hellbent on remaining at left tackle to move inside. Becton did it willfully—and the Eagles liked what they saw enough to keep him there during training camp, when he won the job over second-year lineman Tyler Steen.

"When you have two tackles like Jordan [Mailata] and Lane [Johnson], that's where it came in," Becton said.

Offensive line coach Jeff Stoutland said there was no resistance from Becton to change position and seemed perplexed at the suggestion that there might be given Becton's previous insistence on playing offensive tackle. He relayed the conversation as a simple one:

"Mekhi, there's an opportunity here in the spring to maybe get a week playing some guard," Stoutland said to Becton.

"Let's go, let's do it!" Becton replied. "You're going to coach me on this, too, right?"

"Yeah, I got you!" Stoutland told him.

Reflecting on the conversation, Stoutland explained that Becton was "unbelievable" about the switch. And though guards are not typically known to be Becton's size, Stoutland has long had an affinity for bigger guards. He uses former Eagles All-Pro Brandon Brooks as his prototype at the position, and Becton's 35⅝-inch arms on a 6'7" frame and allows for length to create space against opposing linemen—especially in the running game.

The Eagles introduced six new starters on defense and multiple new contributors. But the headliner of the group might have been Fangio, who came with a time-tested defensive system that includes shell coverage in the secondary with two deep safeties in the middle of the field to limit explosive plays and force shorter throws, among other hallmarks. There have been variations, but the key is Fangio's mind more than his playbook. "We talked about his systems for years and all the people that he developed," Lurie said, "and now we have the guy that fathered the certain approach to defense." If Fangio was unpopular among some players by the end of his tenure in Miami, it did not carry over to Philadelphia—and there was no style change or tact added. On the first day of OTAs, Fangio delivered a message to his group: "It's not your fault you don't work hard," he said, according to ESPN. "It's not your fault, you just don't know how. But that's going to change now that I'm here."

After a few weeks working with Fangio, the reviews were universal.

"Old school," Jalen Carter said.

"No bullshit," Jordan Davis said. "It's straight ball."

The Georgia players on the defense said they were used to that style. Even if players were not used to it, they were expected to get used to it quickly. The defense needed to change. Fangio was the person to make the change, and he had 40 years of experience to show for it.

"It was exactly 40 years ago when I started my pro coaching career across the street at Veterans Stadium [with the Philadelphia

Stars], and I thought it would be cool to hopefully end it here," Fangio said about why he chose Philadelphia. "So 40 years later, here I am. A lot of things change, and a lot of things don't. One of the first things I've done, several times, I still go to the Philadium down on Packer [Avenue] for my meals, just like I did way back then. Phillies are still playing good.... Just to come back, my kids live two hours south of here. My mother, who's 97, lives two hours north of here. So a lot of family considerations. I was a big Philly fan growing up in all sports. It was a thrill for me to go to work every day at Veterans Stadium 40 years ago because I used to go to games there all the time. And now it's a good thrill to come back 40 years later and hopefully finish it out here."

Fangio showed clips of players with single-bar facemasks, tapping into yesteryear to show the way the game was once played. He wanted to practice more than the Eagles typically practiced. He wanted contributing players on the field in the preseason. So old school, yes. But out of touch, no. In fact, he suggested the players have not changed much during his 40 years in professional football.

"What's changed is the people around them," Fangio said. "People are not expecting as much out of players as we used to expect. These players will work and give you everything they've got within reason. It starts at an early age, when they're in high school, college, everybody [has that] less-is-more type of thing, preserve your energy. You guys hear in the NBA, load management. I've talked to coaches from other sports that I know, and it drives them crazy. The players are willing to work. Never had an issue with that. And they're still willing to work. But we as the so-called adults in the room need to push them."

That was the case with Fangio and his coaching staff. Clint Hurtt, the bodyguard-sized defensive line coach who came with Fangio, said from the spring that Carter and Davis needed to work on conditioning to play more snaps. There was an emphasis on physicality and endurance. Fangio went into coaching because he was inspired by his high school coach in Dunmore, Jack Henzes. He likes the practice. He likes the teaching. "Coaching in football has more of an impact on the game than baseball does and most other sports," Fangio said. "There's no other sport where you huddle up, or you're making a call every single time, so you have an important impact."

He said his scheme was flexible based on the players, although there were players that allowed his system to thrive. Linebackers are a good example. It is the position where Fangio has spent most of his time coaching and the position he admitted he best evaluates. He coached Mills and Patrick Willis, both of whom are in the Pro Football Hall of Fame. The Eagles had deemphasized the position in recent years and did not make a considerable investment in the position for 2024. Fangio said "it's hard to play good defense without good ILB play," and that the position has become tougher to play with teams using fullbacks less and third wide receivers more because it becomes more of a space game. Fangio's eyes and instincts told him Zack Baun could play inside linebacker. Baun turned into one of the best at the position in the NFL. "I can do a lot of different things, and if that's where Vic sees me…that's where I'll be," Baun said during the offseason. "No matter where they put me, I'm a football player."

In fact, the competition during the summer at linebacker was not with Baun's spot. He remained a first-teamer all the way through. It was between Devin White and Nakobe Dean. White came with more experience; Dean, a 2022 third-round pick, was supposed to be the top linebacker one year earlier, but injuries derailed his sophomore campaign and he had ground to make up. Early in camp, it seemed Dean was behind. The Eagles held a public practice on August 1—their only time the general audience could watch the team—and Dean was outpaced deep on a wheel route by Kenny

Gainwell. It did not reflect well on Dean that night, although he was dogged in improving against that particular play. Later in the season, he made a game-saving interception while defending a similar route against Jacksonville. That was an example of Dean's development, which was demonstrated throughout the summer. By the end of the summer, the Eagles determined that Dean was the superior option over White despite White's Pro Bowl resume. "From the start of training camp to the end, he won the job," Fangio said.

The other major competition for a starting spot came at cornerback opposite Darius Slay. Quinyon Mitchell was the first-round pick and seemed primed to win the job, although for the early portion of training camp, the Eagles played Mitchell as the nickel cornerback and used Isaiah Rodgers and Kelee Ringo on the outside. Part of this was because Cooper DeJean needed to recover from a hamstring injury suffered while training during the summer and Fangio looked to find his best combination. Once Mitchell was able to take meaningful work on the outside, he distanced himself as a starter. "He's been great since the day we got him," Fangio said. "He works really hard. He's focused in meetings, not just on the practice field. We have put a lot on his plate, like I've said. He hasn't backed down from it at all. He's going to be a good player in this league."

Fangio's preference was to play defensive starters in the preseason, although even their snaps were limited. That was not the case for the offense, who kept their starters on ice until the regular season. This was not the preseason of yore. It also made the joint practice with the New England Patriots leading up to the second preseason game even more important. Even though the Patriots were a rebuilding team, the strong showing from that day—especially from the defensive line—left the Eagles encouraged. "Only way you get better at playing football is to practice football and play in a game," Fangio said. "We got a good day of that. We were able to see new plays, new routes, go against different types of blockers, the way offensive linemen set, the way they protect. Those days are invaluable."

Before that practice, a Patriots fan in attendance yelled at Sirianni that Bill Belichick would take his job next year. It was ribbing from an opposing fan, of course, but it also spoke to the speculation about Sirianni's job security that summer. By the end of the practice, Sirianni could at least say the Eagles were the better team—and that their quarterback did not turn the ball over.

In fact, one of the takeaways of training camp was the lack of takeaways. Hurts did not throw a single interception until the final practice of training camp. He went 15 practices without Fangio's unit swiping one of his pass attempts, a streak that had been tracked by reporters observing practice. When Darius Slay finally stepped in front of Parris Campbell for the interception, he knew he broke the streak.

"I'm aware—the media been talking about it all camp," Slay said. "That's normal. I'm 12 years in. I've been intercepting quarterbacks for a long time—a long time. Some of the great ones. It was fun…. I baited him. I know how to bait Hurts. Made him feel like he was open, and then I'm like, 'Nah, he ain't.' Just a little bait, bait. Throw the rod out there and reel it in."

Slay said Hurts does not talk to him after interceptions, although Hurts said he gave a quick aside to the veteran cornerback.

"About time," Hurts said.

That was August 21. Training camp was finished—after the preseason finale, the Eagles were essentially in game preparation mode—but there was still work to do with the roster. The Eagles attempted to bolster their No. 3 wide receiver spot by acquiring Jahan Dotson from Washington. A 2022 first-round pick from Penn State, Dotson fell out of favor with the Commanders' new coaching staff and joined the Eagles in the

Lehigh Valley-to-Happy Valley-to-Philadelphia pipeline that produced Saquon Barkley. Dotson arrived with his new club in time to watch their preseason finale. Few expected regular contributors played. Interestingly, Nolan Smith was one of those in uniform taking snaps. It was interpreted as Smith's stock sliding. One would not have expected that by the final game of the season, Smith would be one of the team's most important players.

Before each season, Sirianni has a role meeting. In front of the whole team, he defines players' roles. It was an idea he learned from NBA coach Doc Rivers. Sirianni wants each player to have an understanding of his job description. That does not mean that roles will remain the same during the season. He leaves room for evolving roles. But he does not want ambiguity, and he wants players to star in their roles. If they're the gunner on special teams, he tells them to be the best gunner in the world.

"Everybody's role is different, but everybody's role is important," Sirianni said at the start of the meeting in 2024, as seen on footage released by the team. "That doesn't mean everyone's going to like their role. I understand it. But we all have to contribute and do the things within that role for this team to be successful."

He started with Jalen Hurts and looked his quarterback in the eye during the speech.

"Jalen, this is your football team," Sirianni said. "You have final say on what happens at the line of scrimmage because you're the one with the ball in your hand every single time."

Then, the offensive weapons. The Eagles offense is star-centric. It is not a group that tests its depth unless needed. That was clear in the meeting.

"A.J. [Brown], DeVonta [Smith], Dallas [Goedert], that pass game rolls through you guys," Sirianni said. "When we're running well on offense, when we're running well in the passing game, it's because it's going through you three guys."

The Eagles had used committee backfields at times in the past. That would not be the case in 2024—not after they made Barkley one of the highest-paid running backs in the NFL.

"In the run game, Saquon, you're our first-, second-, and third-down back," Sirianni said. "That's why you're here."

Sirianni repeated a phrase throughout the season: *Tough, physical, together*. It was obvious in the meeting where he expected that attitude to start.

"Offensive line, we want to be a tough team," Sirianni said. "That's a core value—physical toughness is set by you and the defensive line."

At linebacker, the starters were identified in the room even before the depth chart was crystallized to the public. Dean won the job next to Baun, who would be relied upon even before he became a popular name among Eagles fans.

"Linebackers—Zack, I want you to be the most physical linebacker on the field every time we step on the field," Sirianni said. "Nakobe, you're the vocal leader. Get everybody on the same page. People follow you. Lead!"

There were more call-outs in the meeting, but those clips showed why Sirianni considers the meeting important.

"We can't be elite unless we're all elite," Sirianni told them. "And it takes us all knowing our role, embracing our role, and being determined to grow in our role."

That was a version of a phrase Sirianni used often throughout the season: "You can't be great without the greatness of others." It became a team motto. Barkley described it as a favorite quote, even using it later in the season when he won Offensive Player of the Year. It came up during the Super Bowl parade. It had never been attributed to anyone before, so it could be considered a Sirianni original.

"It's real. You can't be great without the greatness of others," Barkley said. "I didn't really hear that quote until I got here, but we give all the praise to everybody—whether it's the quarterback, whether it's me, whether it's A.J. [Brown]—but you can't do it, we play the ultimate team game. The way you win championships, the way you do special stuff, is together.... I'd be a fool not to realize that. I play running back. You can hand me the ball, but I don't care how great you are, if I have five guys in the backfield, I'm not Superman. I can't make all those guys miss. That's the reality of it. Guys got to get open. Jalen has to make the throw. A.J. has to make the catch. That's how the game works. And I think we've lost that in today's world with how much we all get paid. You have stats of Tom Brady vs. Peyton Manning, like it's those two guys going against each other. That's not the truth. It's a team sport."

This was also the time of year when the Eagles elected captains. Sirianni thought they had too many captains in 2023 when there were nine. In 2024, the players voted on seven: Hurts, Brown, Johnson, Mailata, Brandon Graham, Slay, and Jake Elliott. Of those seven, Mailata was the only first-time captain—and it was an especially emotional moment for him. Mailata, who has described his life like a movie, became a seventh-round pick in 2018 without ever playing organized football. He was a 6'8", 346-pound rugby player from Bankstown, Australia, who tried learning how to play football. Stoutland cut short a golf trip with friends to scout Mailata in Florida and left floored by Mailata's potential. The Eagles needed a long runway, and they remained patient. It took three seasons for Mailata to play meaningful snaps in a game. By 2021, he became the franchise left tackle. By 2024, he signed a lucrative contract extension that made him one of the highest-paid offensive tackles in the NFL—and, in addition to being a valuable member of the offense, he was a respected figure in the locker room. "It means everything to me, man," Mailata said. "You look at how your teammates see you and I'm honored to be seen like that."

It was a productive offseason and training camp for the Eagles, yet there was still much unknown. Most of the starters did not play in the preseason. The offensive and defensive schemes remained a mystery. When Fangio was asked what he was most curious to learn in the season opener, he answered, "How good we are." There was promise. There were expectations. But the Eagles did not break camp looking like they would finish the year in conversation for one of the best teams in modern history. If the Eagles were to leap to greatness in 2024, it would need to start in Brazil.

Time Out: Nick Sirianni

Nick Sirianni approached Milton Williams during an otherwise unremarkable 2022 practice and asked the then-reserve defensive tackle to speak to him after the session. For a quiet, be-seen-and-not-heard player, this could be a worrisome invitation.

Turns out, it was Sirianni being human. The Eagles coach heard that Williams' mother had breast cancer. Sirianni's father, Fran, is a three-time cancer survivor. Sirianni shared his experience with Williams. He offered hope and understanding. The gesture resonated with Williams. Throughout the locker room, players share similar stories—anecdotes of handwritten notes, of compassion that goes beyond how the player can help on the football field, of empathy during trying moments.

"Find any possible way to connect with the guys," Sirianni said. "And sometimes when that thing in common is an adversity, that bond can be even stronger."

Sirianni discusses these concepts often. Connection is one of his five core principles and is fundamental to his coaching style, and his ability to maintain trust and belief in the locker room has been a key reason for his success as a coach. He was a punchline after a clumsy introductory news conference, and he was able to mock himself in his first meeting with the team. It became an example of confronting issues with players. There was a time in Sirianni's first year when he gave a speech about planting roots that drew public scrutiny. The Eagles responded with their biggest win of the season. "Roots on three!" Jason Kelce said when he broke down the team in the locker room. The Eagles rebounded to make the playoffs.

Sirianni likes to discuss how adversity can be formative—for both himself and his team—and to embrace it rather than run from it. In fact, one week after the Eagles won the Super Bowl, Sirianni was inducted into the Chautauqua Sports Hall of Fame in his native Jamestown, New York. He could not attend and offered his acceptance speech via video. His first message was about hard work. His second message was about embracing adversity.

"This life is filled with ups and downs," Sirianni said. "I can see now all the adversity that I went through in my life has been for a purpose and has made me and shaped me into the person I am today."

The adversity for Sirianni included losing in his first Super Bowl and the 2023 collapse, after which he ceded responsibility of the offense and rebuilt his coaching staff. Or during the Eagles' 2–2 start when his job status kept sports-talk radio stations busy and he barked back at a fan at the end of a Week 5 win over the Browns.

There was little to criticize when he hoisted the Lombardi Trophy. He has the best winning percentage among active NFL coaches, has made the postseason in all four seasons as head coach, and reached the Super Bowl twice.

"At the end of the day," Sirianni said, "we'll be scrutinized for wins and losses."

But Sirianni is often scrutinized for more. Sirianni once gave a spirited defense of Jalen Hurts in which he pushed back on rationalizations of Hurts' success because Hurts plays with high-level talent, noting that the same was true for Joe Montana or Tom Brady. He might have subconsciously been defending himself, because the credit for the Eagles' success often goes to the roster more than the coach.

Yet Bill Walsh had talent. So did Bill Belichick. It might just look different when Sirianni is on the sideline.

Sirianni's animated (and at times brash) style can also be off-putting to opposing fans—and, in challenging times, his own fans. He does not have Andy Reid's stoic sideline demeanor. He'll chew out officials. He'll high-step after touchdowns.

"I definitely think that I have no doubt that I am different than other head coaches. But I am myself," Sirianni said. "I think that's why I'm unique, too, right? I don't try to conform to anything other than who I actually am. I know that that's sometimes looked at—I can be judged that way. And that's OK. The only people I'm trying to lead…is this football team, and so I don't think you can get wrapped up in that."

Sirianni's sister-in-law is from one of his rival high schools. When they go to family gatherings, his extended family members tell him that their former classmates still do not like him. Sirianni wears it almost like a badge of honor. He is unapologetic about his competitiveness. His loyalty is to his team.

"I also know that every good coach I've ever talked to talks about bringing the energy every day and showing your love for the game and your love for the players and how important that is," Sirianni said, "and figure out the way that you do it, the way you go about it."

He's developed callouses along the way. After fans booed during a *preseason* game in Sirianni's first year, he asked his wife in the car if she could believe that reaction in the preseason.

"Well, what did you give them to cheer about?' Sirianni said.

"That was fair," Sirianni says now.

He's learned about pressure. And he's learned about looking inward.

"If you want your guys to get better, you have to get better yourself," Sirianni said. "And I think that I feel like I have in that aspect. None of us that are in these positions are going to live in a utopia where everybody likes you and everyone agrees with everything. That's leadership, though. No matter what form of leadership you're in, you have to do what you think is best, and you got to lead the way you know how, and you got to get better as you lead and not really concern yourself with outside noise or outside criticism that comes with the job."

"He grows all the time," Jeffrey Lurie said. "As connected as he gets as a human being and as genuine, he's also connected to himself and he goes, 'What was I thinking?' or something like that. It's a great quality. We all know people that can't be self-deprecating. They take themselves too seriously. Those are not the people that are the best leaders. I always find people that are self-deprecating have an ingredient of leadership that's special."

The operative word is leadership. So much attention gets paid to coaches who call plays or the schemes of a coach, but the fundamental part of coaching is leading the team. Sirianni's role as "CEO coach" was viewed almost as a demotion, yet of the seven teams that won at least 12 games in 2024, only two had coaches who called plays on offense and defense. Sirianni's job is to lead the entire team. Upon reflection following the 2023 collapse, his focus was on how he could improve the culture. During the summer, when he was considered a coach on the hot seat, Sirianni suggested his prevailing emotion was "joy." He was back working with the entire team, connecting with players, focusing on what he felt was needed for the team to win big. He wanted his team to feel that type of joy.

"We know that it's not easy and nobody in the NFL has it easy and everybody is cutthroat.... We are, too. We want to go win, and that's the main goal. You don't get to have the joy of being a coach if you don't win, right?" Sirianni said. "But I do, I'm finding that joy in it. And that makes it lighter on your burden.... I've really appreciated that this offseason, being able to lead and lead men and have the relationships."

It carried into the season. Vic Fangio, a no-nonsense coach for four decades in the NFL, credited Sirianni's week-to-week messaging as key for the team. Sirianni started each week showing highlights of the players celebrating and included players "talking and showing our culture." He wanted the culture to lead to the results—not the other way around.

"It's very much a college-team feel here," Kenny Pickett said. "Everyone cares about each other.... It's not like that everywhere."

That was why on the morning after the Super Bowl, Sirianni focused on adversity. He focused on connection. He mentioned the collapse. He did not run away from the problems.

He embraced them—just as he embraced the Lombardi Trophy.

"I think that when you embrace adversity, it does something to you," Sirianni said a few steps away from the trophy. "Each and every individual on that football team, the adversity does something to you. And it does something to you as a football team, as well. So our guys, I think that could be the biggest attribute."

CHAPTER 7

EAGLES VS. PACKERS IN BRAZIL

A SEASON THAT FINISHED on Bourbon Street started in Brazil. That was a long way to go for a home game, but the NFL mandates each club hosts international games at least once every eight years. It was the Eagles' turn. Given that they would need to play abroad, Jeffrey Lurie welcomed the chance to become the first team to host a game on South American soil. It would help spread the franchise's popularity to the fifth-most populated country in the world—and one with burgeoning football fanaticism. The game was played in São Paulo, which is the largest city in the Americas.

"It's probably the biggest area of growth for the [NFL]," Lurie said. "We are not a sport that has had tremendous global expansion, global growth. It's about to happen. The sport—its popularity in the United States is like a rocket ship. It's extraordinary in every single metric, every single way—whether it's women, minorities. The entire country has adopted the NFL in a way like we've never seen for any sport. Internationally, I think it's really important. I'm proud that we will be taking the first game to South America.... Proud to be an ambassador for the NFL. I think it's America's most incredibly potential export. Most things in America that are really popular become extremely popular globally. The NFL hasn't yet.

It's about to have a chance to be. To be a part of that, to represent our really good football team that's exciting to watch will be great for Brazil, South America, and for the public to see down there."

Of course, there were logistical hurdles for such a game. The Eagles sent team officials to São Paulo for an advance scouting trip in April, four months before the game. Almost every day thereafter, there were discussions about the trip. The Eagles played in London in 2018, and there is an understanding of best practices for countries that host an annual series. This was the first game in Brazil, so the Eagles were creating their own template. That freedom could be liberating or daunting, depending upon how effective the planning would be.

"I think the cool thing about this trip has been that without the precedent...we've been able to chart our own path on it," Eagles assistant general manager Jon Ferrari said before the trip. "That was true of the first European games, some of the first games in the UK, but we've been able to, 'Hey, we think we should do it this way.' And the Packers agreed, so they let us do it this way, as opposed to like, "Hey, it's like paint by numbers in Europe.'"

The time difference was negligible—one hour later, no different than if the Chicago Bears played in Philadelphia—but the 10-hour flight was atypical. The NFL assigned the game on Friday, a fact that Nick Sirianni played up in his messaging with the team: *How cool is it to play under Friday Night lights again?* Not that the message left all players enthused about the trip. The long flights combined with warnings of safety concerns in Sao Paulo left players such as Darius Slay critical of the trip. Other players were more diplomatic about it. "My personal perspective is I'm a kid from East Houston that used to play this game in the streets," Jalen Hurts said. "Any piece of grass I could find, I'd go throw the ball around and really just enjoy the game, have love for the game. Just having the opportunity to come this far in this journey and be where we are. My spirit is full of gratitude to be here. Really just reflecting on how the journey has come for me. It's a blessing to be able to play an international game and enjoy this moment with the people of Brazil."

The Eagles left on Wednesday morning and flew throughout the day to avoid an overnight flight. The instructions called for the players to mostly stay awake on the flight and remain hydrated, and then to go to sleep soon after they checked into their hotel near the Sao Paulo airport. The Eagles made sure players were not tucked into seat 32E. They flew American Airlines' biggest aircraft, which included more than 50 lie-flat seats.

"We worked with our doctors. We looked at this from a lot of different perspectives," Ferrari said. "This isn't like going to London or going to Germany or any of the other even further East countries that they're looking at playing. We get there with a one-hour difference, right? So we felt like the best thing to do was get there, get a good night's sleep…and then hit the ground running."

Hitting the ground running included a walkthrough in Corinthians Arena the day before the game. This was not a typical walkthrough. C.J. Gardner-Johnson played the drums. The defensive linemen danced in a conga line. Saquon Barkley was presented with a custom No. 10 Brazilian soccer jersey. Third-string quarterback Tanner McKee, who served a mission trip in Brazil and speaks Portuguese, was a popular interview. There was a spectacle surrounding the game, although the players were not there to sip on Caipirinhas. This was a business trip—a far way away for a business trip, but a business trip nonetheless. As it turned out, though, it was a business trip on a slippery field. It might have brought back memories of the Super Bowl turf 19 months earlier. Later in the season, when the Eagles played in the snow in the NFC divisional round, Josh Sweat said he would prefer the snow-covered field to the turf that seemed like an ice skating rink in Brazil.

Despite the turf, there was uncommon electricity for this game. It seemed like a big event. That was apparent from before the game, when the Brazilian crowd joined local singer Luisa Sonza for her rendition of Brazil's national anthem. The spectacle also prompted the Eagles to wear a uniform combination for the first time: black helmet, white jersey, black pants. There was no green. The speculated reason for this move was that green is loathed in Corinthians Arena because it's the color of the soccer club Corinthians' cross-town rival, Palmeiras. The stated reason was that the Eagles were wearing the color combination as a nod to their hosts—not because wearing green would be dangerous. The Packers wore green.

"We chose the color. We sort of looked, and again, Jeffrey [Lurie's] leadership on this: [Corinthians] is the host team, right? They're black and white. That's their color scheme," Ferrari said. "And all throughout that stadium is black and white there…. So we thought the uniform combination that we've never worn before was a unique nod to them, and it got us away from the green jersey."

It was a special uniform for a special opener—and for what the Eagles expected to be a special season.

"Have some fun today," Kellen Moore said to Hurts, as captured by the team's footage.

"Start of something special," Hurts responded.

You could not tell at the beginning of the Eagles' 34–29 season-opening victory. Barkley, the high-profile offseason acquisition, slipped on the turf on the offense's first play from scrimmage. Hurts, who went almost the entire training camp without throwing an interception, was picked off on the third play from scrimmage. It was a sloppy start for the Eagles, who fumbled the ball on their second possession. Two drives, two turnovers. This was Moore's new offense?

The good thing was that Vic Fangio's defense exhibited stingy situational defense, forcing the Packers to a punt and two field goals in the first quarter despite three drives into Eagles territory and two drives into the red zone. The Eagles trailed only 6–0 instead of 14–0 by the time Moore's offense found momentum. The first touchdown of the season came when Hurts connected with Barkley on an 18-yard pass down the left sideline in which Barkley caught the ball while spinning his body back toward the quarterback and tapping his toes in the black paint of the slippery turf. Welcome to Philly—or Sao Paulo.

"Hey, perfect ball, man," Sirianni told Hurts. "Championship mindset right there. Go take care of business. Shit goes wrong, keep coming back."

That was just the start for Barkley—in the debut, and during the season. He rushed for an 11-yard touchdown in the second quarter and a two-yard touchdown in the third quarter. How was this for an opener: 24 carries for 109 yards and two touchdowns along with two catches for 23 yards and a score. "Three piece? Welcome to the Birds, baby!" Dallas Goedert told him on the sideline. It called to mind Terrell Owens' debut with the Eagles two decades earlier. Owens also reached the end zone three times in his first game.

"I think a hat trick is never a bad thing," Barkley said after the game, playing to the Brazilian reporters. "There is so much that I can do, and that's the kind of player that I am."

"He played really well tonight," A.J. Brown said. "Should have had four touchdowns, and I told him."

"You almost did a poker," a Brazilian reporter told Barkley, referring to four goals.

"Today might have been my day scoring touchdowns, it was never no hate [from teammates], no none of that. It was like, 'Go ahead, go get four,'" Barkley said. "That's what you need with a team like this that has so many stars."

This was a star-driven game for the Eagles. Brown finished with five catches and 119 yards, including a 67-yard touchdown at the start of the second half. DeVonta Smith led the Eagles with seven receptions. That feeling Barkley had in the huddle during the first practice in the spring? It was apparent in the opener.

"I mean, on the scouting report I'm probably not even top three you've got to worry about," Barkley said. "Makes my job a lot easier."

This was also the introduction of Moore's offense, which included a player in motion on 65.8 percent of the offensive plays—a sharp increase from a league-low 35.1 percent of the plays in 2023. The problem? Hurts was inconsistent in the opener. There were three turnovers. The quarterback-center exchanges were problematic in Hurts' first game without Jason Kelce. It was not a bad performance—he went 20-of-34 for 278 yards, two passing touchdowns and two interceptions, plus 33 rushing yards—but it was not consistent with the clean football he had played during the summer. Then again, let the lessons come in a game with 34 points—and they could have scored into the 40s.

"As many balls that were on the ground, as many turnovers that I had, finding a way to win the game," Hurts said before the 10-hour flight home, "those are things that I'll learn from, we'll learn from, address those things."

The defense remained a work in progress, with too many missed tackles while the group was still adjusting to Fangio. But one thing that was clear to Howie Roseman watching from the box above the field: Zack Baun was turning into a difference-maker at linebacker. He led the Eagles with 15 tackles and two sacks, including the game-clinching takedown on the final play of the game. Baun totaled only two total sacks in his four-year career and never topped seven tackles in a single game. If he was a surprise starter in the spring, he looked like one of the best players on the team in the opener. By the end of the season, he would be considered one of the best players in the league.

When he packed his bag to fly home, it included a football. He was awarded the game ball from the television crew. This was someone who had never been a full-time starter in the NFL. Now, the Milwaukee-area native was starring on an international stage against his hometown team. And it was just the beginning.

"I don't know if I had anything to prove," Baun said from his locker after the game. "I think I was proving it to myself, like I know I can do this, and I know I'm a baller, I know I can go out there and do a lot of different things. And I proved it to myself. I'm not on Twitter, barely on Instagram, so I don't know what people are saying, but I proved a lot to myself."

Maybe it was fitting that Barkley and Baun were the stars in the season opener. They were signed the same day, and by the end of the season, they were both player of the year candidates on their respective side of the ball. But that night, all that was known was that the Eagles were 1–0—a tough, sloppy game, but a needed victory to start the season. It would have been a long, vexing flight home had they lost the opener. Instead, the players celebrated by listening to "Birds" by Migos over the speakers in the Corinthians Arena locker room. And the party in Brazil was nothing compared to the party that would later come near Bourbon Street.

"It's not easy to win football games in the NFL, especially when you travel 10 hours," Sirianni said. "I know the Packers traveled 10 hours, too. It was a good, good win against a good, good opponent..... What I'm really proud about is it was sloppy, it was definitely sloppy, and both sides, there were things on both sides that looked sloppy. But we were able as a football team to persevere through some dark moments, right? There was going to be some good stuff that happened in that game, some bad stuff that happened in that game, and our guys just kept coming back.... We're not going to be prisoners to—basically what I'm going to say is we're going to enjoy this journey and not let anybody tell us that wasn't good enough. We won the football game."

CHAPTER 8

EAGLES VS. FALCONS

EVEN THOUGH THE SEASON OPENER in São Paulo was technically a home game, there was no D Lot tailgate to visit, and the Broad Street line would not get to your seats. The true home opener was in Week 2, when the Atlanta Falcons visited on *Monday Night Football.*

It was an anticipated debut—especially after the way the Eagles won the season opener. This would be the first time Philadelphia fans could cheer for Saquon Barkley. (It was also Barkley's first opportunity for a victory at Lincoln Financial Field, where he was winless with the New York Giants and even at Penn State.) The festive crowd also had two additional reasons to cheer—Eagles icons Nick Foles, Jason Kelce, and Fletcher Cox would be in the house.

Foles, theretofore the only Super Bowl MVP in franchise history, officially retired with the Eagles and was honored against the Falcons. He had not been back in the stadium since he left the Eagles, never seeing the statue depicting him calling the "Philly Special" in the Super Bowl seven seasons earlier. (Foles nonetheless maintained a strong connection to Philadelphia, even starting a line of baseball caps with "Philly Philly" as a catchphrase. And he felt the love whenever he returned to Philadelphia—even from former teammates and coaches. Eagles offensive line coach Jeff Stoutland will randomly text Foles a photo from the Super Bowl in the hallway at the team facility at 5:30 AM with "I love you" as the accompanying message.)

In Jason Kelce's first year of retirement, his blossoming media career included a spot on ESPN's *Monday Night Football* pre- and post-game shows. Those are filmed on location, so it turned out the Eagles' first home game without Kelce included Kelce in the crowd. In his 13 seasons with the Eagles, Kelce never had the chance to experience the South Philadelphia tailgates. This night gave him a chance to make up for lost time. Kelce roamed the parking lots, tossing beers to admirers. He danced to "Million Dollar Baby" while dressed in a green jumpsuit embroidered with the Italian flag—attire that would earn the approval of Eagles security chief Dom DiSandro, a Philadelphia cult figure who even appeared in a *Monday Night Football* promotion with Kelce that evening. He caught up with former teammates, including Cox—the other high-profile retiree who returned to watch his former team in their first home game without him.

An anticipated prime time home opener during a season with Super Bowl aspirations that included franchise icons in attendance? That should lead to an atmosphere that would energize a team. Instead, the Eagles appeared lackluster. They played without A.J. Brown, who injured his hamstring in a practice the week before the game. The offense reached the end zone only once in the first half, in part because Nick Sirianni's decision to go for a fourth down at the 9-yard line resulted in an unfruitful attempt. The Eagles defense had limited Atlanta throughout most of the game, and a Jalen Hurts Tush Push (with an accompanying two-point conversion) gave the Eagles an 18–15 lead midway through the fourth quarter. When C.J. Gardner-Johnson stonewalled Falcons running back Bijan Robinson on a fourth-and-1 attempt at the

Falcons' 39-yard line on the ensuing drive, it seemed the Eagles made the game-clinching play they needed to preserve the victory. All they needed to do was wind down the clock (or score a touchdown) in the final six minutes.

The plan seemed to be working. Then came the sequence that will be the enduring memory of the game.

It was third-and–3 with 1:46 remaining in the game, and the Falcons used all of their timeouts. A first down would end the game. Even if the Eagles ran the ball and were stymied short of the first-down marker, the clock would tick below one minute. The Eagles had one of the best running backs in the NFL—and one they paid handsomely to bring to the team. Everyone in the stadium expected the ball to be handed Barkley.

That included the Falcons.

The coaching staff saw the way the Falcons tried to defend the run. They were "junking up the middle," as Sirianni explained, and the flats were open. So the Eagles had an idea. The decision was to go with a play-action pass. Hurts faked the handoff to Barkley, who leaked outside and was wide open along the right side.

The plan worked. The play did not.

Hurts sailed a pass to Barkley. The ball slipped out of Barkley's grasp.

"Dropped the ball. Let my team down today," said Barkley, who added: "I make that catch, game's over."

The clock stopped at 1:42. And on a fourth-and-3, Sirianni sent Jake Elliott on the field to attempt a field goal. That would give the Eagles a six-point lead, but it would still allow the Falcons to win the game with a touchdown. The decision sparked debate in Philadelphia. If the plan was to pass, why not try running the ball on third down and then attempt the pass on fourth down? Why not run the ball twice and let the clock tick? The Eagles took only seven seconds off the clock on third and fourth downs and gained three points out of it. The nature of being the head coach is your decisions are praised when they work and scrutinized when they do not work—and usually, the scrutiny is louder than the praise. This is even more amplified in Philadelphia, and especially when the coach is billed as a "CEO coach" whose game management decisions are a major part of his responsibilities.

"Any time it doesn't work out...that's why I'm sitting in this seat, the head coaching seat. I've got to be ready for the consequences of whether it works or doesn't work," Sirianni said after the game. "In that scenario, obviously didn't work. Obviously, I'm going to second-guess myself in those scenarios that it doesn't. Same thing on the third-and-3. It was an incomplete pass. Sometimes that works; sometimes it doesn't work. All I can do is go back and review those and say, 'Did I like what we did here? Would we do it again or would we change directions next time?' Everything is thought out of what we want to do, but that's this game of football. Sometimes it works and sometimes it doesn't. In those cases, it didn't, so I got to rethink it."

Sirianni did not back off the decisions. But the scrutiny only grew louder because of what the Falcons did in those final 99 seconds. Knowing they needed a touchdown, they could play more aggressively. Quarterback Kirk Cousins, a longtime nemesis of the Eagles, had his crowning moment during an ill-fated season in Atlanta. He completed four consecutive pass attempts to bring the Falcons inside the 10-yard line. The Eagles defense, which had contained Cousins throughout most of the game, appeared soft in coverage. After an incompletion, wide receiver Drake London beat Darius Slay to find wide open space along the right side of the end zone—the same spot, coincidentally, where the Falcons could not convert an end-of-game touchdown when playing the Eagles in the NFC divisional round seven seasons earlier—and the Falcons took a one-point lead with 34 seconds remaining.

"That's for sure my fault," Slay said. "I really just fucked that up. I got to be better at that. I should have made the play."

The Eagles still had enough time to try to reach field-goal range. On the second play from scrimmage, Hurts threw the ball deep from the 43-yard line and the pass was intercepted by safety Jessie Bates. The Eagles lost a game in which they had a 99.3 percent chance of winning after the two-minute warning, according to the NFL's Next Gen Stats win probability model. The loss left the fan base in disbelief. Sirianni's game management was under scrutiny. Barkley's drop became a (short-lived) punchline for Giants fans left rationalizing his departure. The defense, which had been stout for most of the game, resembled 2023 at the worst possible time.

"I could sit here and complain and be upset about it or I could be a professional athlete and go back to the drawing board and take the lick and move on and get better from it," said Barkley, who took responsibility. "I've made that play multiple times. I've missed that play before, too. I just got to be better. I let my team down. I got to man up to it, I got to own it, which I'm doing. I could promise those guys in this locker room that I'm going to be better from it.

"It definitely sucks. Any loss sucks. But the game comes down to a few plays and it hurts a little more when you're the one who's making a mistake on that play."

Sirianni responded by asking the team's analytics department to give him a model of every fourth-down decision in the final four minutes when a team is up one to five points to help him analyze and assess what he elected to do.

"The chart is one thing. You guys can punch in the numbers," Sirianni explained in the days after the game. "There are about 20 websites that you can punch in a number and say, 'What did it say here?' You all can see that. But I don't—I base it off of what my studies have been and my conviction in my studies."

Sirianni memorizes his game management sheet and said the decisions are often made during the week, something he learned from reading famed coach Bill Walsh's book. When Sirianni was growing up, one of the popular television shows was "Saved By the Bell" and the main character, Zack Morris, could call a timeout and everyone would freeze.

There's nothing like that that you can do," Sirianni said. "That's why you have to have it memorized, and that's why you have to put the work in, quite frankly, to do that."

But there's no spot on the record for losses in which the coach had conviction in his decision. It's a zero-sum game, and when the team loses, there's often one place to turn—especially when the coach is already under fire.

"Is every decision I make going to be successful? No. But every decision I make has been thought out," Sirianni said. "Is every decision I make going to be glorified? No, not even a little bit, because I know the other end of it. You're going to fail on some, and you're not going to be perfect on fourth-down decisions as far as converting them. But that is my job as the head coach, and that's just something that comes with—that's the price of doing business. It's the business that we chose. However you want to say it. I'll gladly take the criticisms because I know they're coming."

It came that week. It was up to the Eagles to respond.

CHAPTER 9

EAGLES AT SAINTS

THE LOCKER ROOM was never more energized after a regular season victory than it was in Week 3 in the Superdome—maybe it's something about New Orleans, after all?—when the Eagles rebounded from a heartbreaking loss to Atlanta with an improbable, come-from-behind 15–12 victory in the final two minutes. The Eagles had struggled on offense and were missing three of their best players against an opponent that was one of only four teams favored against the Eagles all season.

"To come in here and win like that is special," Nick Sirianni said. "We'll remember this."

C.J. Gardner-Johnson, who had been traded by the Saints to the Eagles two years earlier, was especially vocal. Well after the game had ended, the postgame speeches were recited, and other teammates had showered and changed, Gardner-Johnson reclined by his locker stall still in his full white jersey and green pants, with one leg crossed over the other ready to respond to anyone who had spent the previous five days ridiculing the Eagles and praising the (what seemed to be) high-powered New Orleans offense.

"Listen, we keep receipts," Gardner-Johnson said. "When we do our job, we can't be fucked with."

Here's what happened. The Saints, who had averaged 45.5 points per game during the first two weeks and scored on 16 of 20 drives, only scored on three of nine drives against Vic Fangio's defense. A run defense that was gashed in Week 2 limited New Orleans to 3.1 yards per carry. The Eagles challenged Jalen Carter, who had been benched at the start of Week 2 for being late to a meeting, to play the way the Eagles needed him to play—and how they knew he could. "'JC, why not today, bro? Make you a mark, dawg. I'm telling you, I played against you.... They are scared of you, bro. They are scared of you,'" Saquon Barkley said to Carter, as captured by team footage. He finished with two tackles for a loss, two pass deflections, and one quarterback hit. Carter was a force—and he let the opponents and fans know about it. In fact, defensive line coach Clint Hurtt, team security Dom DiSandro, and Sirianni needed to hold Carter back at the end of the game while he was...outspoken about the way he played.

"Completely dominant," Nick Sirianni said.

"He's a pretty special player for us—he changed that game for us," Jordan Mailata said.

The problem for most of the game was the offense's scoring. The Eagles scored only three points through the first three quarters. Jalen Hurts' turnover issues continued with an interception in the end zone. The fourth-down scrutiny from one week prior remained, and the Eagles missed a pair of attempts in field goal range. Five of their first six drives reached New Orleans' territory, but the points did not follow. They played the game without A.J. Brown. Lane Johnson and DeVonta Smith both exited the game with concussions. Right guard Mekhi Becton left with a finger injury. The offense missed four of 11 starters—including three of their top-of-the-league players. The first touchdown didn't come until Barkley's 65-yard run in the fourth quarter gave the

Eagles a 7–3 lead in one of the season's early signs of Barkley's brilliance, but the Saints built a 12–7 lead with two minutes to go.

The Eagles needed Hurts to play like a franchise quarterback without his top receivers and his best offensive lineman. Facing a third-and-16 at the Eagles' 35-yard line, it seemed the Eagles were on their way to a 1–2 start and more scrutiny on the coach and quarterback. Then the Eagles ran a perfectly designed mesh concept with Jahan Dotson setting a "legal pick" with the Saints in man-to-man defense. That freed Dallas Goedert across the middle, and Goedert sprinted down the sideline for a 61-yard gain that changed the game and the Eagles' season.

This was their version of Jake Elliott's 61-yard field goal from 2017.

"I caught the ball, looked, and said, 'Where is everybody?'" Goedert said. "I ran as best as I could as long as I could."

"Shallow routes like that are so critical that the ball is out in front of him, so that he can have a ball to run with," Sirianni said. "I don't want that to be overlooked. If Jalen puts it [behind Goedert] and he has to slow down at all, then the guy gets to come back and make that play. The pursuit comes. Jalen put it [in the perfect spot] and Dallas could just go."

"Make it happen," Hurts said of his approach on the drive.

Saquon Barkley punched in a four-yard run and converted a two-point conversion to give the Eagles a 15–12 lead with 61 seconds remaining, and Reed Blankenship's game-clinching interception on the Saints' second play from scrimmage sealed the Eagles' victory. That's when Carter needed to be held back, when Gardner-Johnson started gloating, and when it sunk in for Sirianni that the Eagles escaped against a hot team while missing their best players. That's part of why Sirianni was so emotional after the game—seemingly more than is typical for a regular-season game, although not the last time he would be that emotionally charged after a victory.

"We were a resilient team. There are resilient men on this team," Sirianni said. "Last week was rough. Last week was something that our guys had to pick themselves up off the mat. Every one of them did. You get better from your work, and you get better from your experiences. Sometimes losing, you grow a little bit more from that. Not that you want to do it, but you grow a little bit more from that. These guys got better this week. When we talk about handling adversity, we talk about having the right mindset. You can have the victim mindset, which I think the world wants you to have, which is essentially looking at the negatives, or you can have a purpose mindset. A purpose mindset is knowing that through bad things that happen that if you let it then you will get better. You control what you can control. We can't think about what anyone thinks about us. We can't control what anyone says about us. All we can control is our daily work and they did that. When you do that, then you're going to be an example for somebody else. Our guys did that. All of our guys showed how they handled adversity. Adversity happens in life all the time over and over and over again. You are going to have small losses in every single game whether it's an interception or a fumble or me going for it in a fourth-down scenario and we don't get it. You have to overcome those things, and I am so proud of those guys that they did that. It shows resilience. A team plays together. A team has each other's back. I can't tell you how many times Saquon and Jordan Mailata and Chauncey Gardner-Johnson came up to me and said, 'We got your back. We got your back, coach.'"

That was true; the players had Sirianni's back. And that would be amplified more than ever in the coming weeks.

Time Out: Jalen Hurts

The first time Jalen Hurts was congratulated for winning Super Bowl MVP, he responded: "Super Bowl *champ!*" The next day when he was presented with the Super Bowl MVP trophy, he asked for the Lombardi Trophy to be included. One month later when he visited Nike's headquarters in Beaverton, Oregon, the employees chanted, "M-V-P!"

"I hear the MVP chants," Hurts told them, as captured on social media, "but you've got to put 'champ' after that now."

This is how Hurts wants to be known—as a winner. It might not have come with the prolific statistics of some other quarterbacks. The path to this point included obstacles. But it's how he measures himself.

"I've been able to mentally transform to this place of trying to do whatever it takes to win," Hurts said. "These different moments sometimes require a different version of yourself. As a leader, that's something accepted and I submitted to. Because when it's all said and done for me, I won't measure myself off of any numbers or statistics or passing yards or touchdowns or anything like that. I measure it off of rings and championships. That's how I look at it."

How did Hurts learn to think this way?

"By losing," he said.

Like the previous Super Bowl.

In the fourth quarter of the Eagles' Super Bowl victory, NFL Films footage caught Hurts telling Grant Calcaterra that the Super Bowl loss two years earlier "changed my soul." In a team speech the night before the game revealed by team footage, Hurts told his teammates how the game "changed my life and changed my mentality." A central part of Hurts' story had been that he was benched in the national championship game in college. His response to the benching has been viewed as a credit to him—the Eagles were impressed with it during the pre-draft process; baseball Hall of Famer Derek Jeter remarked on it in an essay for *Time* when Hurts was voted one of the most influential people in the world—but Hurts had always imagined how he would play when he started again on the biggest stage. "I didn't get benched. I put on a good show," he said. Yet he also said that he left the game empty. Because it does not matter if you do not win. Hence the image on his phone wallpaper of the Chiefs-colored confetti. He said after that loss that "you win or you learn," and he learned.

"It was just a transformation for me," Hurts said. "For so long, I put tons of effort into improving and trying to be the best I can be. But going through everything I've gone through, you learn the value of winning. Winning is beating the opponent. Learning is improving yourself. Both are required to be great and to be remembered in history. The desire to win just burned like it's never burned before."

The burning analogy might have been intentional. (Of course, everything with Hurts seems intentional. Intentionality is one of his marked characteristics.) At the Maxwell Awards two years earlier—and one month after the Super Bowl loss—Hurts told the crowd during his acceptance speech, "I know I didn't walk through that fire just to smell that smoke." He needed to walk through the fire again. It burned inside of him.

That's also why Hurts' victory cigars have become synonymous with these big wins. It's Hurts letting himself loose—he lit the cigar after both of his NFC Championship Game victories and then in the Super Bowl locker room. And he does not just puff the cigar. It's almost demonstrative, as if part of it is for effect. Consider this anecdote from Jordan Mailata on 94.1 WIP about Hurts in the Super Bowl locker room: "I go up to J and I just look at him, shaking my head, and he was like, 'What?' And I go, 'How do you do it, man? The bigger the moment, the greater your performance.' And he looked back at me, he had a cigar in his mouth. He took a breath in, blew out the smoke, and he said, 'That's what the fuck I do,' and walked off."

A common debate among football analysts is whether wins are a quarterback statistic. You can think whatever you want. You will not sway Hurts.

"The standard is to win," Hurts said. "That's my standard."

The Eagles were a run-first offense in 2024. Hurts' production waned. There were games in which Hurts left more to be desired. He did not make the Pro Bowl. He won the Super Bowl.

"I don't play the game for stats. I don't play the game for numbers, any statistical approval from anyone else," Hurts said. "And I understand that everyone has a preconceived notion on how they want it to look, or how they expect it to look. I told you guys that winning, success, is defined by that particular individual, and it's all relative to the person. And what I define it as is winning. So the number one goal is always to come out here and win."

This also leads to popular debate among football analysts: whether a player can be "clutch." Jeffrey Lurie has been perhaps Hurts' biggest supporter in the organization—he advocated for the Eagles to select Hurts in 2020 even though Carson Wentz was considered the franchise quarterback, he wanted Hurts to have the chance to start in 2021, and he authorized a $255 million contract extension for Hurts after three seasons. ("Money is nice," Hurts said. "Championships are better.") From Lurie's perspective, the "clutch gene" is real—and Hurts possesses it. He showed it in both Super Bowls.

"Going into this game, it was the least of my worries," Lurie said after Hurts was named Super Bowl MVP. "I knew he would play great—just as he did two years ago. You worry about almost everything. That's one thing I didn't even worry about. I just said, 'We got the quarterback.' He's 26, incredibly clutch, he knows what correlates with winning. Sometimes it's through the ground game. Sometimes it's through the passing game. You gotta be able to do both. They did a really great job against Saquon [Barkley] today, but Jalen's a great thrower of the football, a quick decision-maker when he needs to be. And he has the clutch gene."

Sirianni also gushed about how clutch Hurts has been and how often he's been in the winner's circle. He praised Hurts for not caring how it looks. And he scoffed at the idea that Hurts is a byproduct of the talent around him.

"You don't win consistently unless you have great players around you," Sirianni said. "Sometimes I feel like it's a negative on him. It kind of blows your mind. He wins. He's a winner. I don't want anyone else leading us other than Jalen Hurts.... He doesn't care about anything other than winning, and I know that and that's selfless."

Hurts said that when you hoist a trophy, you think about the journey more than the result. He called his journey "unprecedented"—starting as a true freshman at Alabama, two championship games in his first two years as starter, getting benched in the national championship, losing out on the starting competition the following year, entering in relief to help win the SEC Championship Game, transferring to Oklahoma and becoming a Heisman Trophy candidate, getting drafted by the Eagles behind Carson Wentz, taking over as starter late in the season.... It's been well documented by now, and it's part of the Hurts persona. In Hurts' locker at the team facility, he keeps a Michael Jordan sign that reads: *Some people want it to happen, some wish it would happen, and others MAKE it happen.*

Super Bowl MVP—no, wait, Super Bowl champion. He made that happen.

"You put so much work in and you work 364 days of the year just for one moment," Hurts said. "And now the mission is accomplished."

During a Leap Year, the work is even 365 days, for one moment. It was worth it this year.

CHAPTER 10

EAGLES AT BUCCANEERS

THE NADIR OF THE NICK SIRIANNI era came in Tampa Bay on January 15, 2024, when the Eagles' humiliating loss in the post-season opener punctuated the end-of-season collapse that seemed to put Sirianni's job in peril.

On September 29, 2024, it was difficult to feel much better about the Eagles in Tampa Bay.

Maybe it's something about visiting Raymond James Stadium, as if the pirate ship behind the end zone shipwrecks the franchise. There were legitimate football reasons for the Eagles' 33–16 loss to the Buccaneers—A.J. Brown, DeVonta Smith, and Lane Johnson were all out of the lineup—but this was without compare the worst performance of the season from the Eagles. They were down 24–0 in the first half. The offense went three-and-out on its first three drives. They muffed a punt when Isaiah Rodgers pushed an opponent into returner Cooper DeJean when he was trying to field a kick in his debut in that role. They committed two penalties on third-and-long. Their tackling looked to be in preseason form. It was the Eagles' fourth consecutive game with a negative turnover differential, and they were as undisciplined as they were unsound.

"Our fundamentals weren't what we needed [them] to be," Sirianni said.

For as much talent as the Eagles proved to possess, it seemed theoretical in Week 4. They had spurts in which they looked like the best team in football. They had spurts in which they looked like they were on track for a midseason coaching change.

The new-look offense was nowhere to be found in the first quarters of the loss. By the end of the game against Tampa Bay, the Eagles were the only team in the NFL without a point in the first quarter of a game. They had one first down on their four opening drives of the season. That also meant they were playing from behind. By this point of the season, they had played behind more than all but three other NFL teams. Without the top receivers, the offense was a shell of itself. Saquon Barkley continued to star—he rushed for 84 yards on only 10 carries, including a 59-yard rush—but Jalen Hurts did not look like the Super Bowl MVP. He lost a costly fumble, continuing turnover woes that dated back to the previous season—from Week 15 of the 2023 season through Week 4 of the 2024 season, Hurts committed more turnovers than any quarterback in the NFL—and he threw for only 158 yards.

"I clearly didn't do enough," Hurts said. "You can point fingers wherever, but I own all of that. I touch the ball every play and I take pride in that."

It was a stark contrast to the quarterback on the other side of the field. Bucs quarterback Baker Mayfield threw for 347 yards and two touchdowns, and he was barely touched. He released the ball in 1.95 seconds—the quickest from any quarterback in the NFL at that point in the season. The secondary did not play press coverage, and the Bucs wide receivers took advantage of the space. The quick throws and unthreatening coverage created a bad combination, and when the ball was in the Bucs' hands, the Eagles missed 15 tackles—which, as Vic Fangio called it, was "way too many."

"A lot of times, we left our feet too early. Sometimes, we didn't wrap up well enough," Fangio said. "You emphasize it through film study, through practice drills, and better technique."

The scorching Tampa heat was a problem for the Eagles. Reed Blankenship left with a heat-related illness. Multiple players were treated for cramps. C.J. Gardner-Johnson could be seen in the corridor outside the locker room in an ice tub receiving intravenous fluids. The description from one player? "Hot as fuck."

So was the emotion of the fan base.

Hurts said the Eagles needed to find their offensive identity. And if Hurts was cryptic after the Tampa Bay loss at the end of the previous season, that did not compare to how he seemed after this defeat. The loss came before the bye week. An early bye might often be unwelcomed, but in the Eagles' case, they had traveled to São Paulo, New Orleans, and Tampa in a 25-day period. The itinerary had worn on them. The injuries mounted. The scrutiny bubbled. Hurts was asked if he and Sirianni would discuss the plan for the team during the bye week.

"We have our moments," Hurts said.

That was a challenging answer to interpret. And the Eagles, at that point at least, were challenging to interpret. They oozed with upside, yet they were hindered by inconsistencies.

In other words, they had their moments.

What was unknown at the time was that the bye week was the perfect moment for the team. It proved to be a turning point, and the group that returned two weeks later discovered an identity and became the best team in the NFL.

CHAPTER 11

THE BYE WEEK

THE EAGLES LEARNED THE DETAILS of their 2024 schedule on May 16. When Howie Roseman saw the 17-game slate, he was unenthused about a Week 5 bye.

Ugh, Roseman thought to himself. *We're going to have such a long run after that. It's terrible.*

Plus, early October is beautiful in Philadelphia. The bye week is often a chance for those who work in professional football to take a breath and get away.

"It's not even cold in Philly if you wanted to go away," Roseman said, remembering his thoughts at the time.

Turns out, the bye helped change the season.

"The bye week was a huge turning point for our football team," Roseman said.

The Eagles were at their low point entering the bye week. They looked like they did at the end of the previous season. Internally, there was not the same angst as there was among the fan base. The Eagles expected the first month of the season to be a period in which they were learning themselves.

"We had a lot of new pieces on and off the field, and when you're really going through training camp, September has really become almost an extension of the preseason, and figuring out what you have and who you are," Roseman said.

Figuring out who they were was a priority. There was much discussion going into the bye week about finding the identity of the team—especially on offense. Key leaders from the offensive line, including Lane Johnson, Landon Dickerson, and Jordan Mailata, met with Nick Sirianni to implore him to call more run plays. It was a Philadelphia talk-radio caller's dream suggestion. Lean on the linemen. Lean on Saquon Barkley.

"It was an offensive-led movement. We knew we had to make some adjustments," Johnson said. "Some of the leaders on the O-line had our fair share of talk in helping it. We want our offense to be the best version of itself, win some games, and score points in the fucking first quarter. That would be nice."

Mailata was impressed with Sirianni's willingness to listen. "Changed the trajectory of the team," he said. Kellen Moore said the coaching staff conducted a "deep dive on so many things"—the players were off, but the coaches were in until the weekend—and there was a focus on the offensive identity, reducing turnovers, and starting quickly in games. From a big-picture perspective, there was a better sense of how to maximize the roster.

Hurts bought into it, too. Remember the cryptic response before the bye about how he and Sirianni have their "moments"? Hurts, who can be sly in his callbacks, noted how productive the bye week had been when practice resumed one week later.

"This is probably one of the most efficient bye weeks I've been a part of, share those moments, talk through some things," Hurts said. "Some great moments."

It included extended conversations with Sirianni, both in person and over the phone. It was more of a work week than a bye week. The Eagles wanted to cut down on turnovers. They turned to a run-based offense.

"It was hard, because in the offseason, we're still trying to figure it out, right? You're still putting stuff together, and we've taken what we had done, what we wanted to do, and [trying] to put together how things want to look and what it's going to look like," said Kevin Patullo, the associate head coach and passing game coordinator in 2024 who worked closely with Moore in putting together the offense and who is also Siranni's right-hand man on the staff. "You could see it in training camp start to evolve where we wanted to go. The biggest piece was Saquon, right? So now there was a new dynamic with the run game. It wasn't always [shotgun] runs and stuff like that. And then from [there] I would say, just a couple games. I know the bye week, and we can talk about that. But it really was kind of like a moment where Kellen, myself, Nick, we all kind of were able to look at it. Because you don't know when you're in it, you're just going. So it was kind of a good moment for us to sit back and evaluate what actually we were doing and where we wanted to go. And we knew coming out of that bye, it's going to be baby steps to get going. It wasn't just going to be the Cleveland game, they're going to explode."

Sirianni tried playing down the significance of the bye week as an inflection point in the season. He called it "very business-as-usual" and there was "no panic." The idea of listening to his players was something he always welcomed. It was why there's a leadership council, and for all of the quibbles that fans might have about Sirianni, his connection with the locker room was undeniable going back to 2021.

Then again, it said something that the leaders of the team felt something needed to be said.

"It's not really like me standing up, 'Hey, look at me. I want to change.' It's more of a conversation," Johnson said. "If I get tired of seeing something or something needs to change, I voice my opinion. That's what I like about playing here. Nothing's ever going in one ear out the other or kind of seen as a nuisance. I just think mutually with some of the conversations that we had, that we could get better, we can start producing like the team that we're meant to be. So I want to continue to do that. I want to win. I don't want to lose, and I want everybody to succeed here.... I work my ass off. I don't say a whole lot. I will when I have to, but most of the time I'm working."

Hurts needed to be a part of it, too. The quarterback was open to the offense's in-season evolution. Hurts said he was "not directly" involved in the change in the offense, but he said "everyone has a voice," and there was an understanding that every season calls for a different way of approaching the offensive identity.

"It's about the vision and the mission—the vision of saying 'this is who we are' and going out there and being that," Hurts said. "When you're capable of doing so many different things, you're capable of trying to do it all and you can root yourself to something and be able to adjust when you need to adjust."

On defense the major adjustment was a lineup change. Cooper DeJean was inserted as the top slot cornerback, which had seemed inevitable but was delayed because of DeJean's offseason hamstring injury. Because DeJean did not start practicing until midway through the preseason, the Eagles slow-played his entry into meaningful defensive snaps. After four games, the decision to make a change was settled. DeJean provided size, physicality, and athleticism and was an immediate upgrade over veteran Avonte Maddox. Roseman thought that was one of the more underrated developments of the season.

After the Eagles played Atlanta on a Monday night, the team had two walkthroughs and four practices over the next two weeks and then came the bye week, with no practice. "So you've got to practice, and the only way to really get him ready in practice was to put him in there and get him the reps," Vic Fangio said. "Because if he's the backup, you can't get many reps when reps are at a premium, anyway. So it was just, in my opinion, time to put him in there, and let him get all the preparation, and see what he can do."

Fangio repeated later in the year that the Eagles did not practice during the bye week, so it was not as if there were any major improvements made on the field. However, there was an emphasis on tackling that was apparent when the Eagles returned to practice leading into Week 6. After the bye week, the improved tackling was noticeable and a major part of the sound defensive performance under Fangio. Jim Mora, a coaching mentor of Fangio's from their time together with the USFL's Philadelphia Stars (and the New Orleans Saints thereafter), told Fangio that if something is emphasized, a team ought to do it well. With the Eagles, that was tackling.

Jeffrey Lurie recalled a conversation he once had with Bill Belichick about how Belichick's best Patriots teams were still trying to figure out who they were during the first month of the season. Lurie's point was that a team is not trying to maximize success in September. "I optimistically felt our culture was right. Our talent level was right," Lurie said. "We weren't performing to the level we thought we could, and it was so early in the season. And so my feeling was, could we get from 2–2 to something special? And I thought we could."

It is hard to say if the changes would have been made in time or with the same effectiveness had the bye week been in Week 8 or Week 10 or Week 12. It was not conducive to Roseman's vacation plans, but it proved to be outstanding for his football teams. And the players did not mind the timing, either, because some of them—like Johnson—viewed it as the halfway point from when they reported to training camp. He said he's had bye weeks later in the season and "you still feel terrible" upon returning, so the rest is not always the purpose.

The Eagles needed a chance to reset. That's what the 2024 bye week permitted.

"It just worked out that that was a really good time for us to kind of all get together, have honest conversations, and move forward," Roseman said upon reflection in February. "There are a bunch of turning-point moments in the season.... When you get the opportunity to play in the Super Bowl, there's probably 20 moments you could look at that if they would have gone a different way, you're probably not sitting here. But certainly, in hindsight, the timing of that bye and getting together was a huge part."

The Eagles went 16–1 after the bye week with a point differential of plus-238 and a turnover margin of plus-29. That version of the Eagles is one of the most successful teams in NFL history.

"If I could bottle that," Lurie said, "I would just say that collectively, everybody knew. I think the roster that we had, and to be 2–2 with that roster at that time didn't feel right. So there's a self-evaluation on everyone's part, coaches, players, 'What is preventing us from being the team that we just expected to be?' And I think it was a combination of a lot of growth-minded players and coaches and everybody.... I think that was good timing, and it was put to great use. But a lot of it's resilience, toughness, connectivity, unselfishness on the players, humility, all that kind of stuff evolved to make that possible. Because you can say, 'We're not as good as we should have been, blah, blah, blah.' You've got to have all those qualities to max out. And so that's what happened. We maxed out."

Time Out: Lane Johnson

When Lane Johnson was named second-team All-Pro during the 2024 season behind Detroit Lions offensive tackle Penei Sewell, he posted a chart on the wall next to his locker room for anyone who passed by to see. It showed how Johnson measured against Sewell in multiple categories, including sacks allowed, hits allowed, hurries allowed, pressure allowed, win rate, "island rate" (the amount of times he blocks a defender one-on-one), the quarterbacks' time to throw, and team rushing yards. Johnson was superior in every category. This was not meant to diminish Sewell, one of the most promising offensive tackles in the NFL. It was a combination of Johnson's pride and competitiveness—plus a creative way for him to convey his message.

"I'm an extreme competitor," Johnson said, "so I take every little thing you can personally."

When Johnson was a Pro Bowl snub in the 2018 season, he drove to the team facility and slept there before meetings because he was so miffed. After there was an ESPN article that suggested his popularity was tied to a loud voice, he kept a low public profile as a response. Pass rushers still didn't get past him. In fact, Johnson once went three seasons without allowing a sack.

"Best offensive lineman in the world," Nick Sirianni said.

Johnson was once the young guy on the offensive line. He was the No. 4 overall pick in 2013, joining an established offensive line. He had played the position for only two seasons, having moved from quarterback to tight end to defensive line to offensive tackle in college. He was an athlete who added size and learned the position—when former Oklahoma coach Bob Stoops asked the strength coach if Johnson could get from 270 pounds to 300 to play tackle, the answer was he needed "a cheeseburger and a week"—and first-year offensive line coach Jeff Stoutland was convinced of Johnson's ability to develop into a high-end player after overseeing a private pre-draft workout. When Jeffrey Lurie asked Stoutland about the visit, Stoutland responded with, simply, "Wow"—a word he said he does not use often—and was left in awe of Johnson's quickness, flexibility, and length.

So it stood out that Johnson starred in his third Super Bowl in his 12th NFL season as the old man on the offensive line. Jason Peters wasn't here anymore. Neither was Jason Kelce. Johnson looked around the locker room in 2024 and reflected on the life cycle in the NFL.

"When you're about to turn 35, you tend to reflect a lot—especially in the league," Johnson said after the season. "It's been a fun ride. Coming into the NFL, you don't know what to expect. This fanbase has really embraced me through the good and the bad. The culture has been a certain way for a long time. I feel like I've been introduced to something special, and in some aspects, I was able to carry on the tradition. I think that's what I'm most proud of. With new teammates, show them what Philadelphia is about, what this team is about, and what it's like in this building."

Johnson has become one of the great players in Eagles history, a six-time Pro Bowler who has made first-team All-Pro or second-team All-Pro six times. And sometimes—as the sign by his locker demonstrated—that's not good enough. But the Eagles know.

"I can't tell you how many times I'm watching the tape and I'm like, 'Man, this guy is one of the best football players in the world. This guy is the best offensive lineman in the world,'" Sirianni said. "I can't tell you how many times I've watched the pass protection and said that to myself or paused it and said it to the offensive staff when we're watching tape together because he does things that are so, like, crazy athletic and for how big he is. One thing I like to say to guys on the offensive staff, too, is when you watch him move his feet in pass pro and get his hands on a guy, but just how he moves his feet, I go, 'If you guys think you can score one bucket on Lane Johnson in basketball, you are dead wrong. He would lock you up. I don't care how many points you averaged in high school.'"

And Johnson has shown no signs of slowing down. Early in Johnson's career, he missed time because of suspensions for performance-enhancing drugs. (He was critical of the NFLPA because he took what he was told was an approved supplement, but it included a banned ingredient.) He vowed to stay clean and was even better upon returning. Injuries affected him during the middle portion of his career, when ankle surgeries left him questioning whether he would keep playing. He also missed time in 2021 while dealing with symptoms of anxiety. Johnson has since become the best version of himself—on the field and off it. He wants to keep playing. There's some irony to this, considering Johnson was drafted to replace Jason Peters and Peters kept returning long beyond what anyone thought. Johnson signed a three-year contract extension after the Super Bowl, and he hoped to finish the contract. He's inspired by athletes who go past "perceived barriers" to maintain their ability, citing LeBron James and Olympians who push into their forties.

"I thought my body was going to start going downhill," Johnson said. "I feel really good. As long as I'm feeling good and can contribute, I think I'll continue to play. It's all I've ever known. I love my football family. I'm an only child, so my brothers are here."

Those bonds also keep him playing. Kelce once said the cafeteria kept him returning—he was referring to the relationships, not the food—and there's merit to it when you hear Johnson discuss his teammates. He's formed bonds with players of all ages. He's taken on a louder voice publicly with Kelce gone, but his leadership has also been valuable behind the scenes. It's not in speeches, but often in one-on-one conversations and knowing when to use his voice.

"Actions speak a lot louder than what words can," Johnson said.

Or signs by your locker, too.

CHAPTER 12

EAGLES VS. BROWNS

THE ENDURING MEMORY OF WEEK 6 against the Cleveland Browns will not be anything that happened during the 20–16 victory that started a 10-game winning streak—a game, by the way, in which the Eagles did not yet appear to be the juggernaut that would emerge later in the regular season and in the postseason run.

At this point of the year, there was still fan unrest. The skepticism from before the bye week had been boiling. And it was mostly directed at the coach. A win itself would not unburden Sirianni, but he was lighter for this game—literally. On the Friday before the game, Sirianni buzzed his hair. He tried explaining it was a summer cut. Regardless, it was a visual difference for a coach whose temperament had long been a subject of intrigue. Even during a game that the Eagles won, there was audible booing from the fan base. There were jeers for Sirianni—and even chants of "Fire Nick!" Harping on the displeasure of the vocal minority of a crowd of 69,879 would be like listening to talk radio on the way home from work and thinking that a few callers (or hosts, for that matter) are speaking for the entire fan base. But it's hard to dismiss what is heard, and Sirianni did not ignore it. When the Eagles had the victory in hand, he turned to the section behind the Eagles' bench and engaged in an animated shouting match.

Different fans in the area where the shouts were directed have different versions of what compelled the behavior—one version was that Sirianni was being playful with a fan who told him to the run ball, and Sirianni noted his compliance—but the viewing public at home did not know context. They saw Sirianni firing back at the fans, cupping his ear as if he could not hear them, and the visual was at least of an embattled coach unhinged against his own fan base.

"We thrive off the crowd when they cheer for us. That's all I'll say," Sirianni said after the game. "When our crowd cheers for us, we thrive off of them. You know, we hear them when they boo. We don't necessarily like it. I don't think that's productive for anybody. When they cheer for us and we've got them rolling, we love it."

One day later, Sirianni apologized for his behavior.

"I would say this about that: what I was really doing was trying to bring energy, enthusiasm yesterday. And I'm sorry and disappointed about how my energy was directed at the end of the game," Sirianni said "My energy should be all in on coaching, motivating, and celebrating with our guys. And so I've got to have better wisdom and discernment of when to use that energy, and that wasn't the time. We have the best fans in the world. There is no place like this."

Certainly, screaming at one's own fans is not the type of energy sought by Jeffrey Lurie, who had been honest during the offseason about Sirianni's demeanor. He likes the emotion but also wants it channeled positively. Lurie's sentiment in the spring of 2024 was mostly how the most animated version of Sirianni could compromise the Eagles with officials, and Sirianni had admitted to trying to be more controlled when dealing with officials. Of course, it is also difficult to envision how Sirianni acted after the Browns game when the conversation occurred seven months earlier. Lurie has become well-versed to the volume of disagreeable populist views in his 25 years, but there is an expectation of decorum.

It was unknown to the fans—and the viewing public—that one of the pleas from Sirianni's players before the game was *more* emotion from Sirianni. "We need you back, Nick. We need your energy. We need your focus," Sirianni relayed as the feedback from the players. Remember the conversation about joy from the summer? This is how Sirianni exhibits joy. The swagger is part of it. "If I want the guys to celebrate and be themselves after big plays, then I should probably do that myself, right?" Sirianni explained. "There are times for that and times that are not for that. I have to have wisdom and discernment of when to do that and when not to do that." Like him or dislike him, Sirianni believes in authenticity. And a staid version of Sirianni seems almost inauthentic.

"I told him to be him. I need him to be 2022 Nick," Brandon Graham said. "We want people to be themselves. Coach has been taking a bunch of heat, and I understand he got a lot of stuff on him. We got his back. Because Philly can be hard—I know all about it. How I do it every day, I say, 'They're going to eat the words that they say.' And Nick's probably saying it, too. And every chance that you get, you let them know. That's what I would do."

The Eagles did not look like the 2022 version of themselves against the Browns. (They did not look like how the 2024 version would eventually look, either.) But they showed signs of progress—especially compared with how they played before the bye. The offense remained hindered by slow starts, toiling through another scoreless first quarter. Their opening drives through five games combined to total 16 offensive plays and 12 yards. That was not what the Eagles spent the offseason trying to improve. Lane Johnson said the offense felt "constipated." The Browns did a better job bottling up Saquon Barkley than any other team throughout the regular season—he rushed for only 47 yards on 18 carries—but the return of A.J. Brown was critical for the Eagles. He finished with six catches for 116 yards and one touchdown, and the Eagles sealed the game with a 40-yard deep pass when Hurts and Brown made an adjustment based on Cleveland's coverage. (It was a bold call in that situation, although as DeVonta Smith explained by his locker a few minutes after the play, "If you don't have no nuts in this game, maybe you shouldn't be in it.") Smith, who returned from a concussion in this game, also caught a touchdown. When the Eagles were not sluggish, as Johnson might suggest with different word choice, they could be potent. But too often they appeared unable to flow, backing up Johnson's suggestion.

"I feel like two years ago, we were a very explosive team, a team that took a lot of shots down the field and made a lot of explosive plays," Smith said. "I think that the humbling thing about it is we know teams are not going to give us those looks to go out there and just chuck the ball down the field, so we have to be patient. I think that that's good for us. It teaches us patience, and I think we're getting very good at it."

It helps when the defense keeps the opponent from scoring, which Vic Fangio's unit did during a sterling response to the Tampa Bay debacle. The defense allowed only nine points, three third-down conversions, and one trip to the red zone. They totaled five sacks, their most of the season to that point. The tackling improved with additional emphasis. The change in personnel was inserting Cooper DeJean as the slot cornerback, an expected move with DeJean adjusting to the defense following the offseason injury that kept him out for part of training camp in the preseason. DeJean's athleticism, size, and physicality were an upgrade from Avonte Maddox, a respected veteran in the back end of his career. Cleveland's only touchdown of the game came on a blocked field goal that was returned for a touchdown, continuing an early season trend of special teams miscues that the Eagles would later rectify. But if you watched the Eagles play—albeit against a Cleveland offense that proved to be feeble with Deshaun Watson at quarterback—you would at least be encouraged by their progress.

It was a much-needed win, especially given the cacophony surrounding the team during the bye week. And some of the encouraging signs were taking root—especially the offense avoiding turnovers and the pressure from the Eagles defense. But you would not have encouraged Eagles fans to book their February travel to New Orleans based on the Cleveland game.

"Did we play like a championship-level team today? No, not by any means," Sirianni said.

That would come. And Sirianni would be cheering with his fans—and not against them—by the next time they played in Philadelphia.

CHAPTER 13

EAGLES AT GIANTS

SITTING ON THE VISITORS' BENCH at MetLife Stadium under the New York Giants' Ring of Honor that he once seemed primed to join, Saquon Barkley was only 14 yards from setting his single-game career high in rushing yards. The Eagles built a 28–3 lead. Nearly 10 minutes remained in the game. There was ample time for Barkley to make history on a day when he was the center of attention.

"You're 13 yards away from your career high," Nick Sirianni told Barkley, as caught by the team footage. "I would love for you to get that, but that's up to you."

Sirianni made it known that the decision was Barkley's to make, but the plan was to take the starters out of the game.

"You good," Barkley responded. "Let them eat."

"You sure?" Sirianni said.

"I promise," Barkley said.

"All right, listen to me: I want you to do it if you want to do it," Sirianni said.

"It's all good," Barkley said. "I'd rather see the young boys eat."

The exchange was first described by Sirianni after the Eagles' 28–3 win over the Giants, and it seemed too good to be true, like it was ripped off from the script of a sports movie. The on-sideline audio confirmed the conversation, and it instantly became synonymous with Barkley. Maybe *he* was too good to be true. The organic moment showed that he values his team over himself (it allowed the offensive linemen to get needed rest) and the type of teammate he was to the other running backs (the "young boys," in this case, were Kenny Gainwell and Will Shipley). Barkley finished his anticipated return to New York (or, better said, East Rutherford, New Jersey) with 17 carries for 176 yards and one touchdown. A career high and his first 200-yard game would have made for a rich story, but this was the NFC East rivalry version of the punch that Muhammad Ali never gave George Foreman.

"Numbers don't do it for me," Barkley said after the game. "Of course, I want to be great and I'm all about my legacy. But at the end of the day, I'm all about the team."

During the week leading up to the game, it seemed all about Barkley. In Philadelphia, there was leftover discussion about Sirianni's decorum at the end of the Cleveland game. Nationally, there was one story. This game had been anticipated from the moment the NFL schedules were released on May 15. It was known then that Barkley's return to his former stadium would come on October 20. It's not unusual in the modern NFL for high-profile players to face their former teams—A.J Brown's game against Tennessee two years earlier also carried considerable anticipation—but what made this unique was the nature of Barkley's exit. He was the franchise player with the Giants and insisted he wanted to be a "Giant for life." It was the Giants who seemed less enthused about keeping him—or least paying him market rate. Then he did not sign in Houston or Chicago but with a division rival 90 minutes down the New Jersey Turnpike. That's happened before, too. Just look at James Bradberry across the locker room. The additional fuel came when HBO's *Hard Knocks* documented the offseason, and the negotiations and subsequent departure played out like a soap opera. Giants general manager Joe Schoen's rationalization for allowing Barkley to leave was apparent for all to see. Giants owner John Mara's disdain for the possibility that he could lose Barkley to the Eagles became a meme.

"I don't have to prove anything to them," Barkley said in the days before the game. "I'm thankful for the opportunity [with the Eagles]. That's the people I got to prove it to—and to my teammates. And at the end of the day, the most important thing is winning. Whether I go and have 300 yards or I have 10 yards, as long as we win…I don't have that big of pride or ego that I have to go out and ball and looking at those guys over there, 'Look what you guys let go.' There's no hate over there."

Barkley was honest that he did not know what his emotions would be, and he tried insisting it would be like any other game. His teammates did not believe him. "I think he's handling it the best he can," Brown said during the week. "Of course, I think the beast will be let out on Sunday." Sirianni is a New Jersey resident who runs into Giants fans in his community. Those fans often make comments about the Eagles to Sirianni when he's out during the summer months. Sirianni has become accustomed to laughing them away. During the 2024 summer, Sirianni added a new retort: "We got your best player!"

As much as Barkley prepared himself for what awaited in front of the fans for whom he played for six NFL seasons, he was still startled when the team bus approached the stadium. Barkley is used to seeing smoke billowing from grills for tailgaters. Usually, it's burgers or sausages on the grates—not a No. 26 Giants jersey.

"That was crazy!" Barkley said. "I've seen my jersey get burned before on social media, but the timing of it, I'm locked in, I'm listening to my music, and I see the fans, and all I see is fans just pointing, and I look and I'm like, what are they pointing at? I see smoke and I'm just like, where's my jersey at? That was definitely different. I don't know if I've ever experienced anything like that in my life and hopefully, I don't experience that again. But in that moment, I was ready for third-and-1. I'll just say that."

In the tunnel before the game, he heard taunts of "traitor." There were even No. 26 Giants jerseys with TRAITOR where it once read BARKLEY. Once the game started, Barkley was booed whenever he touched the ball. "How long that last?" he asked on the sideline. "I'm going to shut them up." Barkley's extra juice for the game was apparent on the opening drive, when he lowered his shoulder into safety Dane Belton at the end of the run. "Don't worry, I'm coming!" he told the Giants defense.

At the beginning of the game, that was not necessarily the case. The Eagles' slow starts continued for another week. The defense was pummeling Giants quarterback Daniel Jones—Barkley's old friend—so the Eagles avoided a hole. And it seemed just a matter of time before Barkley would break through for a big run. "When I break a long one," Barkley told his former teammates, "don't come get me!" That was tested in the second quarter, when Barkley sprinted down the familiar field for a 55-yard gain. Three plays later, Barkley found the end zone. That touchdown was all the Eagles needed. "They can't fuck with us," running backs coach Jemal Singleton told Barkley on the sideline. He was right. The difference between the two teams showed why it was such a boon for Barkley to cross state lines in the first place.

As outstanding a player as Barkley is, he would tell you the best player on the team is Brown. One can entertain that debate. Supporting evidence for Brown would come on the following drive, when the Eagles kept their offense on the field for a fourth-and-3 from the Giants' 41-yard line. Typically, a high-percentage play would be a quick pass. When the Eagles see Brown in man-to-man coverage on the outside, though, they like that matchup. They closed the game against the Cleveland Browns with the play one week earlier, and they were unafraid to throw deep on this fourth down. Hurts placed a perfect pass downfield to Brown, who outmaneuvered the defender for the touchdown. This was not a check at the line of scrimmage like the play one week earlier; this was the actual play call from Kellen Moore. "It was just a great opportunity. One-on-one in that situation in the game," Hurts said. Watching from the sideline, Barkley marveled at the guts of the call—and the spectacle for Brown. "Goddamnit A.J. Brown is fucking good at football!" he said. He never played with someone like Brown in New York.

The Eagles did not need to pass much more for the rest of the game. They did not need to score much more, for that matter. The Giants totaled a mere 119 net yards—the fewest allowed to that point in the Sirianni era—and the eight sacks were the most of the Sirianni era, too. (Jalen Carter and Nakobe Dean both recorded a pair of sacks, with Josh Sweat, Nolan Smith, Bryce Huff, and Jalyx Hunt each joining the party.)

Hurts only needed to pass the ball 14 times, with the Eagles rushing for 269 yards. What was not known at the time was that the Eagles were in the process of becoming a ground-heavy offense. "It's what we needed to do this week to win," Sirianni said about the recipe. "You want to be able to win in multiple ways," Hurts added. When Barkley is the running back and he's finding yards behind perhaps the best offensive line, that becomes a productive way to win. Barkley added yards in bunches—he unleashed rushes of 51, 41, and 38 yards in the game—putting him in position to break his record in the fourth quarter. That was when he "let the young boys eat," as he said. The record against his former team would have been poetic, although the

Giants—and those fans burning the jersey—already knew what they were missing.

"I don't think it's this week. It's every week," Barkley said. "Howie [Roseman] took a chance on me. The whole organization took a chance on me, and I'm thankful for it. Stuff like that means a lot to me. That's why there's no hate in my heart for the Giants organization. They drafted me, brought me in, helped the kid live his dream. I'm the same way with the Eagles. I didn't know how things were going to shake up. I was able to find a home and a place I love. I'm excited to be here. It's not about proving anybody right, proving anybody wrong. It's about going out there and being myself."

That sounds nice, but even Barkley admitted he "talked a little more shit" than in most games. The on-field microphones backed this up, and Barkley was especially animated when Hurts pushed in for a touchdown and he let the Giants know they could not stop the Brotherly Shove (or Tush Push or push sneak; whatever you would like to call it), even when they knew it was coming. In these types of games, it is good to have the last laugh.

"He held it in all week," said Brown, who had a similar game against the Titans two years earlier. "If he said otherwise, he's lying."

"The first time was like an incidence. The second time it's coincidence. And the third time might be a precedent," Hurts said.

The dominant performance quieted some of the heat on Sirianni. It is hard to complain about the coach after a 25-point victory. This was the Eagles' first time winning by more than 20 points since the NFC Championship Game in January 2023. "Winning cures it all," said Brandon Graham, and the players knew well the type of conversation surrounding Sirianni since the Cleveland game.

"I think what I said to our team, just to let you know a little bit of that, is obviously you try not to listen, but you do media seven times a week. I think the thing that I learned this week, and I just told the team it happened a bunch of different ways. There was a bunch of different ways that I learned this week," Sirianni said. "It wasn't just through the situation that I was in. I'm not even going to go into all that, but it's like, you can be angry, but all anger does is cloud your ability.... If you really are holding onto anger, all anger does is cloud your ability to get better and control the things that you need to control. So what I said to the team is I put my head down. When you have criticism when you have those different things, you put your head down and you work even harder. The thing about that is the hard work that the team had and that we had throughout the week helped put us in position to be successful today. The other thing it does, to be quite honest with you, is it unites. You can look at it as a positive if you allow yourself to do that. I think that this game is constantly teaching us things, and that's what it taught me this week."

Here is something else that could be learned: Hand the ball to Barkley, and good things will happen.

The big rushing performance from the Giants-turned-Eagles star? It became common.

The dominant defense effort by Fangio's unit? This was not the last one.

The huge blowout of the opponent with the reserves playing in the fourth quarter, allowing those young boys to eat? It would happen again.

Barkley broke down the team and gave the postgame speech in a visitors' locker room that he did not know before that day.

"Let's keep building on this. There's so much more out there!" he told his teammates. "At the end of day, it's all about the team."

Time Out: Saquon Barkley

Go to Coplay, Pennsylvania, look catty-corner to the ground-floor apartment that was Saquon Barkley's childhood home and across the street from Samuel Owens Restaurant & Bar, and you'll see a rock with a plaque that features Barkley's likeness. Underneath the face is Barkley's accomplishments as of 2018, when he was the No. 2 overall pick by the New York Giants.

Saquon Barkley
Running back
Whitehall High School
2014 Mr. Pennsylvania Football
1st Team All-State
Penn State University
2-time Big Ten Offensive Player of the Year
2017 Consensus All-American
March 24, 2018
Coplay, Pennsylvania

They might now need a bigger rock.

Barkley signed with the Eagles, who could technically be considered his hometown team—Coplay is about 65 miles from Philadelphia and Barkley says he can do the ride in 45 minutes—and produced one of the most magical seasons in football history. He earned Offensive Player of the Year honors. He rushed for more yards when including the post-season than any player in NFL history.

Most importantly, he won a Super Bowl.

During training camp, rookie running back Will Shipley turned to Saquon Barkley and asked him what keeps him going. Barkley was a bona fide star in Year 6, one of the highest-paid running backs in the NFL, and he pushed through a practice in August.

"I just want to be great," Barkley told him. "I want to take it to the highest level I can take it."

That's what happened in 2024. There will be kids in Coplay who type Barkley's name in the YouTube search function the way he once did Barry Sanders and Walton Payton. Barkley watched Marshall Faulk, too—more the St. Louis Rams version than the Indianapolis Colts version. Faulk started his career with the Colts, but he is better known for his time with the Rams, with whom he won a Super Bowl and became an MVP candidate. Sound familiar?

Barkley himself made that comparison when the Eagles gave him a contract extension after only one season that made him the highest-paid running back in the NFL. They would only do that if he is, to use Barkley's qualification, "great."

"I want to be the best of all-time," Barkley said. "It's kind of weird because we don't really get to say who's the best of all-time.... Emmitt Smith has the most rushing yards all-time, but I don't think he's my one. He's up there.... I know Barry [Sanders] didn't rush for 18,000 yards, but to me, Barry [Sanders is] the best [of] the best with the ball in his hands. But all around—tough, pass pro, in between the tackles, outside—you have to go Walter [Payton]. Now, in the [present-day] game, how Christian [McCaffrey] is more like a Marshall Faulk...we're more in that mode. It's hard to say. When it's all said and done...hopefully you guys decide for that, and I'm mentioned in that category."

Barkley's physical characteristics portended greatness from a young age. The Whitehall High School wrestling coach received a call about a third-grader in the school district whose "calves are unbelievable." Yet he did not even start in high school until his junior year. Rutgers offered him a scholarship based on junior varsity film and a football camp during the summer. Before he made the leap to the best high school player in the state and the best running back in college football and the highest-drafted running back in over a decade, Barkley still needed to learn to *think* like one who was great.

"He always had a lot of questions," said Bob Hartman, the athletic director at Whitehall who grew close to Barkley and even allowed Barkley to babysit his kids. "He doesn't like it when I say it, but I think part of his questions were out of self-doubt, self-confidence. If there was a flaw he had outwardly—he would tell you inwardly he was always confident, I believe that to be true—but outwardly, he had doubt, confidence issues."

"I think the things that I was able to do in my career so far at a big stage…I hear the jokes now…like, 'Oh, that's just God-given,'" Barkley said, agreeing with Hartman. "I agree with all that, but I feel it's like a negative connotation behind that when people say that, because I feel like it takes away my work, too…. I have this conversation with my boys all the time—because a lot of them didn't get to see me until I was 18, 19 years old, and they see the stuff that I was able to do at Penn State, but it wasn't like I was the best high schooler, the strongest high schooler. I just had a shift in my mindset. And I always had the passion for football. I always had the love of football, but my mindset kind of switched when I wanted to quit. And my dad told me, 'Once you quit one thing in life, you're gonna be a quitter for the rest of your life.'"

That was how Barkley took the leap—and his many leaps. His highlight reels from high school and college include enough hurdling players that the backward leap Barkley made against Jacksonville in Week 9 that turned into the highlight of the year would not have been a surprise. He even drew penalty flags in high school for leaping defenders, which was forbidden by state football rules. It was not a rule that typically needed to be enforced. (If you ask those back in Barkley's hometown for Barkley's best hurdling story, it actually has to do with somebody else. In a 2015 track meet, Barkley won a gold medal for the 100 meters. Two hours later, a hurdler was disqualified for a timing malfunction in her race even though she won. Barkley offered his medal to her. "I just thought that was the right thing to do," he said.)

When the Eagles signed Barkley, they thought he could take another leap from the way he had played with the Giants. They figured his talent combined with their offensive line and offensive weapons would bring Barkley closer to those great running backs he studied—like Faulk, and, of course, like Eric Dickerson. Barkley was chasing Dickerson's single-season rushing record and needed 101 yards to surpass Dickerson in Week 18. Nick Sirianni elected to sit Barkley. There were people close to him who wanted Barkley to break the record. His response? "We didn't come here, I didn't sign here, to break Eric Dickerson's record," Barkley said. "We came here to win the Super Bowl."

That has something to do with greatness, too. Barkley appreciates the rock back in Coplay. He wants his children to see it. It makes his family proud. Want to know what matters more to Barkley? At Whitehall, Barkley's jersey is retired next to Matt Millen and Dan Koppen. They won six Super Bowls between them. Barkley felt like there was something missing when he saw his jersey. Maybe the description on the rock will be extended. But whenever a Whitehall football player passes his jersey, they'll need to know Barkley was also a Super Bowl champion.

Isn't that great?

"The coolest thing is—don't get me wrong, the rock is cool, too—but being on the wall with those guys," Barkley said. "Hopefully one day…there's a kid playing and I'll have that same impact on him."

CHAPTER 14

EAGLES AT BENGALS

THE EAGLES BUILT A ROSTER teeming with stars—they are not a team of the franchise quarterback and everyone else. During the 2024 season and the post-bye shift to a run-heavy attack, that was especially the case.

But there were also games when Jalen Hurts flexed his muscles and reminded anyone watching—or talking, for that matter—of his standing. One such week was a 37–17 victory over the Cincinnati Bengals in Week 8. On the other sideline was Bengals quarterback Joe Burrow, who earned his distinction as one of the NFL's elite players. He was the No. 1 overall pick during the year that Hurts was a second-round pick. Burrow was the Heisman Trophy winner during the year that Hurts finished second in the voting. Hurts' final game in college was a playoff loss to Burrow's Louisiana State team. Hurts tends to play down the quarterback versus quarterback narrative that generates before these types of matchups, and he offered a terse, chilly response when the topic was raised four days before the game—"We crossed paths in college," he said—but maybe there was something to the Eagles and last laughs this season. Because Hurts' best game (of the regular season) came on that Sunday in Cincinnati, when Hurts went 16-of-20 for 237 yards and one touchdown to go with 37 rushing yards and three rushing touchdowns. He did not commit a turnover for the third consecutive game. He had the best expected points added per drop back of his career and his second-best completion percentage. Burrow is a special player, no doubt. But Hurts outshined him that day.

"I have standards for myself, as well," Hurts said.

So do the Eagles. Even though the Bengals entered the game with a 3–4 record, they were viewed as a legitimate Super Bowl contender entering the season and the presence of Burrow (and top receiver Ja'Marr Chase) offered a formidable test for the Eagles defense. Vic Fangio's group held Burrow to his worst passer rating at that point of the season and his fewest yards per attempt since the season opener. After the Bengals scored a touchdown on their opening possession, they scored only 10 points in their next seven possessions and turned the ball over twice. That was the day the defense appeared worthy of being considered among the best in the NFL.

"Y'all thought they'd score that much on us?" Nakobe Dean answered when asked what his reaction would have been before the game if informed that the Eagles would limit the Bengals to 17 points.

Cooper DeJean, who was in his third week as the starting slot cornerback, made a critical fourth-down stop when he upended Chase short of the first down. It was the type of smart, physical, athletic play that the Eagles envisioned when they targeted DeJean on draft weekend, and it was notable that it came against one of the best receivers in the NFL. It would be one of a number of highlights the rookie made during the season.

Speaking of best receivers in the NFL, this was also a statement game for DeVonta Smith. He had only one catch for minus-2 yards against the Giants during the week when the Eagles barely passed, but it was the least productive game of his career. It can be difficult for the Eagles to ignite everybody each week, although Smith often sacrifices his individual statistics relative to what they might be elsewhere. In a group of Eagles stars, Smith should not take a back seat—the Heisman Trophy winner has 4,011 receiving yards through his first four seasons with the franchise and is one of only four NFL receivers with at least seven touchdowns in three consecutive years. The "Slim Reaper" is praised for his smooth route running and endless toughness, and his voice carries weight in the Eagles locker room. Against the Bengals, he finished with six catches for 85 yards and a 45-yard touchdown that he caught over his back shoulder. Smith, who wore the microphone during the game, was crazed after the touchdown. "I fucking do this shit!" he shouted with glee, as captured by team footage. It was a reminder that he is, in fact, one of the best receivers in the NFL.

Also, A.J. Brown finished with five catches for 84 yards and Saquon Barkley's ho-hum day included 108 rushing yards. The stars shined, led by the quarterback.

"It's tough, man," Smith said. "It's going to be tough for teams. We go out there and try to establish our identity to run the ball. We take our shots when we get one-on-ones and make the most of it. We know how the flow of the game will go. Some weeks that could change based on how teams play us, but I think it's a good thing we have a running back, two receivers, a quarterback, [and] an offense who could go out there and make something out of nothing."

In Sirianni's postgame speech, he highlighted the full-team effort required by spotlighted players who made unheralded contributions. On Smith's long touchdown catch, reserve tight end Jack Stoll held a block for eight seconds. When Darius Slay left the game with an injury, Isaiah Rodgers stepped in and even tipped a ball to C.J. Gardner-Johnson for an interception. The Eagles were plus-2 in turnover differential, a trend of remaining in the green in that department that would carry through the Super Bowl season. Sirianni pointed out that when the Eagles win the "double positive"—the turnover differential and big-play differential—they "win the fucking game!" He then told them that they would return to work the following day. The "Victory Mondays" were a relic of 2023. The Eagles came to work after wins.

"Success takes what it takes," Sirianni said.

The postgame music of choice was seemingly atypical for a 2024 locker room. Earth, Wind & Fire and Michael Jackson songs reverberated from the speakers, throwback music apparently requested by Howie Roseman. Sirianni sang "P.Y.T."

The Eagles were finding their groove.

CHAPTER 15

EAGLES VS. JAGUARS

IT MIGHT SEEM LIKE A LEAP to suggest that a 14-yard gain in the second quarter of a 28–23 victory over the Jacksonville Jaguars in Week 9 was the signature play of a Super Bowl season, but that would only be the case if you did not see Saquon Barkley's leap.

Excuse me—his *backward* leap, hurdling a defender in midfield after a spin move in one of the most jaw-dropping moments one could witness on a football field.

"It was the best play I've ever seen," Nick Sirianni said. "What I think is so cool is there are going to be kids all over the country and all over Philadelphia—I really think about that—trying to make that play and talking about that play and simulating that play as they play backyard football or Pee Wee Football.

"They aren't going to be able to make it because I think he's the only one in the world that can do that. I'm speechless. It was unbelievable, and the way the crowd—when I looked up, like, I thought I saw what I saw. As a coach you're looking at the line sometimes, looking at the secondary, looking at the defense. And so I thought I saw it, but when I looked up at the big screen and the crowd reacted to it, it was unbelievable."

The term *unbelievable* could be used loosely when describing football, but this type of play was hard to believe when it occurred.

With the Eagles nursing a 7–0 lead and the game turning from the first quarter to the second quarter, Jalen Hurts threw a pass to Barkley in the flat. Barkley made a quick cut and a spin move to find space, and had those been the only parts of the play, it would have made highlights from the game. At the end of the spin move, Barkley's back faced Jaguars cornerback Jarrian Jones. He considered another spin, but Barkley thought Jones was going low for a tackle at the knees. So his body took over, just like his golf swing three days earlier when he played at Merion Golf Club with President Barack Obama and Jeffrey Lurie (with Hurts joining them for the afternoon). There are some moves that could be explained, and there are times when the muscle and the mind meld at the right moment to make the gridiron a canvas. Barkley leaped in the air, crunching his knee toward his chest, and hurdled Jones—a 5'11" cornerback in position to tackle Barkley. It is one thing to hurdle someone. But to do it backward?

This was not just the crowd in disbelief. Even players were speechless, raising eyebrows or putting their hands over their mouths to cover gasps. They looked at each other, wondering what just happened.

"Did he just jump from behind?!" Nolan Smith asked Nakobe Dean.

"This shit's crazy!" Dean said upon watching the replay on the big screen, even narrating the play. "I ain't never seen no shit like that!"

"He's a special son of a bitch, just like you," Lane Johnson said to Hurts on the field.

All Hurts could do was laugh. The man who takes pride in a stone-faced, stoic demeanor actually smiled on the football field.

In the broadcast booth, Eagles Hall of Famer Mike Quick could not contain his disbelief on the live radio call. "What was that?" Quick said. "I've never seen that move, and I've been watching football all my life.... How do you jump over a guy—*backward*?"

This was Michael Jordan at the slam dunk contest in 1987 with the dunk that spawned the iconic silhouette logo. A silhouette of Barkley's jump has since been created. The image has been a memorable part of the Eagles' season.

"I feel like—not in a cocky way—I feel like God blessed me," Barkley said. "I feel like God gave me the ability to play this position, gave me some instincts, and sometimes you've got to let go and let God take over."

Talk about a leap of faith.

Lane Johnson was blocking during the play and could not fully grasp and appreciate it until he watched the replay on a cell phone in the locker room. "I saw the spin. How the fuck did he see him?" he asked. "That right there. I don't know, man. Some guys are blessed."

There might not be a better measure of brilliance than when peers are impressed.

"I ain't gonna lie: I felt like a fanboy for a quick second," Josh Sweat told reporters. "I had to snap back to who I was, but I was like, 'Yeah, that was crazy.'"

LeBron James gawked at the play on social media. Barkley was even wearing James' signature shoes. It was dubbed the highlight of the year by commentators. As it turned out, Barkley had made a similar play before—his sophomore year at Penn State against Iowa. "But it wasn't as cool," he admitted. This one did not fade from memory. Barkley kept seeing video of the play. It became a feature in Madden. And it remained associated with him, part of his iconic Eagles season.

The play happened on the night that LeSean McCoy was inducted into the franchise's Hall of Fame. McCoy was the last Eagles running back to make those types of gasp-worthy plays. He was the last running back that Howie Roseman had paid to be a franchise running back. Barkley finished the night with

159 rushing yards and a touchdown and 40 receiving yards and a touchdown, and the performance put him over 1,000 yards from scrimmage through eight games. Only McCoy and Brian Westbrook had achieved that feat in Eagles history, and the history book would continue to be rewritten by Barkley. But Barkley could not stop and revel in the play. He still had a game to finish. So did the Eagles. And that was not the only play of the Jaguars game that inspired awe.

In the fourth quarter, with the Eagles clinging to a 22–16 lead, the Eagles were backed up with a third-and-22. Hurts threw a deep pass to the back corner of the end zone. DeVonta Smith, with his defender trailing him, extended his right arm to fingertip the catch into his body. While falling down, he made sure his toes tapped just a few grass blades away from the white paint. The play was confirmed a touchdown. Had it not been for Barkley's leap, this would have been an enduring memory of the game.

"Oh my fucking God!" Dean said on the sideline.

Once again, a divine interpretation of a play.

This was also an example of what made the Hurts–Smith connection special. Hurts did not have a line of vision to Smith when he made the pass. But the two have played together for four seasons. When Smith visited Alabama, he eschewed parties on Alabama's downtown strip and caught passes from Hurts. This was, as Smith described, a matter of "trust."

"Sometimes, I think people don't take notice of how much of a lack of vision a quarterback [has] in certain situations," Hurts said. "And I didn't have great vision on him, but I think it's the number of times that we've repped those types of routes. [I] have a feel for him. I think it's a thing of connection as well. And then put it in a spot where he can only get it, and then him making a hell of a play."

Smith is not necessarily a physical marvel, but part of his brilliance is his body control. He is so precise in how he plays the positions and so graceful in his movement that a sliver of space in the back of the end zone is all Smith needs. A few days later, Smith called the catch the finest of his career.

"We do our catch circuit, and in our catch circuit is making those one-handed, over-the-shoulder catches," Smith said. "So that's part of it. And me just having a good feel of where I am on the field, when I'm close to the sideline, just letting my legs go dead and be ready to drag."

And that one-handed catch might not even have been the most memorable catch of the night. (Yes, it was an indelible evening in Philadelphia.)

Barkley caught a touchdown earlier in the game on a wheel route—a popular play for running backs in the passing game. "I wouldn't be surprised if they tried to hit us with that," Dean said. "We might get that in the red zone. Running back, stutter and go. I've been waiting for that all week."

He might have been waiting for it all season. During training camp, Dean was outpaced for a touchdown when Kenny Gainwell beat him on a similar play in a public practice at the stadium. It might have been Dean's worst session of the summer. Dean had been working to improve on the play ever since, even conferring with Hurts about how to adjust on the play. On the sideline against Jacksonville, Dean told safeties coach Joe Kasper that he expected the Jaguars to challenge him with the play. "Keep your eyes on his hips," Kasper told Dean. "Keep your feet active. Don't let your feet die."

With the Eagles holding a 28–23 lead, the Jaguars had one last chance for a go-ahead drive. The defense needed to make a stand. Jacksonville drove into the Eagles' red zone with under two minutes to go. The Eagles' chances of winning appeared in peril.

On first down from the 13-yard line, Jacksonville was ready to test Dean. They lined up a three-by-one formation, isolating Dean on a running back. Dean knew that was the matchup the Jaguars craved. Quarterback Trevor Lawrence tried sailing the pass over Dean's head. Dean remained tight in coverage, timed his jump, and grabbed the pass before it dropped into the running back's hands. It was the first interception of Dean's career. He called game. He was the hero.

"You're a fucking dawg!" Zack Baun told his fellow linebacker.

"You know what the fuck I do!" Dean screamed toward the crowd before jumping in the first row, a Philadelphia version of the "Lambeau Leap." (Another memorable leap during the Eagles' Leap Year!)

"I've seen it quite a bit. I remember it from college. Got beat on it a couple times in practice, too," Dean said. "So I was waiting on it. It was an opportune time."

Teammates knew how much time Dean spent preparing for that play—and knowing how to defend it.

"Hell of a fucking play," Hurts told Dean on the sideline. "I'm so proud of you, man."

"I've been waiting for that all game, man!" Dean told Baun.

"Perfect. Perfect," Baun said. "You were calling for that shit in the first quarter!"

In the locker room after the game, Sirianni gave the game ball to Dean. "Unbelievable catch," he told him with the whole team applauding.

Of course, that could not be the only game ball Sirianni rewarded. The win mattered. But the Barkley backward leap endured.

"Saquon," Sirianni said, holding a game ball up for his running back. "You made the best play I've ever seen in my life."

CHAPTER 16

EAGLES AT COWBOYS

WHEN YOU JOIN THE EAGLES, you learn quickly about the fan base's disdain for the Dallas Cowboys. The nature of playing in the NFC East is that all the teams are rivals, and the proximity to New York and Washington (or New Jersey and Maryland, respectively) allows for more of a geographic crossover in those rivalries. But there is history with the Cowboys, from their run of Lombardi Trophies in the '70s and '90s, to their once-recognized designation as America's Team, to the spectacle that is a Cowboys game.

In 2024, the Cowboys were expected to be the Eagles' top competition for first place in the NFC East. They were the defending division champions and had won 12 games in three consecutive seasons. Injuries (and a stagnant roster) sidetracked Dallas' plans of contending with Philadelphia, though, and by the time the Eagles visited the Cowboys in 2024 in Week 10, the Cowboys were 3–5 and on a three-game losing streak. They started a backup quarterback. The Eagles were seven-point favorites—the most they were favored for a game in Dallas since 2013. In fact, the bigger rival in the NFC East awaited four days after the Cowboys game when the Washington Commanders visited Philadelphia on a short week.

This meant the Eagles–Cowboys game did not necessarily shine with the same luster as other games in the rivalry, but no matter. It was still "Dallas Week."

"Let's go fuck the Cowboys, on three!" Landon Dickerson said in the pregame huddle, as captured by team footage. "One, two, three, fuck the Cowboys!"

"This shit don't gotta be close!" Darius Slay told his fellow defensive backs.

It was not close. The Eagles' 34–6 win over the Cowboys was their biggest margin of victory at that point of the season, the Eagles' fifth-consecutive victory after the bye and another sign that the team was on their way to, as Nick Sirianni told them the night before the game, do "special shit."

"We got really good coaches. We got really good players. We got a really good front office and GM. And with great talent, and with great coaches, and with great physicality, and with great detail, you can win a lot of games," Sirianni said in his Saturday night speech. "You can win 10, 11, 12 games. But you can't do shit special unless we come together as a football team. I ain't in it to win 10, 11, 12 games. We've done that here.... I want to do special shit! And you can't do special shit alone!"

They did it together against Dallas—winning in Jerry World (er, AT&T Stadium) for the first time since 2017, and you would not have been out of line to start thinking of what happened in 2017 with this Eagles team. The key was an Eagles defense that dominated an undermanned and overmatched Cowboys offense. It was the third time in five games that Vic Fangio's group held the opponent out of the end zone. The Cowboys totaled only 146 yards and 2.6 yards per play.

"You could say that, because we got five turnovers," Jalen Carter said when asked if this was the best the defense played all season.

"Our goal was to get more and more turnovers, and coaches told us that it's gonna happen.... To find out we have five, that's a big accomplishment. Try to get seven next week."

The key was Zack Baun, who continued his unexpected ascension into one of the NFL's best linebackers. He led the team with eight tackles, forced two fumbles, and recovered one. They were running out of turnover celebrations, even attempting handstands after one fumble recovery. Baun joked after the game that they would need to pile up the footballs they kept from turnovers because they were running out of places to put them. Baun might have been the ringleader, but the tackling was sound at all three levels. The defense that played against Tampa was unrecognizable compared to how the Eagles looked in November.

"We've emphasized it in practice, which is always good," Fangio said. "I had an old coach when I first started in pro ball who said, 'If you emphasize something, you've got a chance to get it.' That's what happened there. Plus we've played better overall, and the ball hasn't been in the open field as much."

The defense's performance bought time for the offense, which scored only once on their first five drives. In the second half, there was a stretch in which the Eagles scored two touchdowns and kicked two field goals on four consecutive drives. It was not their most consistent offensive performance—this was one of the only games after the bye when turnovers were an issue—but they were efficient. The Eagles scored on four of their five trips to the red zone. They were 3-of-3 on goal-to-go opportunities. Jalen Hurts completed 14-of-20 pass attempts for 202 yards and rushed for 56 yards.

"We haven't scratched the surface. That's the scary thing," Saquon Barkley said after the game. "We just beat Dallas by

[28] points...in Dallas, and we're still sitting here and saying we didn't do enough."

By the fourth quarter, the Eagles had built such a big lead that Sirianni pulled his starters. That was especially important with the Washington game waiting in four days. In the visitor's locker room, where the Eagles had too often dressed for a moribund flight back to Philadelphia in recent years, there was dancing. Jordan Davis was the headliner. But there was also the quick shift to what awaited in four days.

"It shifted right now," said Lane Johnson, who was in Year 12.

"It's right now," said Brandon Graham, who was in Year 15. "I mean, you got to enjoy the win. But when we get on that plane, we're gonna be talking about, 'Alright, y'all, it's a big one right here.' I ain't saying this [is] our season, but if we are first right now, we got to stay in first. So we got to make sure that we separate ourselves."

"I'll watch the tape on the plane, meet with the coaches briefly on the plane and dive through, process it, and as soon as we lay foot back in Philadelphia, it's over," Hurts said. "We're moving on. Usually, we put a 24-hour rule on it. I do. But it's obviously something that will be lessened. So we'll get going."

A win over Dallas would usually prompt a long celebration. Not this season, and not this week. The Eagles had their sights set on something bigger.

"We said we want to do special shit!" Sirianni said in his post-game speech. "And to do special shit, we've got to do it together! And that's complementary football. Continue to find ways that we grow close together.... Keep coming close together as a team. I feel it. I know you all feel it. It's a great win. But we're going to have to move on quick."

Time Out: Zack Baun

Before the season, Zack Baun told an Eagles assistant coach he set only one personal goal for 2024.

"I told him I wanted to have 100 tackles and make an impact on this team," Baun remembered.

In Baun's first four years in the NFL, he totaled only 88 tackles and was never a full-time starter. At the time, reaching 100 tackles might have seemed ambitious. He quickly realized he was selling himself short with that goal.

"Shoot, that was probably Week 6, Week 7," Baun said of when he broke it.

It was Week 11, but who's counting? Because by that point, it was clear that Baun had become one of the NFL's elite off-ball linebackers—a position he had not played full-time until joining the Eagles on a one-year, $3.5 million contract. By the end of the season, Baun was a Defensive Player of the Year candidate—not to mention first-team All-Pro and Pro Bowler.

Could you imagine that as a goal?

"That's really cool, really special," Baun said. "Honestly, not even on the spectrum of a goal of mine. I really just try to be the best player I can be and try to maximize my potential, my ability. So for that to be—not the end result—but an outcome of the work I put in, I'm really proud of myself."

Baun was considered an undersized edge rusher in the 2020 NFL Draft after a college career in which he was the first consensus All-American at linebacker in Wisconsin history. He amassed 12.5 sacks during his junior season, and rushing the quarterback is an appealing trait—although there aren't many top rushers who are 6'2" and 238 pounds.

After Baun's Pro Day, he went for a meal with then Houston Texans linebackers coach Bobby King at a Madison, Wisconsin, restaurant. It was his only meeting with a position coach before the COVID-19 shutdown. Baun did not want to hear it at the time, but King saw him as an off-ball linebacker. By coincidence, King now coaches inside linebackers in Philadelphia and was critical in Baun's transition to the position.

"We were having the same conversation," King said. "I was the inside 'backers coach, and it was like, 'Can this guy play inside 'backer?' He's got the body type we like, the speed, the length. Really hadn't seen much to say he could do that totally, but Wisconsin had had a track record of having those tweener OLBs that converted and became good players. There have been three or four of them, and so that kind of sparked the light in my head. Just getting to know him talking football over dinner—'What are you seeing here and there?'—and you're like, this guy's talking the right kind of lingo to possibly maybe make the transition to ILB or be a versatile guy."

"I remember him telling me he could see me at inside linebacker. He told me some of his guys—Zach Cunningham, in particular—he sees me like him," Baun said. "I'm like, 'In my mind, I'm going to be an edge,' this and that. Everything he preached to me that day, he's preaching to me to this day."

He went to the Saints, who could never quite find the right role for him. He was mostly a special teams contributor. When he hit free agency, it was a career crossroads. Baun said money was not the priority. It was fit and opportunity. The Eagles targeted him early in the process. They say how Andrew Van Ginkel thrived in Vic Fangio's defense as a hybrid edge rusher and envisioned Baun potentially playing a similar role. He could provide depth at edge rusher, as a floor, be a special teams contributor. Plus, giving Baun a chance to rush the quarterback was what Baun wanted to hear, so it was a good pitch by Roseman. The Eagles signed him on the first day of free agency.

Yet when Fangio watched him, he did not see an edge rusher. There were plays when Baun played on the edge in New Orleans but needed to follow a tight end in coverage, so Baun would need to back off the line or motion elsewhere on the field. Seeing the fluidity of Baun's movement, Fangio had an idea.

"After I watched it, I said, 'No, I think he's an inside linebacker,'" Fangio said.

Fangio has coached Hall of Famers and All-Pros, from Sam Mills to Patrick Willis to Roquan Smith. Of all the positions on defense, Fangio has the most confidence in his ability to evaluate linebackers. There is hubris to think you can see a few plays and make that type of assessment, but Fangio has "watched a lot of linebackers over the years" to "trust my own eyes, my own experiences."

"Was I going to bet my life savings on it?" Fangio said. "No, but I had a good feeling that he could do it."

Plus, the Eagles had not placed a premium on linebacker during Howie Roseman's time as general manager. It's seldom a position in which they invest major resources. The barrier for entry to the lineup as an off-ball linebacker was easier than edge rusher. During offseason workouts, Fangio assigned Baun to the new position. It was explained then as something to assess during a non-contact camp heavy on seven-on-seven work, so pass rushing is not as prominent. But Baun would ask Fangio when he would have the chance to rush the quarterback.

By training camp, it was clear that Baun wasn't just in line to earn a starting position—he was their top linebacker and might not come off the field. Devin White had a more distinguished football resume. Nakobe Dean had draft pedigree with the Eagles. Baun was the best of the group. To those outside of the building, that said something about the group. Baun and

Dean reminded themselves during the season of a preseason article that ranked the Eagles No. 30 at linebacker—and that was with White expected to be a key player. (He was released midseason.)

"We took it personal," Baun said. "That's the kind of people me and Nakobe are. Someone's going to say something—good or bad—we're like, 'OK, we'll show you.'"

By Week 1, there was little doubt this experiment would work. Baun finished with a team-high 15 tackles and two sacks, including on the final play of the game. He took every defensive snap. He was one of the best players on the field, and his flight home from Brazil included a game ball to show for it.

"You saw it from the first game," Roseman said. "He played phenomenal in that game."

There had been only six players since 1982 with 15 tackles and two sacks in a game. Two of them were Willis and Smith, Fangio protégés whom he considers his prototype at the position. Baun studied Smith while working on the transition to off-ball linebacker.

Even after Week 2, when Baun fell victim to cut blocks, he adjusted and did not have problems thereafter. By Week 10, he was named defensive player of the week. There were few linebackers in the NFL who compared to Baun, and inside the front office, the payroll projections started to change. This was a special player—and if they would keep him on a long-term contract, it would stretch them beyond what they usually pay at the position. Roseman deferred that conundrum to the offseason. Meanwhile, Baun's price kept rising each week. By the end of the season, he was the NFL's highest-rated linebacker by Pro Football Focus and was an invaluable chess piece for Fangio on the NFL's top-ranked defense.

"He just doesn't play ILB for us," King said. "We move him around to where we have him rushing at three technique, and that's the standard of Vic Fangio defense, and that's how we kind of saw him in Houston.... He is a freaking Swiss Army knife, and that's his tool set, and that's what we expected from him."

Baun had a takeaway in every postseason game, including an interception in the Super Bowl. It was a play he (and teammate Nicholas Morrow) predicted he would make on the sideline.

"Honestly, probably the last six games, I was going into games very confident and confident I'd make a play in each game," Baun said. "I couldn't tell you if it was a forced fumble or a pick. I was just playing so confident."

When Baun was named as a first-time Pro Bowler, Fangio congratulated him and asked, "Remember in the spring when you asked me, 'When am I getting outside linebacker reps?'"

There was a lesson in Baun's story about players misplaced on NFL rosters who simply needed a chance and the importance of fit and circumstance in a player's career. And Baun, who turned 28 toward the end of the 2024 season, might just be scratching the surface of what he can do with the Eagles at that position.

"If I can move off the ball and play inside linebacker and do what I do, and that was my starting point, I'm excited for this team and this defense moving forward," Baun said.

After the Super Bowl, the Eagles made him their priority in the offseason and signed him to a three-year, $51 million contract. Like the Eagles making Saquon Barkley the highest-paid running back at a position, the Baun contract was an example of the Eagles making an exception on positional value for an exceptional player. He remembered walking into the building one year earlier with Barkley when they signed on the first day of free agency. Barkley became the Offensive Player of the Year. Baun became a Defensive Player of the Year candidate.

"It's cool to see the evolution of the mindset Howie has and the way he values positions," Baun said.

In Baun's initial contract, there was an incentive for making the Pro Bowl. He laughed at the thought of it in a deal.

"Because I didn't think that was necessarily a goal of mine," Baun said. "Obviously, it's a goal of mine, but I didn't think I could reach it at this point of my career."

Sounds like it's time for Baun to make new goals.

CHAPTER 17

EAGLES VS. COMMANDERS

C.J. GARDNER-JOHNSON STRUTTED through the tunnel after the Eagles' 26–18 victory over the Washington Commanders with a message ostensibly for the assembled media, but presumably for the rest of the NFL

"Washington, respect y'all, but y'all know this shit runs through us!"

All games count the same in the standings, but they do not all carry the same significance. There was something more to this win—a nationally televised game on Thursday night between two division rivals that would determine the top of the NFC East standings. The Eagles entered the game 7–2. Washington entered the game 7–3. Had the Eagles lost, they would have lost control of the division. Instead, it was clear after the game what Gardner-Johnson colorfully confessed—the division ran through them. (And, as it turned out, much more than the division.)

The dialogue before the game indicated that they knew what this game meant. "We the big dawgs!" Nakobe Dean told the defense in a pregame huddle, as captured by team footage.

The defense received the message. It was another standout performance from Vic Fangio's group, and their reputation as one of the NFL's elite groups was established. Washington entered the game with the NFL's second-ranked offense in defense-adjusted value over average (DVOA) and 29 points per game. The Commanders scored 1.8 points per drive, punted five times, turned the ball over once, and missed a critical fourth-and-short. Rookie sensation quarterback Jayden Daniels could not surpass 200 passing yards or 20 rushing yards; Gardner-Johnson said the game plan was to force Daniels to "play quarterback" instead of becoming "very dangerous" with his athletic ability.

Jalen Carter dominated at the line of scrimmage while playing all 66 defensive snaps of the game. It was his first time playing every snap of an NFL game, a clear indication that conditioning was not an issue. The Commanders' interior offensive line had no answers for Carter, and he was especially disruptive on a critical stand in the fourth quarter when the Eagles nursed a 12-point lead for their first advantage of the game and Washington had driven the ball into the Eagles' territory. Carter stymied Washington on a second-and-1 and was disruptive again on third down. Facing a fourth-and-2, Commanders coach Dan Quinn eschewed a 44-yard field goal that would have given the Commanders the lead and instead tried to gain those elusive yards. It seemed a reasonable decision if not for the way Carter disrupted the game. Sure enough, Carter busted the play on fourth down by pushing the interior linemen back into Daniels—penetrating with such force that Carter might have collected the snap himself. He made Daniels stumble, and that left the play out of sync and gave Zack Baun and Reed Blankenship enough time to chase Daniels down when he tried rushing to the edge. The box score would indicate Baun and Blankenship play. Anyone watching the game saw that Carter was the difference-maker. You could not judge his impact by statistics.

"When Jayden tried to keep the ball, [Carter] could see the O-Line lean and different things were going on when he could take a chance to go and shoot a gap," Eagles defensive line coach Clint Hurtt explained, "and just have that kind of disruption that can cause issues with quarterback-center exchanges. Because think for a center, I gotta snap the ball and I gotta block this guy? You can cause issues like that. And just being aware of what's getting ready to happen and what people are trying to do, it could be a formation that maybe he didn't see over the course of the game that they want to play out of, and he sees it, and he can attack him in a way that can be disrupted to it."

That fourth-down stop helped the Eagles keep momentum that had not swung in their direction for much of the evening.

"That was huge," Sirianni said. "That's a turnover in our eyes.... We're an athletic defense that flies around and hits. As that play got strung out, you could see the effort to the football and also you could see the athletic ability to the football to make that play. Jayden Daniels is obviously a really good athlete, really good football player, and it was good to be able to string that thing out and get the stop. It was huge."

Another standout on defense whose influence on the game could not be measured by his own statistics was Quinyon Mitchell. The rookie cornerback had been so steady throughout the season. Few matchups appeared to be more challenging than Washington wide receiver Terry McLaurin, a savvy veteran whose consistent production shows up even against accomplished cornerbacks. McLaurin recorded only one catch against the Eagles that night—and that catch did not come with Mitchell in coverage. On the 20 routes when Mitchell covered McLaurin, the receiver was not even targeted. Future Hall of Fame cornerback Richard Sherman attended the game and watched Mitchell up close. He spoke to Mitchell after the game and told the rookie cornerback, who theretofore had no interceptions, that he needed to "catch the ball"—fair advice, but not possible on a night when Washington did not even test him.

"At the beginning of the season and the preseason, a lot of people were underestimating this defense and the guys we have," Baun said. "We set out to change the narrative."

The defense needed to keep the Eagles in the game, because the offense struggled to score for most of the night. The Eagles totaled three points in the first half. Jake Elliott missed two field goals, which contributed to the lack of scoring, but they also punted three times. The Eagles were 0-for-2 in the red zone. Jalen Hurts was briefly monitored for a concussion and passed the examination—that was not the case during the rematch against Washington—and he misfired on completions the Eagles needed.

Sirianni's message to the team at halftime? "Hey, this is going to be a grimy, gritty game. Just keep going. We know we are grimy and gritty," he told his players. "It's a street fight and it's not about who is tougher, but about who is tougher longer."

With the passing game inconsistent, the Eagles could turn to Barkley. When the star running back prepared to leave the locker room after the game, Stevie Wonder's "Don't You Worry 'Bout a Thing" offered the soundtrack—as if the song was a message directed to Eagles fans. Barkley rushed for 146 yards and two touchdowns—both in the fourth quarter to help extend the Eagles' lead. He reached 1,000 rushing yards in this game, joining Miles Sanders and D'Andre Swift to become the third different running back in three years to reach that mark. But this came before Thanksgiving and on his sixth 100-yard rushing game of the season—more than Sanders and Swift *combined*. Barkley wore down Washington, with 76 of his rushing yards coming in the fourth quarter alone. Lane Johnson explained that the power of the run game is if the Eagles stick with it, "eventually it's going to break open for you." This was the recipe that the Eagles had found in November.

"It energizes me," Johnson said. "The whole game, even when it wasn't good, he was like, 'Keep attacking with the O-line, it's going to break open for us.' And eventually, it did. That's the kind of guy he is. When things aren't going good, that's when you really tell a lot about a person. He never wavered."

"It comes down to will, the want-to," Jordan Mailata said. "We showed out there…we wanted it more."

Washington left the game eager to see the Eagles again. As it would turn out, they would play each other *two* more times. But on this night, the Eagles showed they were the "big dawgs" of the NFC East. They showed that "shit runs through us," as Gardner-Johnson said. Barkley showed you don't need to worry about a thing. But they also knew it was not yet time to book tickets to New Orleans.

"You don't get trophies for midseason," Barkley said.

CHAPTER 18

EAGLES AT RAMS

SAQUON BARKLEY ARRIVED at his locker stall after the best game of his career and saw a half sheet of paper above his locker—a common sight for players, and one Barkley had seen too often throughout the season. It is the league's notice for a drug test.

It would have seemed a version of gallows humor for Barkley to get drug tested after he rushed for 255 yards and totaled 47 receiving yards in a 37–20 win over the Los Angeles Rams.

As it turned out, it was just Goedert humor.

Eagles tight end Dallas Goedert took the slip off his locker and taped it on Barkley's locker room as a practical joke.

"I've been drug tested enough," Barkley said. "Hopefully I get away from that for a little bit."

With the way Barkley ran the ball against the Rams, one might seek answers for how or why he could play like this. Nobody in Eagles history has accumulated that many rushing yards or total yards in a game. It was the ninth-best single-game rushing performance in NFL history and the ninth-most scrimmage yards in a game.

"I ain't never seen nothing like that before," Mekhi Becton said. "He's different."

There were multiple instances for Barkley's teammates to make that comment.

The first "wow" play came after halftime, when Rams coach Sean McVay told NBC coming at the break that the Rams "need to get a stop here"—and then Barkley sprinted through the line of scrimmage for 70 yards on the first play of the second half.

"On the first play of the second half, he makes a cut that I didn't think anybody else could make," Nick Sirianni said. "He just stopped on a dime. We blocked it really well and Jordan Mailata did an awesome job on the backside. Landon Dickerson did an awesome job on the backside because we ran an outside zone and we were able to cut the backside off, and so first and foremost to get into the open field, it started up front. It started on the front side then obviously what we did on the backside, and then he made this cut where he put his left foot in the ground and went around the edge, and then he just hit the gas."

You would expect a 70-yard gain to be the longest rush of the game. It helped propel him to 183 yards in the fourth quarter—a superb performance, but not yet a career high. He needed seven more yards to top 189 yards from December 2019 with the Giants against Washington. That was the mark he bypassed one month earlier against his former team when he "let the young boys eat."

This time, Sirianni let Barkley eat while the Eagles built a 30–14 lead late in the fourth quarter. The Eagles were trying to wear down the clock. Barkley had already worn down the defense. He looked up at the halo video board circling above him and glanced at his in-game statistics, noticing he was closing on his best rushing performance.

"I wish I never saw that," he said to himself. "That's just the devil talking."

On a third down, Barkley took a handoff from the 28-yard line. He cut to his left and found full speed before the defenders could spot him. By the time they did, Barkley raced 72 yards to the end zone. He reached 21.91 miles per hour on the run, per NFL's Next Gen Stats, which was the fifth-fastest total of any player all season. (No. 4 on the list was Barkley against the Giants at 21.93 miles per hour.)

"What a night! What a season! What a player!" Mike Tirico said on the NBC broadcast.

That performance was the first time the discussion about Barkley winning MVP became a national debate. When you perform that way in Los Angeles on national television, it raises eyebrows. For Barkley, it was what he expected with the Eagles.

"Yeah, to be honest, I'm not surprised," Barkley said. "I didn't know I would have *this* type of success...but I'm thankful to be here, I'm thankful for the fresh start.... [My family and I thought] this was a spot I could rewrite my story and show everyone the type of player I think I can be and I was meant to be, and it's working out right now."

Barkley rewrote record books—even when he did not realize it. He knew the rushing record when he glanced at the scoreboard. But he did not realize it was his first time topping 300 total scrimmage yards.

"I didn't do it in New York against Washington?" Barkley asked.

That mark was 279 yards. No word on whether it required a drug test afterward.

"That's big," Barkley said, nodding to himself. "But you can't do it alone."

That's where his offensive linemen come into the conversation. Lane Johnson noticed the Rams attempted different strategies in the first half, including moving around one of their versatile players in the front seven each play to attempt to flummox the offensive line. Johnson met with offensive line coach Jeff Stoutland at halftime to make slight adjustments. Barkley did the rest.

"With the run game, it's sometimes not perfect early, it takes a little bit to get in a rhythm, but once we're able to get a hat-on-hat, Saquon found some creases. He's just a dynamic running back," Johnson said.

Johnson blocked for LeSean McCoy in 2013 when McCoy set the Eagles' franchise rushing record. He waited 11 more years to see a similar type of season, and Johnson thought the MVP conversation was valid. After the game, he posted "MVP 26" on social media.

"Hell, I don't know why he wouldn't be," Johnson said in the locker room. "Everyone has known what type of player he is. He's had some ups and downs in his career, but I think now he's having a real year where people can see what type of talent he carries. A guy that size who can do that, it's fun blocking for him, I'll tell you that."

"We start thinking about that when the season's over," Barkley said. "I love being in that conversation—it's cool and all—but it's a team sport. And if you told me I could have the year I'm having, win the MVP but not win the Super Bowl, or I could have the year I'm having and not win MVP or Offensive Player of the Year but win the Super Bowl, I'm going to take the [second] one."

If only Barkley knew what was coming in a few months. If only the Rams did, too, because they would see Barkley again.

One player the Rams did not see again? Brandon Graham. While playing perhaps his finest game during his farewell tour, a running back chipped Graham and he felt a sting in his triceps. At age 36, Graham is used to feeling tendinitis. When team doctors greeted him on the sideline, they all learned that the sting was caused by something more serious: he tore his triceps. Jalen Hurts came over to him to pray. In the locker room after the game,

Graham shared with reporters what happened. His season was finished—or so he thought. He called his wife and cried. Then he wiped away those tears. Graham tried telling his teammates they must stay positive, and at that moment, he suggested he would be "taking my own advice" when revealing the news after the game.

"We pour everything we can into this game. When I say I trust God, I trust God. I'm about to enjoy this little rehab. And I'm about to enjoy leading this team the rest of the year," Graham said. "As soon as I can be back out there [with the team], I'll be back out there. But, man, boy, man, we was having fun out there. We'll still have fun out there. But as a player, I'm out for the year."

"I'm devastated for him, one of the best leaders I've been around, not only how he plays, but how he mentors the guys on and off the field," Johnson said. "He's kind of a father figure to a lot of these guys. His story screams perseverance and resiliency."

Graham, who had said he would retire at the end of the season, did not want to use that moment to declare whether the Rams game would be the last time he played professional football. It was a distinct possibility.

"Hate to have to go like this," Graham said, "but at the end of the day, I don't have any regrets."

He also said the team's mission does not change. Graham is close with Jason Peters, who tore his ACL during the Eagles' run to the Super Bowl in 2017. Peters carried the Lombardi Trophy out of the locker room. At the time, the best-case scenario was that Graham could become the Eagles' next version of Peters.

"Hoping we're holding that trophy regardless in the end," Graham said.

Nobody could have predicted that Graham would play one more time this season—when the Eagles had the chance to win that trophy.

Time Out: Jalen Carter

There were multiple times throughout the Eagles' Leap Year when the defense needed to make a decisive play, and the player who emerged was Jalen Carter. In the NFC divisional round, Carter dominated an opposing guard for a critical third-down sack, then pummeled Los Angeles Rams quarterback Matthew Stafford on fourth down to seal the Eagles' win. In Week 11 against Washington, Carter plowed through the Commanders' offensive line to disrupt quarterback Jayden Daniels and force him out of rhythm on a short-yardage fourth-down run to halt a critical drive.

"The special ones are looking for the three or four plays that happen in the game where they can change the game," said Eagles defensive line coach Clint Hurtt, the former Seattle Seahawks defensive coordinator who worked with Calais Campbell and Vince Wilfork at the University of Miami.

When Hurtt coached in Seattle, the Seahawks were choosing between Carter and cornerback Devon Witherspoon at the No. 5 overall pick. Carter might have been the most talented player in the draft, but his stock dropped because of his involvement in a car accident that killed a Georgia teammate and a staff member. Carter pleaded no contest on two misdemeanor charges of reckless driving and racing. There were also pre-draft whispers about a questionable work ethic at Georgia. The Eagles, who owned the No. 10 pick in 2023 even though they had just reached the Super Bowl because of a 2022 trade with New Orleans, were eager to take what other teams considered a risk. They swapped one spot to move to No. 9 and gladly select Carter, who they foresaw as the successor to Fletcher Cox as a disruptive force at defensive tackle. They felt confident in their research on Carter. Howie Roseman leans on security chief Dom DiSandro to ascertain off-field concerns. They believed in the infrastructure they had in place, including respected veterans like Cox (who connected with Carter every day during the 2023 offseason) and a collection of Carter's Georgia teammates, such as Jordan Davis and Nakobe Dean—plus later in the draft Nolan Smith and Kelee Ringo. The "Philly Dawgs," as the Athens-to-Philadelphia pipeline became known, offered built-in support for Carter. It was clear to Cox (and other veterans) early during Carter's rookie season that he could be special. Carter showed spurts of excellence but needed consistency—and needed to endure late in the season. Cox retired after the 2023 campaign, and the expectations turned to Carter to become the top player on the defensive line.

"There's probably going to be a lot on my back, but I'm ready for it," Carter said before the season. "New season, new me—I'm ready to play."

The first place to start was Carter's conditioning. That was the message from Vic Fangio and Hurtt even before they started working with Carter.

"The No. 1 thing for him is just being in the best shape he possibly can be in," Hurtt said. "And he's taken huge strides with that this offseason and it's a work in progress but he's off to a really, really good start. If he's in great condition and he can play all out…then he's going to be a hard guy to block. He's a huge man, long arms, strong, he can get up and down and make tackles in the tackle box. The No. 1 thing for him is conditioning. Can he be in great shape?"

"I think he's talented enough that no matter what we do with him, we'll be maximizing him," Fangio added during the spring. "He's got to get in great shape, which I think he's off to a great start here, so we can play him a lot."

Fangio told the starting defensive linemen that they would need to play 70 to 80 percent of the defensive snaps—a departure from the rotation the Eagles had used in the past. Carter played 48 percent of the defensive snaps as a rookie. Fangio emphasized the "box drill," when four cones are placed a few yards apart and linemen run and shuffle between cones. Carter trained against a tackling dummy after practice to improve his hands. He spent the two days after games on stationary bikes with interval training, similar to the short bursts of a play with a rest in between. He labored on the Versa climber. The results were evident. Carter played 84 percent of the defensive snaps in 2024, even outpacing the percentages from Cox's career. It was not lost on the Eagles how many impactful, game-changing plays Carter made in the fourth quarter and later in games.

"It doesn't work unless the player himself has the expectation for himself," Hurtt said. "So credit to him with getting that part of it done."

Opposing offensive lines tried double-teaming Carter, often freeing up one-on-one opportunities for other players on the defensive line. There were times when Carter was egregiously held and did not draw a flag. At one point, Fangio asked reporters if they had any ideas for how the officials would start calling holding against him. His statistics were respectable—4.5 sacks, 16 quarterback hits, 12 tackles for losses—but his effect on the game belied his statistics. That was apparent when he was named to the Pro Bowl in Year 2. The other defensive tackles? Dexter Lawrence and Vita Vea. "Just for my name to be up there with those guys and having watched them before I got to the league?" Carter asked, shaking his head.

He should get used to it—and he knows it. Carter has the talent to become one of the best defensive players in the NFL.

"I get that a lot," Carter said about whether he knows how good he is. "A lot of people be answering it for me."

"Does he have confidence in himself? Absolutely. Is he arrogant or braggadocious about it? No, that's not his way," Hurtt said. "But he knows that he's gifted. He knows that he's talented. So he's aware of what he has. He has gifts. It's my job to keep pushing for more."

Teammates suggest Carter does not get enough credit for his football IQ. It's easy to see the strength and athleticism. He's inquisitive in meetings and he notices subtle indicators in formations or shifts that allow him to play with anticipation. He'll ask about particular plays the opponent presents so he has an idea of how he'll be blocked or where the play will go. That allows him to make plays that other defensive linemen cannot.

"A lot of times when you get big, talented guys like that, they just say, 'Get off the ball and go forward and whatever happens, happens,'" Hurtt said. "For him, he can see stuff."

And the Eagles can see what he's doing. After the postseason win against the Rams, Howie Roseman walked by Carter's locker and asked if he wanted the photo for the Hall of Fame.

It might seem ambitious. It does not seem outrageous.

"Oh my gosh, that dude is just a monster," Zack Baun said. "The best in the league."

CHAPTER 19

EAGLES AT RAVENS

Nick Sirianni stood in front of his team at the Baltimore Marriott Waterfront on the eve of the Week 13 Eagles-Ravens game with a message that was evident during the Eagles' 24–19 victory and became a rallying cry after the game.

"Our physicality will be on display with the things you can see," Siriainni said, as captured by team footage. "Tackling, ball security, blocking, you can see.... What you do when no one is watching will show up when everybody is. Everyone gets to see it tomorrow."

All week long, the Eagles were asked about the Ravens' physicality. It's a brand of football that had long been established from the franchise down Interstate 95 coached by former Eagles assistant John Harbaugh. It's evident in how they play and who they acquire to play for them. The Eagles dutifully answered questions all week, but it might have vexed Sirianni when the question was framed as whether the Eagles could match Baltimore's physicality.

"They had to match ours," Sirianni said after the game. "We know they're a physical team. We know we're a physical team. That was our message going in: They got to match our physicality.... I'd like the question rephrased a little differently."

The question was not just rephrased—it was answered. Saquon Barkley rushed for 107 yards, which is even more impressive when you consider the Ravens had not allowed more than 63 yards to an opposing running back all season. The longest run they had allowed all season was 21 yards; Barkley surpassed that, too. The offensive line overpowered the line of scrimmage. The wide receivers blocked on the perimeter. One mantra that the offensive linemen often repeat is that it's not who's tougher, but who's tougher longer. The Eagles offensive linemen were tougher longer. That was evident in the fourth quarter, when the Eagles extended a 14–12 score to a 12-point lead with Barkley's 25-yard touchdown.

"We have an unbelievable offensive line," Barkley said. "I think week in, week out, you guys are able to see that. Especially our tackles, they are able to move, and how big they are, and being able to move at that size.... I kind of saw the look, and just trusting he was going to make the block, and I just ran through it as fast as I could, pretty much with my eyes closed, and got to the open field. Jahan [Dotson] and Parris [Campbell] did a really good job of running off the DB to open up space for me and get into the end zone."

When Barkley scored his touchdown, the Eagles fans who drove down the highway to see a rare Eagles game in Baltimore on Thanksgiving weekend serenaded Barkley with chants of "M-V-P"—an especially relevant chant this weekend because the Eagles played against Lamar Jackson and Derrick Henry. They were two of the top players during the season and contenders for the league's annual award, but they were outplayed by the Eagles defense. Consider this: the Ravens entered the Eagles game as the NFL's top-ranked offense by yards and the second-ranked offense by points, yet they scored only one touchdown before the final minute of the game. The Ravens went eight drives in the middle of the game with 166 yards and three points.

It was, as C.J. Gardner-Johnson called it, a "want-to game."

"You've got to go out there and tackle one of the best running backs in the game [and] want to chase one of the best [dual-threat] quarterbacks in the league," Gardner-Johnson said.

To that point, no play was more memorable than in the fourth quarter when Cooper DeJean upended the 247-pound Henry. It is rare for any player to body-slam the most imposing runner in the NFL, so DeJean's play led highlight reels after the game. There is some context required when remembering the play, considering Henry caught a pass and was at an unsuspecting standstill while DeJean charged toward him. Somebody taking eighth-grade physics could discuss acceleration and force. But the symbolism was clear. Which team was more physical?

"I think that's what we try to do every week—be the most physical team every week, try to make the opposing team match our physicality," DeJean said. "And when they try to match it, we just go even more. That's been a point [of emphasis].... I love it. Football's a physical game. That's how you have to play it. You have to continue to do that, especially down the stretch. As we get to the cold games, you have to be mentally tough to play a physical game."

"Physicality" is an easy buzzword for a coach to recite, and it goes over well in Philadelphia, although it is easier preached than practiced. Sirianni said with the Eagles, it starts with fundamentals—one of the core principles—and the way they tackle and combat blocks. It requires "relentless effort" with how they hit. But it also comes down to the types of players they seek to add. You cannot make a featherweight a heavyweight.

"Your style of physicality could be through any scheme, but you talk about it through your fundamentals and guys being physical as the nature of who they are as people," Sirianni said. "Nolan Smith is physical. He was physical in college. He didn't just turn physical. He was physical in high school, and I imagine he was physical when he played Pee Wee football. It's huge to have guys like that on your team that seek out hits, and want to hit, and know the way the game changes when you deliver hits."

The way the Eagles played against the Ravens also sent a statement to the rest of the league. If you can do that to Baltimore *in* Baltimore, you can do that to just about anybody. If there were any lingering doubts about the Eagles, they should have been pulverized sometime between Barkley's touchdown and DeJean's hit and the joyous drive back up to Philadelphia

"Hey, listen—you earned the right to play in games like this—because of what you've been doing all year. And you earned the right to play in more of these!" Sirianni said in the locker room after the game, as captured by the team footage.

"What was very clear today—what was so clear—is we're a physical team. We knew it in the first half, and we kept…hitting them, and kept hitting them, and kept hitting them," he added.

When Sirianni went from his postgame speech to his postgame press conference, he had a different message to convey. Yes, he wanted to reinforce how the Eagles were more physical. But he also wanted to stand up to anyone who wanted to beat up his quarterback. Jalen Hurts went 11-of-19 for 118 yards and one touchdown, along with 29 rushing yards and a touchdown. Those are modest statistics, especially compared to Jackson's video game–like productions. The "M-V-P" chants were for Barkley—not Hurts. Teammates told Barkley to put on his cape while Hurts was being labeled as a "game manager"—a term that Sirianni wanted to defend or dismiss, depending upon how you interpreted it.

"You'll say 'Game manager.' That's all bullshit," Sirianni said. "Jalen played an awesome game. His stats [will] say we didn't throw it a lot…. But he made runs when he needed to make runs. He made good checks. He managed the game in [four-minute offense]…. Jalen Hurts deserves to be in the MVP consideration because of how clean of football he's playing. Look at his quarterback rating in the last month and a half. Jalen Hurts is a winner. He may not have the stats, but because his team is winning in the fourth quarter, he doesn't have to make those stats."

This might have been Sirianni simply standing up for his quarterback after a high-profile game. Or maybe Sirianni knew the Eagles would need Hurts to win games like this come the postseason. The Eagles were in the Super Bowl conversation, after all, and the scrutiny surrounding Hurts had not yet reached its crescendo.

CHAPTER 20

EAGLES VS. PANTHERS

THE WINNING LOCKER ROOM was not an especially joyous place in Week 14, which would seem curious because the 22–16 win over the Carolina Panthers was the team's ninth consecutive victory. The win clinched a postseason appearance for the fourth season under Nick Sirianni and saw Saquon Barkley set a franchise record for rushing yards in a season. Most franchises would celebrate those three occurrences. The Panthers might have even thrown a parade!

But in Philadelphia—and especially this season—simply beating the Panthers in December does not beget satisfaction. They should be able to beat the Panthers. What mattered was what it would take to win in January—and perhaps February.

That was the impetus for the dissatisfaction of the offensive players. During an afternoon in which the game plan called for the Eagles to pass the ball, Jalen Hurts finished 14-of-21 for 108 yards and two touchdowns. A.J. Brown was targeted only twice in the first three quarters of the game—the fewest of any game he had been healthy for since arriving in Philadelphia in 2022—and not once on the opening possession. Brown and DeVonta Smith combined for only 10 targets. The passing game is supposed to run through them, yet 18 players in the NFL were targeted more than the duo was targeted *combined* in Week 14.

When Brown was asked what the Eagles must improve, he gave a simple answer: "Passing."

That response was obvious—they had 108 passing yards!—but the interpretation was "passer." The Eagles needed more from Hurts. Nick Sirianni had stumped for Hurts as an MVP candidate one week earlier and cited Hurts' passer rating, but even Hurts acknowledged the Eagles needed "better synchronization"—a Hurts-ian way of echoing the star receivers' sentiment that they needed to get on the "same page." When asked if they should be on different pages after 13 games, Hurts simply responded, "No."

"I think they did a good job. I think we did a bad job," Hurts said. "That starts with me, how I execute, and ultimately you yearn, and I yearn, for better synchronization amongst that, for a more complementary style of ball, in a sense. Some things don't get you until it gets you. And there's definitely been some urgency there, trying to figure it out."

When asked for more details, Smith suggested the players must be in alignment with how they think and the signals they see. There was a disconnect simmering, and winning can sometimes obscure what it will take to win big.

"What we did today won't help us," Brown said. "We know we got the win. But we're trying to do the things we talk about."

Brown's frustration was visible when he threw his helmet on the sideline, which he said was in response to three-and-outs. But it was not an accident that Sirianni told his team in the postgame speech that they cannot be a "prisoner of your expectations" and they must enjoy the win. Sirianni had been harping on joy since the summer. The coach needed to find the right mix between pushing for more and maintaining perspective.

"I think we're all going to come away from this…and say, 'Hey, there are things we got to do better in the pass game,'" Sirianni said. "Our running game was able to do some really good things. I think that's fair that the questions are about our pass game right now."

The running game included Barkley rushing for 124 yards—this had become the norm for the league's leading rusher—and it was part of a historic month for Barkley. He needed 109 yards to break LeSean McCoy's record of 1,607 yards. The record books were rewritten on a nine-yard run in the fourth quarter, and the attention shifted to whether McCoy could then go after Eric Dickerson's NFL single-season record.

"I never wrote the goal down to break [McCoy's record], but you're always aware of it and that's how I train and how I operate in the offseason and in camp," Barkley said. "Because you want to be great. It's something I want to do and something I believe I can do—especially with the men and women in our facility; they make it a lot easier for me."

There was only so much celebration for Barkley, which speaks to how it had become a formality and that there were more pressing issues for the Eagles. The passing game did not receive a pass, and an offense that had once been called "constipated" by Lane Johnson was now lamented by Jordan Mailata for "putting the defense in shitty situations." The defense did just enough to hold onto the win—in part because the Panthers could not hold onto a potential go-ahead pass—and it's true that not all games look like a domination in the Super Bowl.

There's a survive-and-advance element to regular season football, and part of playing professional football in Philadelphia requires weathering storms. The storms that came after the Panthers game, though, were generated by players on the team more than the media or fans.

One day later, on Brandon Graham's radio show on 94.1 WIP, the defensive captain made a comment that stopped Eagles fans in their tracks. It is one thing when talk radio hosts manufacture drama. It's another when a team captain is a talk radio host and creates drama.

"I don't know the whole story, but I know that [Hurts] is trying. [Brown] could be a little better with how he responds to things. They were friends, but things have changed," Graham said on radio. "And I understand that because life happens. But [on] the business side, we got to make sure we don't let the personal get in the way of the business. And that's what we need to do better."

Graham, who was on injured reserve while recovering from a torn triceps, later walked back his comments in an interview with ESPN, but the comments had enough oxygen to survive. There was a team meeting in which the comments were addressed.

"We're good," Hurts said.

"Me and Jalen are good," Brown said.

"In the end, BG knows he spoke out of place," Hurts said. "It's about the team in the end. I think overall, that's where my focus is. I think that's where everyone's focus is at heart."

"Everybody loves BG. He's speaking from the heart. He's giving his perception from the outside," Brown said. "[Others] perceive what I said about passing and think it's an attack on Jalen. I think that's what [Graham] did. Me and [Hurts'] relationship is good."

They tried their best to defuse the speculation about the personal drama, although there was a sentiment that what Graham said was productive because it brought a simmering issue to a head. (After the season, Brown offered this on the *Million Dollaz Worth of Game* podcast: "I'd be lying to tell you we never had any issues. We're two alphas who want to be the best and demand greatness from each other and everyone around us. Some reports are true, some reports aren't true. But me and him are good, man. We just wanna be great and push each other. Sometimes we bump heads, but that's normal, don't nobody sweat it.")

And the personal drama aside, the questions about the passing game were legitimate—and they needed fixing.

"I said that for a reason," Brown said. "Honestly, because we went to the Super Bowl and lost. We tried it again next year. We were 10-and-whatever our record was, and it was a landslide. It's something we can correct right now while we have the opportunity. I was bringing awareness to everybody's attention."

Brown also thought his answer was obvious. Anyone could see the Eagles needed to improve the passing game.

"When he asked the question of what the offense could do better, obviously it's not running the ball. [Saquon Barkley] is about to win MVP, like literally," Brown said. "So what other thing do we do on offense? We pass the ball. And that can go into protection, that can go into picking up a block, us getting open quicker, being on the same page, Jalen reading something—whatever the case might be."

Hurts said he starts by looking at himself: What must he do better as the quarterback? Plus, he had seen how the offense looked when the passing game had the synchronization that he suggested it needed. That should be the standard. And if you know anything about Hurts, you know the standard is not compromised. There was a theory that he played more conservatively because of the team's determination to reduce turnovers after the first four games. Hurts responded he must "saturate" himself in the team's offensive approach.

"That's something people have to accept. It's going to look the way Jalen Hurts wants it to look," Hurts said. "But he's going to win."

Hurts showed as much in 2022. When Sirianni was asked about concerns about the locker room dynamic, he suggested the Eagles exhibited more "2022 vibes." The focus was whether they could look like the 2022 version of the offense—or perhaps better. The next test would come the following weekend against Pittsburgh.

"We are moving on," Mailata said. "It's the Pittsburgh Steelers this week—not the A.J. Brown and Jalen show. It's the Pittsburgh Steelers. That's it."

CHAPTER 21

EAGLES VS. STEELERS

JALEN HURTS HAD THE LAST LAUGH—even if he didn't laugh. Hurts, with the same stoic look as ever, sat down for the post-game press conference after the Eagles' 27–13 victory over the Pittsburgh Steelers that served as the answer to all the questions he heard leading up to the game—about the passing game, about A.J. Brown, about his fitness as the franchise quarterback. Wearing a Kangol-style hat similar to the one he would wear two months later at the Super Bowl parade, Hurts was like Michael Jordan settling old scores.

"So that's what y'all wanted to see, huh?" he asked.

The statement referred to Hurts' best game of the season to date. He completed 25-of-32 pass attempts for 290 yards and two touchdowns, while also rushing for 45 yards and a score. Saquon Barkley was considered the MVP candidate for the Eagles. If you watched the Steelers game, you would have put Hurts in that category.

Of course, the Steelers knew how dangerous Barkley was in the Eagles offense. They appeared hellbent on stopping Barkley, leaving it up to Hurts—and his high-profile receivers—to win the game. The Eagles like to be able to run when they must run and pass when they must pass, and this was a day for passing. So when A.J. Brown said one week earlier the Eagles' "passing" must improve, this was what he meant.

"We always knew there was going to come a time we were going to have to rely on throwing the ball. It happened, and we answered," DeVonta Smith said. "It was a matter of getting that one team that wanted to stop the run and wanted us to win the game through the air."

Brown finished with eight catches for 110 yards and one touchdown. Smith finished with 11 catches for 109 yards and one touchdown. It was the first time they both exceeded 100 yards together since 2022—fitting, of course, because Sirianni had said during the week that the Eagles showed "2022 vibes" more than the warning signs of 2023. This was the way 2022 looked. It even carried over to the celebrations. Hurts and Brown, whose relationship had come under focus throughout the week, choreographed a touchdown dance. It was the "Kid 'n Play" dance from *House Party*.

"That was our moment to tell everybody to shut up," Brown said.

But it was only because they opened their mouths in the first place. The comments from the receivers and Graham's subsequent comment on talk radio led to conversations during the week. Similar to the bye week, the Eagles needed the football version of a therapy session to fix what ailed them.

"A lot of tough conversations, uncomfortable conversations," Smith said.

"It's easy for us to have these tough conversations and call each other out because we know what we want in the end," said Brown, who added the Eagles engaged in "long, repetitive meetings" during the critical week. It is common to categorize anything that does not fall under the company line as a "distraction," but it is also important to remember these are adults in a workplace. It is a high-profile workplace, sure, but sweeping something under the rug for the purpose of a Norman Rockwell–like public front is unproductive. The Eagles were trying to do "special shit"—remember?—and sometimes that can become dirty.

"I said it for a reason," Brown said. "I didn't have ill intentions behind it. It wasn't for me to get the ball. It was just for us to all get on the same page and put our best foot forward. We know what we're capable of, and last week wasn't our standard. It's just crazy, though, because everybody in the locker room said the same thing and I kind of got crucified for it. But it was cool."

Of course, there were football reasons why the Eagles were better in the passing game. Because the Steelers loaded the box, the Eagles used empty formations—no running back in the backfield—to put pressure on the defense. Kellen Moore called more drop backs out of empty formations than the previous seven games combined. When the Steelers played cover-two zone defense on third downs, the Eagles utilized zone beaters to find space. Brown said the "coaches let the game come to them," but passing was the plan from the start. Hurts dropped back on five of the Eagles' first six plays and targeted Brown and Smith on the opening drive.

"I've always said and believed that you want to make sure that all of your tools are sharp when you need them, so when it's time to use them, you can go," Hurts said. "I don't think there's a doubt in that. I think, frankly, there's an effort there. The approach was a little different this week. The grass will be green where you water it. We decided to water it and saw the fruits of our labor in that. Obviously, we've been watering the running game a good bit. It's natural to put emphasis on one thing and take emphasis off of another and see what you guys have seen. We want to continue to be well-rounded, push to be well-rounded, and water all areas of our yard."

The ground game was watered on the final drive. With a two-touchdown lead, the Eagles took over possession on their own 1-yard line with 10:29 remaining in the game. When there's that much time in the game, a two-score advantage is not insurmountable. Except in this instance, the Eagles did not even allow the Steelers to get the ball back. They went on a 21-play drive that finished at the Steelers' 9-yard line with Jalen Hurts taking three knees and included 99 yards of total offense. The Eagles converted four third downs and a fourth down on the drive. It was the Eagles' longest possession by plays since at least the 2001 season—the team's stat data for drives doesn't beyond that period.

"We're not projecting out that far. You take it circumstance by circumstance," offensive coordinator Kellen Moore said when asked if he started the drive even thinking the Eagles could finish the game with the ball. "It started with a backed-up scenario, got a few first downs, played some third-down football. As we approached that midfield line, that's where four-minute football started to present itself, and we had to make those adjustments. Now we're playing the clock and all those situations. I thought it was a really good job by our guys of understanding there were a lot of circumstances that played out throughout that whole drive. A lot of situational football that happens on the fly. And to have it all in one 21-play drive is very rare."

The Eagles defense only played two drives in the entire second half.

"I didn't even get to rush once the whole second half!" Josh Sweat said on the sideline, as captured by NFL Films.

It allowed them to watch the offense for much of the game—and see what Hurts said everyone wanted to see.

Little did Hurts know it would be his last time laughing last in the regular season.

Time Out: A.J. Brown

Ask Saquon Barkley for the best football player on the Eagles, and he won't say himself—even though he won Offensive Player of the Year honors.

He would say A.J. Brown.

"He's a freak of nature," Barkley said. "He weighs the same as me, he's bigger than me, and he can move like me—I just can't run routes like him. The most impressive thing about A.J. to me, you have guys who catch the ball, but when he catches the ball, the ball does not move in his hand. He has the most impressive hands. I kind of knew that in New York seeing him, seeing how he operates. Me and Daniel [Jones] used to talk about that a lot, actually. He's a heck of a player. Hall of Fame–caliber player."

John Ross, a former first-round pick who set a record at the annual scouting combine in the 40-yard dash, spent the 2024 offseason with the Eagles and closely studied the receivers. Turns out, trying to pick up tips from the way Brown plays proved futile.

"I don't think nobody can learn from A.J.," Ross said. "I look at him like a Terrell Owens—he's one of one. You can't replicate that. He's not a super tall guy. He's not a super fast guy. But he'll run by you. He'll jump over you. And he's big enough to move you around. And he'll catch *everything.*"

Nick Sirianni calls Brown the best wide receiver who has ever played in Philadelphia. His production would suggest as much. In three years with the Eagles, Brown has already set franchise records for single season receiving yards (1,496 in 2022) and receptions by a wide receiver (106 in 2023). Since entering the NFL in 2019, his 15.8 yards per reception are the most of anyone in the NFL with at least 300 receptions.

He's caught touchdowns in both Super Bowls. He's on a Hall of Fame trajectory.

Yet he is often misunderstood. If he's emotional on the sideline, he's charged with being a diva instead of passionate. (Brown suggested DeVonta Smith actually requests the ball more!) If Brown reads a book on the sideline, it's interpreted as frustration rather than finding peace (or *Inner Excellence*). Brown once called into a local Philadelphia radio station during the 2024 offseason when there were polls about trading him. At the Super Bowl parade, Brown's microphone drop was, "They said I was a diva, they said all I cared about was stats. You can get all of those things wrong about me, but there's one thing you can get right: I'm a fucking champion!"

"I'm going to continue to be myself. It's not pretend, it's not a facade or anything," Brown said during the playoffs. "Who cares who don't like it? I'm a three-time All-Pro. I'm going to pop my shit. That's just what it is. I do that for myself. I'm not a distraction. Most importantly, I go out and do my job. All the other shit, it doesn't matter."

Inside the locker room, there are no questions about Brown. He's a team captain who is unafraid to speak up when needed. During the 2024 rookie minicamp, Brown came to watch roster hopefuls go through drills. During his Super Bowl eve speech to teammates, he singled out teammates who do not get credit.

"A.J. is one of the best people we have on this team," Sirianni said. "Just know he deeply cares about being a great football player. I know he deeply cares about his teammates. And I get to see that on a daily basis. A.J. has been phenomenal since the day he stepped foot onto this team. I think the way he's played elevates everybody. The way he plays football elevates everybody. Everyone leads a little differently. There is also a reason that A.J. has the 'C' on his chest. So everyone leads a little bit differently. A.J. is a great player, great leader, great person."

The truth is Brown wants the ball when he knows it will help the team. Franchises dream of finding a player like Brown. It would behoove them to use him. When Brown arrived in Philadelphia, he put a sign above his locker: ALWAYS OPEN. "The sign is bold, very bold," Brown said. "But you gotta believe it." It's not belief. It's truth. Brown is outstanding at creating space with his body and catching the ball in traffic, so even when it might seem as if he's covered, chances are he'll catch the ball. He looked up to Julio Jones, a future Hall of Famer with whom Brown played in Tennessee and Philadelphia. There are similarities to the way they play the game. It's easy to look at their sheer physical ability, but Brown points to the understanding of how to run routes. He said what makes a bigger receiver special is when he can get in and out of breaks, running routes like a smaller player. So of course he would want the ball—look what happens when he gets it!

"If you throw the ball to me 100 times," Brown explained during his first season with the Eagles, "I'm going to want it 101 times." The reason, as Brown suggested, is that he "can change the game at any moment."

"That's what you want from your receivers, to want to have the football," Sirianni said. "Part of the reason why receivers are good is because they want and crave the football. They want the ball to change the game."

Brown's first game in the NFL came against the Cleveland Browns. It was the debut of Odell Beckham Jr. in Cleveland. Brown looked across the field during pregame warmups and saw Beckham and Jarvis Landry. But he thought to himself, "They're coming to see me, not them." Brown was the only receiver to reach 100 yards that day.

"I don't think he thinks he's the guy—he *knows* he's the guy," Eagles wide receivers coach Aaron Moorehead said. "That's the difference."

The flip side to this is that Brown has played with 2,000-yard rushers twice in his career. He's needed to block for Derrick Henry. He's needed to block for Barkley. So he wants the ball to change the game, but he does not object when it's working with something else—so long as it's working.

"What we have in the backfield, he's rare. Once you accept that, everything else is easier," Brown said during the 2024 season. "I don't [get bothered] because what I see on a day-to-day basis is very special.... I played with Derrick Henry, that's the same thing. You have to switch your mindset a little bit and not get comfortable with touches. That's not a bad thing. I'm going to give you a little context, because I know guys can run with that. So whenever you get the opportunity, you have to make the most of it. And when guys get a lot of touches in a game, you may not go as hard here or there because you know you got another touch coming. But when you don't know, you're going to make the most of it because of who's in the backfield [and] how special they are."

That's what happened in 2024, when Brown had the fewest targets since his rookie season yet he also had the best catch percentage and success rate of his career. He blocked for someone special when it was needed. But it might be worth asking that special player in the backfield who he considers the special one.

CHAPTER 22

EAGLES AT COMMANDERS

The Eagles' only loss in the final four-plus months of the season (including the playoffs) came in Week 16 against the Washington Commanders, although on that day, it seemed to matter less *that* they lost and more *to whom* they lost.

On the second drive of the game, with the Eagles on their way to a two-score lead, Jalen Hurts ran a quarterback draw for 13 yards and dove to the ground at the end with two Commanders defenders colliding into him. Hurts' helmet hit the ground with force, but in the moment, it seemed unremarkable. He had taken bigger hits before. He had appeared woozier, too. There seemed to be more of a question about a head injury after a hit in the first Washington game. Hurts even tried returning to the huddle. The officials forced him to retreat to the sideline to undergo evaluation for a concussion. Hurts begrudgingly entered the blue medical tent. It was not as if he needed to be helped off the field. After a few minutes in the tent, he returned to the edge of the sideline and put his helmet on his head. That is typically the signal that the player will return to the game.

Head trainer Tom Hunkele pulled him back for more evaluation in the tent, almost like a child trying to sneak out of the house without a winter coat before the parents notice. While Hurts was in the tent for a second time, backup quarterback Kenny Pickett finished the Eagles' drive with a touchdown pass to A.J. Brown. Hurts could not celebrate with his teammates. He jogged inside to the locker room—not walking, not sitting on the front seat of a golf cart—but a full jog. It seemed at that moment like the evaluation was a nuisance. It was actually done in service of Hurts, who was determined to have a concussion. He did not return to the game (and would not play again until the postseason).

With a 14–0 lead and Pickett taking over at quarterback, the Eagles were still in a position to win. They also had a defense that had not allowed more than 20 points in a game since September. The Commanders were a formidable opponent, but it was not as if the Eagles' situation should have been dire.

By the end of the game, the locker room tried to piece together how the defense surrendered a 27–14 lead and could lose a game in which they forced five turnovers; how Hurts' absence affected Saquon Barkley and a running game that decimated opponents throughout the season; and whether Pickett could keep them afloat while Hurts was on the mend.

Start with the defense. They forced four turnovers in the first three quarters, which should have been enough to win the game. But Commanders rookie sensation Jayden Daniels was a menace in the fourth quarter, leading three touchdown drives—including a game-winning drive with a touchdown pass with six seconds remaining. Daniels went 12-of-17 for 139 yards, three touchdowns, and one interception in the fourth quarter, along with 12 rushing yards. This also coincided with the ejection of C.J. Gardner-Johnson, leaving the Eagles secondary exposed in the middle of the field. That was where Washington attacked. It also hurt that the four-man pass rush could not apply enough pressure on Daniels, forcing Fangio to blitz more than he typically does.

"My calls could have been better," Fangio said two days after the game. "I think if my calls were better, we would have had a better result. But give them credit. They executed and they played well."

The defense allowed too many explosive plays and could not get off the field on enough third downs despite the impressive takeaways. And though the game was an outlier, Fangio did not present it to the team that way during the next week. The allure of Fangio is not only his defensive acumen and his astute game plans, but also how demanding he is with his players.

"No, you don't say it's just a blip," Fangio said. You've got to learn from all your experiences, both good and bad, and improve. We've got to get back to playing. Not have three unsportsmanlike or whatever they're called, two times 12 [men] on the field. We've got to get back to playing better football."

The game should have ended a few times before the loss, and the defense would not have been to blame had a Reed Blankenship interception with 3:06 remaining while the Eagles clung to a 30–28 lead resulted in the Eagles running out the clock. One week earlier, they had a 21-play drive to finish the game. This time, it was three-and-out in 55 seconds. The critical play came on third down when DeVonta Smith dropped an open pass from Pickett that would have moved the chains and helped the Eagles run out the clock. It was like Barkley's drop against Atlanta in Week 2; there was no rationalization, no excuse to be made. He makes the catch nine times out of 10. This one time, he dropped it.

"I made all the tough catches today and then the easy one I had, I dropped," Smith said. "Ain't nobody else's fault but mine.… Ain't nothing I can do about it now. I just dropped the ball. Ain't no teaching on it. Just catch the ball. It's simple."

Had that catch been made, there would not have been as much scrutiny on Pickett. The storyline would have been how Pickett helped the Eagles win in relief. Instead, he was the quarterback for their first loss after the bye week. Pickett finished 14-of-24 for 143 yards with one touchdown and one interception, and the numbers would have been even better if two pass interferences that A.J. Brown drew could have been catches. However, the Eagles were 1-of-12 on third downs after the second drive of the game (when Hurts departed), and there were plays when Pickett—who played scout-team quarterback and seldom worked with Brown or Smith—appeared out of sync with the Eagles' stars. He took three sacks and the Eagles' offense success rate with Pickett was 30.5 percent—down from 45.3 with Hurts on the field during the season leading up to the concussion. Pickett also underwent X-rays after the game for a rib injury that would linger throughout the next few weeks.

"It's two different players—Kenny was trying to get situated and get his feet under him," Brown said. "Kenny hasn't played all year. I just think it was a little different. [He tried] to calm down and get comfortable. He did sometimes, sometimes he got rattled.... I thought he did well to handle everything, not playing a single game."

One way the offense looked different without Hurts: Barkley was not as effective with the Commanders selling out against the run and the Eagles lacking the plus-one dimension in the running game that Hurts typically provides. Barkley's prolific stats were built early in the game; he had seven carries for 109 yards and two touchdowns in the first quarter and 22 carries for 41 yards for the next three quarters.

"They were loading the box. We get it each week. The dynamic of Jalen definitely helps," Barkley said. "In our situation, a lot of the things we do in the run game are designed with Jalen. It's hard to run the same stuff without him. We had to adjust."

Even the Eagles special teams had a costly miscue late in the game, surrendering bad field position so that Washington started the game-winning drive on its own 43-yard line. Those hidden yards were almost like two free first downs.

This loss turned into one bad day during four-plus months of brilliance, but the Eagles did not know that at the time. Hurts exited the stadium with sunglasses covering his eyes. It's hard to see the bright side with sunglasses on. And in the locker room down the frigid FedEx Field corridor in late December in Maryland, the Commanders were infused with confidence that they could hang with the top team of the division.

The sunglasses came off by the time the two rivals played again. When they did, the truth was clearer than ever.

CHAPTER 23

EAGLES VS. COWBOYS

THE WAY THE EAGLES offensive line readied for Saquon Barkley to become the ninth player in NFL history to reach 2,000 yards was retold like the script of a sports movie. They gathered in the huddle early in the fourth quarter ahead of what seemed likely to be the final drive for the offense in a 41–7 win over the Dallas Cowboys while Barkley sat 47 yards away from an immortal milestone.

"Let's go get this mother-F-er," Lane Johnson said.

"We have 48 more yards," Landon Dickerson told Jordan Mailata.

"To the real thing?" Mailata asked, referring to Eric Dickerson's single-season record.

"No, you dummy!" Dickerson responded. "2K!"

That was the version described by the players. When the team released the footage and sound from the microphone Mailata wore during the game, only a part of that conversation was replayed. The spirit of it remained the same.

"Saquon needs 47 to break 2K!" Landon Dickerson told his teammates in real time.

Barkley entered the game needing to gain 162 yards to reach 2,000 yards and with Eric Dickerson's single-season record a possibility, so time was of the essence. One of Barkley's friends on the Cowboys told him on the field before the game, "You're going to have to break that record next week."

Given the standings, there was no guarantee that Barkley would play in Week 18.

"We definitely knew what the number was to at least get to 2,000, and we weren't leaving this field without at least accomplishing that," Barkley said. "Those aren't the words from me, those are the words from the guys up front. So that means a lot to me. When you see that, and those guys are like, 'This mother-F-er needs this to get it. Let's go get it,' it puts a little pressure on you too, but at the same time, it's pressure that you want."

There was much memorable about the victory, including Kenny Pickett living the dream of every kid who wore an Eagles jersey on Halloween by starting against the Dallas Cowboys at home and helping lead the Eagles to the NFC East crown; Tanner McKee stepping in and showing the type of poise and promise that eventually made the Eagles rethink their backup quarterback situation; and the defense rebounding from the Washington loss with a dominant effort against an overmatched Cowboys offense. But the legacy of the game will undoubtedly be Barkley reaching the 2,000-yard club.

"I'm not going to lie, but just being a fan of the game and the running back position, to reach a milestone and put myself up there with eight other backs that I respect, and some of them I grew up watching, definitely means a lot," Barkley said. "But at the same time, I wouldn't be able to do that without this team. Like I said, you can't be great without the greatness of others, and I'm just happy I was able to be a part of the team and be able to reach a milestone like that."

"It's special. What did you say, nine people have done that? Nine total," Sirianni said. "I imagine they're pretty special names.

Saquon is pretty special. This offensive line is pretty special. This offense is pretty special. I know the guys were excited when that happened. Yeah, it's just a cool thing to be a part of. Any time you can be a part of something special, that's what's cool about being part of a team."

Barkley was stuck at 40 yards on 15 carries at halftime while the Eagles built a 24–7 lead. The game was getting out of hand, and it seemed the goal was reaching 2,000 yards. Barkley carried the ball six times on the first drive of the second half, then five times on the second drive. By the fourth quarter, the Eagles were determined to set the mark. So was Barkley. On the fifth play of the drive, after rushing the first four times, Barkley broke loose for a 23-yard gain to reach 2,005 yards. It came on his 31st carry of the game. The crowd serenaded him with "M-V-P" chants. He joined O. J. Simpson, Eric Dickerson, Adrian Peterson, Jamal Lewis, Barry Sanders, Derrick Henry, Terrell Davis, and Chris Johnson in the record books. The offensive linemen reveled in it as much as Barkley, who did not know until Sirianni called a timeout that he reached the mark.

"It was just special, the fact that going out there, you knew what you needed," Barkley said. "And then it's like, in your mind, you're like, 'Alright, damn. I want to get this.'"

By that point, McKee was in the game. He took over for Pickett, who re-injured his ribs—but not before Pickett went 10-of-15 for 143 yards and a touchdown in his only start of the season. He grew up an Eagles fan in Ocean Township, New Jersey, going to games with his father. There was something surreal about wearing the vintage Kelly green and beating the rival Cowboys to clinch a division crown. When McKee came in and completed 3-of-4 pass attempts for 54 yards and two touchdowns, there were reminders of how much he had impressed in training camp and the preseason.

The Eagles did not need the offensive fireworks, considering Dallas turned the ball over four times and scored only seven points. C.J. Gardner-Johnson, who was ejected one week earlier, had two interceptions. One was returned for a touchdown. The Eagles were back to appearing like a juggernaut in what proved to be the final game for the starters. The only intrigue was whether Sirianni would allow Barkley to try to break Eric Dickerson's record. Otherwise, the Eagles would soon learn they were entrenched in the No. 2 seed, and their postseason position could not change in the season finale.

The new division championship hat is old hat for established Eagles who are used to a hat and T-shirt game. ("It's kind of normal at this point," A.J. Brown said. "We expect more. It's low-hanging fruit.") For newcomers unaccustomed to the postseason, such as Mekhi Becton, clinching the division crown was an emotional moment. Becton shed tears on the sideline.

"You've been working so hard…we're going to do some good shit for ya, baby," Landon Dickerson told him on the sideline, as captured by team footage. "You just won your first division championship!"

"That was pretty special for us to be able to share that," Mailata said after the game. "But you just have to let him feel it out. Just let him cry, let him be happy, whatever it is. Just gotta be there for him. And then you have to remind him, 'Hey, let's enjoy this moment, because we got more to go for.'"

That was the chord Sirianni struck in his postgame speech. There were no victory cigars for the NFC East championship—those would come next month—and the scrutiny from September had long faded. The Eagles had a 2,000-yard rusher and had become a Super Bowl contender. This day proved both.

"We said together we can do special shit!" Sirianni told his team in the locker room while wearing an NFC East championship

T-shirt and holding a championship cap. "[Rushing] for 2,000 yards is special shit. Winning the NFC East.... Turning the ball over four times, again, is special shit. But I want a lot more! Think about how special this journey has been so far."

That was at the heart of the decision Sirianni needed to make in the next 48 hours—whether he would play Barkley in the final game.

"I came here to do something special, and obviously breaking the record is special," Barkley said. "But I want a banner up there. I think we all do."

CHAPTER 24

EAGLES VS. GIANTS

Saquon Barkley entered Week 18 just 101 yards shy of breaking Eric Dickerson's single-season record, and a national debate ensued about whether the Eagles should play their star running back. With the Eagles entrenched as the No. 2 seed and hosting an opening round playoff game the following week, the season finale would seem like an opportune time to rest starters without a bye week since Week 5. But this was also the chance for history.

Nick Sirianni weighed the decision after discussions with Barkley and veterans on the team. He conferred with Howie Roseman. The coordinators and position coaches offered their input. Sirianni elected to sit Barkley and bypass the chance of breaking the record in a game against Barkley's former team—the one that undervalued him, let him leave, and watched him have a historic season.

"It's a very special record that's been standing for a very long time by a great player. It's a team record that everybody's involved in. So you weigh in all those things, but at the end of the day, you just try to do what's best for the team," Sirianni said. "It wasn't the easiest decision to go through.... We have just selfless guys that want to do what's best for the football team. Get some guys some rest."

Barkley was conflicted. After the Cowboys game, he admitted he did not care too much about whether he would break the record. After sleeping on it, he felt stronger about playing.

"It was like an opportunity to imprint my name in football history. You may never get an opportunity like that again. So I'm down,'" Barkley said. "But at the end of the day, I don't care for putting the team at risk. [Sirianni is] the head coach for a reason. He makes those decisions. And whatever decision he wanted to make—if he wanted to play, I'm going to make sure I go out there and get it. And if we don't, I'm OK with that, too."

The challenge with playing Barkley is it's not *just* Barkley. The starting offensive linemen would need to play, too. There's more risk of injury and exposure to fatigue for the rest of the team. In Week 18 of the 2023 season, A.J. Brown suffered a knee injury that kept him out of the postseason loss to Tampa Bay. How would the team feel—how would the fan base feel—if someone suffered an injury because the Eagles were trying to rewrite history books?

"The record would be cool. But we want guys who have had a long season to rest up or you have a chance of a player getting injured," Lane Johnson said. "I look at [Brown's] situation last year. He didn't play in the Tampa game last year. So you try to learn lessons from past experiences."

Jordan Mailata called them "tough conversations"—it did not seem unanimous, and Mailata had said he wanted to break the record—because it is a team record, too. The Eagles offensive line would have been the group that blocked for the record-holder. Back in Week 14, when Barkley broke LeSean McCoy's single-season franchise history, Mailata remembered Barkley giving his offensive linemen a new goal: "Let's go get ED's [record]." It was something that had been a target behind the scenes.

The person who might have taken it the hardest was Barkley's father, Alibay. The two spoke on New Year's Day, one day before

Sirianni made the news public. How special would it be to see the Barkley name attached to a prestigious record?

"Selfishly for him, you got to think about it. For however long, if it took a year for someone to break it or another 40 to 50 years, our last name would have been attached to that," Saquon Barkley said. "So I see it from that side, too. But at the end of the day, the most important thing is to win football games. And he's the one to raise me to be about the team, too. So he can have his little selfish moment, but he'll get over it."

There were different rationalizations, too. Dickerson set the record in 16 games. Barkley would have set it in 17 games. Does that water down the record at all? It's like the Roger Maris conversation from 1961. Johnson thought reaching 2,000 yards was significant in its own right. When a baseball player reaches 3,000 hits, he's in the club—the hits thereafter are not always remembered.

"If I play next week and break ED's record, which, one, would be phenomenal. But I'm not into like, 'Oh, if you do it in 17 or 16 games,'" Barkley said. "I'm a fan of the position. If that's the case, then O.J. [Simpson] got the record. O.J. did it in 14 games. I know we don't really speak about that, but in reality, he rushed for 2,000 in 14 games. ED, it took him 15 to do it. So if anything, it's like, why are we even having the conversation? Or if you're trying to get ED's record, if that's the conversation, it should be, you've got to do it in 14. The way football is right now, it's kind of hard to rush for 2,000 yards in 14 games. So whether it's 16, whether it's 17, it's a feat that you can never take away from what I was able to do with the O-line. And only eight other players did it, so it's a special moment."

In an interview with the *Los Angeles Times*, Dickerson said he did not want Barkley to break the record. Barkley did not hold it against the Hall of Famer.

"If you had a record, would you want me to break your record?" Barkley said. "I don't look at it that way. I haven't broken records—I guess I have this year, technically, with the Eagles franchise—but if 10 years from now, or next year, three years, however long when I'm done playing football, if a back is able to beat my Eagles franchise record, or say, if I did break ED's record, I [would say], 'Go ahead and get it, it's fun.' You want to be that. It's an honor to have your name attached to that record and having guys chasing it. Guys have been chasing that record for 40 years. So I don't see it as a shot. I don't see it as throwing shade. You shouldn't want me to break your record. That's how I look at it."

Of course, Dickerson never won a Super Bowl ring. The two aren't mutually exclusive, but the ultimate rationalization for Barkley was that he was not pursuing the rushing record because there were bigger goals in mind—and anything that could be remotely impeding that goal goes by the wayside in January.

"That's what I tell my family: We didn't come here, I didn't sign here, to break Eric Dickerson's record," Barkley said. "We came here to win the Super Bowl."

This was also the week when Pro Bowlers were named. The Eagles had six on the initial roster: Barkley, Johnson, Landon Dickerson, Cam Jurgens, Zack Baun, and Jalen Carter. It was the first time Jurgens, Baun, and Carter earned that honor. For Jurgens and Carter, it was seen as an example of the team's successful succession plans after the retirements of Jason Kelce and Fletcher Cox.

"I feel like before the season, every day I was getting questions about what it's like taking over for Kelce, this and that," said Jurgens, who had created his own name and reputation after an enormous shadow preceded his entry to the lineup. "Then the season started, and I feel like I was playing good, and I didn't get a single question about that until just now. I feel like I did good my first year. There's still room to improve, but I'm happy."

Dickerson gave the response that was common for any Pro Bowler on a contending team: "I hope I don't go." That would mean the Eagles were in the Super Bowl. However, he seemed mystified by the voting because it didn't include Mailata. "I don't know how the voting shit works or whatever, but that's probably the most rigged, flawed shit in the world," Dickerson said. "Because I think that's the best left tackle in the league right now."

It would not be evident in the season finale, at least. Without Barkley on the field—and most other starters—there was less buzz for the Week 18 visit from the Giants. Jalen Hurts remained in the concussion protocol and Pickett nursed a ribs injury, giving Tanner McKee his first career start. If there was anything memorable from the game, it was the way McKee played. He went 27-of-41 for 269 yards and two touchdowns. Jahan Dotson, who had modest contributions since the August trade, excelled as the top pass catcher with a 94-yard effort. The defense limited the Giants to 238 yards and 13 points, ensuring that they finished the season No. 1 in total defense and No. 1 in scoring defense. It was the first time they had the league's top defense since 1991—a stark turnaround considering the way the defense had played one year prior. They were now in the same category as a group that featured Reggie White, Jerome Brown, Clyde Simmons, Seth Joyner, and Eric Allen.

That group was historic. But they never won in the playoffs. It was a good reminder of what mattered for the Eagles.

"I think it's a good honor for the players," Fangio said. "They are the ones that did the work. They deserve it. But we are on to the playoffs now."

In the postgame locker room, what was ahead mattered more than what they had accomplished. It was the 14th win of the season—the second time in franchise history they had achieved that mark, both under Sirianni. It was the 300th win of Jeffrey

Lurie's ownership, something Roseman noted in front of the team when he threw the game ball to Lurie. The owner and the architect embraced, and when the players called for a speech, Lurie focused on the 301st win—and then 302nd, 303rd, and 304th.

"This is for all you guys," Lurie said, as captured by the team's video crew. "We have a lot more to accomplish. Fourteen wins, be proud of it. But you know where our goals are. It starts next weekend."

Time Out: Darius Slay

Darius Slay's locker was next to Quinyon Mitchell's locker at the team facility. Slay requested it this way. He remembered the way veterans treated him, guided him, mentored him when the Detroit Lions selected Slay early in the second round of the 2013 draft. He vowed to do the same for Mitchell, the Eagles' first-round pick who Slay acknowledged was there to one day take over for him as the team's top cornerback.

But not in 2024. No, this would be Slay's final season after five years with the team. The Eagles acquired him from Detroit in 2020 to give them a No. 1 cornerback—an elusive distinction in Philadelphia, as Slay noted in his Super Bowl speech. He made three Pro Bowls during that span and thrice served as team captain. He went to the two Super Bowls. He won one. When the Eagles traded for Slay, Fletcher Cox—Slay's teammate at Mississippi State—told him that Philadelphia is different and he would win if he went there.

During the playoff run, anyone who went to Slay's locker—or Mitchell's locker, for that matter—could see a red plastic gas can, like what you use to fill up your car when it goes idle on the side of the road. On the gas can, there was a yellow Post-It note. It was from Eagles defensive backs coach Christian Parker, who at age 32 was actually younger than Slay.

How much gas do you have left in the Big Play tank? CP

The answer proved to be enough to win the Super Bowl.

"It went by fast," Slay said before the NFC Championship Game, which was his final home game with the Eagles. "I'm thinking, 'Dang boy, Slay! Five years here, four times playoffs, two times NFC championship [game].' And it went by in a blink of an eye."

Cornerback is a position in which its inhabitants don't age gracefully. You lose a step, you lose your game. Slay is an exception. He was one of three cornerbacks age 33 or older in 2024. He still made plays, including a highlight-worthy interception in the postseason opener. (Slay did not go by "Darius." If you didn't call him "Slay," he would otherwise answer to his nickname, "Big Play.")

"Well, he's like some good Italian Dago red wine," defensive coordinator Vic Fangio said. "Gets better with age."

"The only time I feel 34 is on a Wednesday," Slay said. "You can feel 34 today. But on Thursday, Friday, Saturday, Sunday, I feel 25."

Fangio noted how Slay takes good care of his body—Slay said he's never had a sip of alcohol, so he cannot attest to the red wine—and that Slay still enjoys playing football. That cannot be overlooked—or overstated. Walk by Slay's locker on a Friday and ask him about the game from the night before, and chances are he watched it. Quiz him on a cornerback prospect in the draft, chances are he's watched his film. Discuss an opposing wide receiver, and Slay will reel off a scouting report. He used to find local high school games to attend. He trains young cornerbacks during the offseason.

"He has an appreciation and an energy level like he's a rookie," Parker said. "He has more energy than a rookie, to be honest with you."

If energy is indicated by volume, then yes. Mitchell is more mild-mannered. Slay has never met an audience he did not want to make laugh. Earlier in his career, he felt his light-hearted manner made him misunderstood, as if he did not take football seriously. He likes to laugh, joke, and smile. But you better believe he likes to play football.

"I'm already wealthy enough to be chilling," Slay said. "I won't be playing this game for free…but I do love this game. I do love and appreciate this game, what it's taught me, what it's done for me."

That's felt in the locker room—"Locker room [talk] is the best talk," Slay once said. "That's what you really miss in the football world"—and his contact list stretches a decade-plus of teammates for whom he'll vouch. They'll vouch for him, too. He used to bring homemade banana pudding around from his wife on Fridays to feed the players. When former Eagles safety Marcus Epps opened a gym in California, Slay flew out to work out at the gym as a sign of support.

"He doesn't just talk about football; he talks about life," Isaiah Rodgers said. "He cares about the guys around him. He cares about the guys in the room. He treats practice squad players like they're playing this week."

In 2022, Slay's peers voted him team captain. He cried when the announcement was made. Sirianni could not contain his excitement for the announcement. Jalen Hurts declared he wants Slay leading.

"As a teammate, he's one of the best teammates in the locker room," A.J. Brown said. "As a player, I think he's a Hall of Fame player."

The Hall of Fame might be ambitious—"I did enough to get a big toe in it," Slay said—although he was one of the best cornerbacks of his generation and a Super Bowl run helped. The Eagles moved on from Slay after the 2024 season, as Slay expected. Mitchell and Cooper DeJean took his place, just as Slay once took over Rashean Mathis' spot as the top cornerback. Slay left for Pittsburgh, but his legacy remains in the Eagles' locker room. Slay remembers when Mathis told him after a few weeks, "Hey Slay, all I'm here to do is be your guide, but this is your DB room. You're the future." Slay did the same for Mitchell. Howie Roseman even said when Mitchell was drafted that he wanted Mitchell to live next to Slay.

As Cox was fond of saying, everyone's just renting space. Slay emptied the tank in Philadelphia. It was someone else's turn to ride.

CHAPTER 25

NFC WILD CARD GAME

THERE WAS A SYMMETRY to the postseason opening against the Green Bay Packers, just as the regular season did, although the way the Eagles were viewed entering the two games differed. In Week 1, the Eagles were expected to be an offensive juggernaut while the defense was the unknown variable. Come January, the Eagles had solidified themselves as the No. 1 defense in the NFL. It was a ranking they earned—and they still felt as if they were not given due respect, probably because their ascent into the NFL's elite unit was unexpected and their best players were still not yet household names. They had proven themselves against top quarterbacks—Green Bay's Jordan Love among them—and the group was far superior to the one Love witnessed in Brazil. The questions about the Eagles were focused on the offense, especially because Jalen Hurts was not cleared from his concussion until two days before kickoff and the Eagles were not the pass-heavy team that the Packers prepared for in September.

Throughout the week leading up to the game, the Eagles heard how they drew a tough matchup for a No. 2 seed. Because the playoff seeding favors division champions, a third-place team in the NFC North with 11 wins (as the Packers were in 2024) was seeded below 10-win division champions from the NFC South and NFC West. So the Eagles, who were the No. 2 seed, drew a superior team than the other opening-round teams in the NFC. In fact, five of the Packers' six losses during the regular season had come against 14-win teams. They were ranked No. 4 in DVOA (defense-adjusted value over average, a metric that analyzes every play and compares a team's performance against the league average). The Eagles drew a bona fide Super Bowl contender in the first round. The Eagles were still a 14-win heavyweight in their own right—and they entered the game 5.5-point favorites, even greater than the point spread on a neutral field in Week 1—but it was not difficult to encounter upset picks from some daring pundits. And it was not hard to find precedent, either. One year earlier, the Packers were the No. 7 seed and had upset the second-seeded Dallas Cowboys in the opening round of the playoffs. Love was sensational, offering compelling evidence to a deal he signed months later that made him the highest-paid player in the NFL.

The 2024 Eagles were better than the 2023 Cowboys. Playing in Philadelphia in January is more daunting than playing in Dallas.

By the time the Eagles completed a 22–10 victory over Green Bay, it was clear why Vic Fangio's group was No. 1 in the NFL. The Packers' 10 points were their fewest of the season—and their fewest since November 2022. Green Bay did not score a touchdown until the fourth quarter. The Eagles intercepted Love three times, part of four takeaways in the game. When Darius Slay was asked after the game how they performed so well against a top 10 offense, Slay was surprised there was any surprise.

"What are we ranked as a defense?" Slay asked. "We come out there to play, too."

The Eagles showed their fangs from the opening kickoff. "From the jump, make 'em feel you!" special teams coordinator Michael

Clay told his group, as captured by team footage. "Get 'em down, get the fucking ball out!"

Sure enough, when defending the kickoff, linebacker Oren Burks popped the ball from returner Keisean Nixon's grip and Jeremiah Trotter Jr. recovered the fumble. (Burks was fined by the league for use of a helmet on the play. No flag was thrown during the game.) The forced fumble resonated even more because kickoff coverage had been a point of emphasis during the preparations leading up to the game. They even sprinkled in starters on the unit to add more teeth to the group. The upgrades included Nolan Smith.

Three plays later, Jalen Hurts threw a touchdown to Jahan Dotson. Hurts was back. The offense scored early. The Eagles never trailed.

The dominant performance from the defense included an interception by Slay, who ran stride-for-stride with a Packers receiver and looked like a receiver hauling in a highlight-worthy catch when the Packers were trying to intrude on the Eagles' 10–0 lead.

"You know what they call me!" Slay shouted toward the fans on the sideline, referencing his "Big Play Slay" moniker.

It was the first interception by an Eagles cornerback all season—Slay had been suggesting in the film room all week that an interception was coming—and it was the first Slay ever made in a postseason game. It also proved to be his final interception in an Eagles uniform.

"I was like, 'Oh shit, Slay, this motherfucker [is] right here in front of you,'" Slay colorfully described his interception after the game, "and then I just caught that motherfucker."

Perhaps a more impressive interception came at the end of the quarter—and take it from Slay, who called it "one of the best plays I've seen in a long time by a linebacker." The Packers had entered Eagles territory for only the second time all game and the score had been locked at 10–0 throughout the quarter. Love thought he had an open receiver in the middle of the field. He did not see Zack Baun drop deep into coverage, drift off his man in improvisation, and break on the ball. Baun, a Wisconsin native, described it as a "dream interception" because of "the situation and the coverage and the play that it was against"—although it was not nearly as memorable as an interception he would make one month later in the Super Bowl. This interception came days after he was named first-team All-Pro and was evidence of the trust that Fangio had developed in his emerging star.

"Just trusting my coverage responsibility and playing free within the system to seal backside dig," Baun said, describing the play. "I have a list of dream interceptions I want to make, and that was one of them."

Baun's role also evolved in the game. Nakobe Dean, who had been such a steady sidekick all season for Baun, exited the game with a serious knee injury. It prematurely ended his season, and it seemed grim on the field. Baun assumed the duties of defensive signal-caller. Dean's absence was especially devastating to Smith, his college roommate and close friend. Smith tried to help Dean up after the play; Dean could not stand.

Smith finished what had heretofore been his best game in the NFL with a heavy heart. He recorded two sacks and two tackles for a loss against an offensive tackle that Lane Johnson described as one of the best in the NFL. Sirianni, who awarded Smith the game ball for the way he played in the game, said afterward the Eagles have "seen Nolan grow into this player with the things he was able to do today to help us win a playoff football game." It didn't happen right away, and it was not the way Smith was discussed entering the first Packers game, when he had just been one of the few regulars playing in the preseason finale.

"I want my sons to play football like Nolan Smith," Sirianni said. "Before my kids go out to play any sport, I say, 'Have fun, play hard, be physical.' That guy is the definition of those things. He has fun out there. He has fun with his teammates. His teammates love him. He plays as hard as I've ever seen anybody play, and this dude is a physical, physical, physical guy."

That was why Smith embraced playing special teams during the game. It was more football for someone who shared the perspective that he could be back on the docks in his native Savannah, Georgia, latching down boats on a 12-hour shift. Think that way and running down on kickoff coverage doesn't sound so arduous. And after the game, he said he just wanted to find his mother. "I go out there and I just want to make my mama proud and make the 10 guys next to me proud," Smith said. "When they turn on the film, they know [No. 3] gonna fly around to the ball. I just try to do that every day, even in practice."

The final interception of the game came on the Packers' final offensive play, when the Eagles had a 12-point lead and looked ready to advance. Quinyon Mitchell, whose outstanding rookie season included the lone knock of no interceptions, finally finished a play with the ball. He had been so close so often—*too* often—and his teammates had razzed him about his near misses. Finally, on a Love deep shot for the end zone, Mitchell forced the Eagles' fourth turnover. The celebration on the sideline was not just for the Eagles advancing, but also because of the elusive interception for the first-round pick.

"A lot of excitement," Mitchell said. "All year in the cornerback room, we hadn't had an interception. So it was real nice for both of us to get it."

"I'm so happy I almost cried," Slay said. "I know it don't count on his record, but this is way bigger—a playoff pick in a big-time game to end the game."

The problem for the Eagles? As dominant as the defense played, they did not turn any of the three interceptions into points—although Saquon Barkley could have scored after the final interception had he not slid to let the clock wind down. The offense totaled 290 yards, they went 2-of-11 on third downs, and they had six drives of fewer than 20 yards. It was a one-possession game in the second half despite the defense stifling Green Bay. But the Eagles did not turn the ball over and did enough for the victory. Johnson said it would not help the offense's Yelp review.

"We have to do a better job making plays when they create turnovers," Barkley said. "We've got to score points off of that."

"We don't win that game without the defense playing lights out," Jordan Mailata said.

It was a tough day to get a read on the offense. The biggest story was a key player reading.

In the second half of the win, FOX television cameras caught Brown on the sideline bench reading a dog-eared copy of *Inner Excellence*, a self-help book by former minor league baseball player Jim Murphy that had been transformational for Brown. He carried it so often that teammates started calling it the "recipe," although it was nonetheless striking to a national audience seeing a professional football player reading during the game.

"That's a book that I bring every single game," Brown said. "That's the first time I heard that y'all got me on camera. But it's not the first game. It's got a lot of points in there. It's a lot of mental game, a lot of mental parts about it. For me, this game is mental."

The book was recommended by Eagles defensive lineman Moro Ojomo. Brown tries to read two books per month, leaning toward nonfiction. He highlights different sections, like the second page of the book that reads:

> In the pursuit of extraordinary performance, it's easy to succumb to anxiety and pressure, because so much is out of your control. When you learn to live a life that is fully engaged, however, then you can perform your best and love the challenge.

"I always revert back to the beginning of the book," Brown said. "It states that if you can just have a clear mind, if you have a clear mind and remember that nothing else matters. Clear mind and clear conscience, [then] nothing matters, negative or positive. You're willing to take risks. I go back to it. It also says if you're humble, you can't be embarrassed. So no matter what happens in a game or no matter what happens, I'm just going to stay free and play free, keep going, take risks."

For those who do not know Brown—or for those who try to typecast a wide receiver—the leap was made that his literary retreat was born from frustration. He laughed off that suggestion, having heard it before. The storyline was exhausted.

"I was not frustrated at all," said Brown, who had one catch for 10 yards on three targets when cameras caught him mid-chapter. "I figured that's what y'all probably thought. I wasn't frustrated. Why y'all always think I be frustrated?... I like to read!"

Brown had read the book against Washington when his production was prolific. The book was in hand at the Super Bowl, too. The frustration angle was a poor leap to make. Plus, the behind-the-scenes footage from the game revealed how locked in Brown was on the postseason victory. This was apparent in the final two minutes of the game, when Barkley burst through the Green Bay line of scrimmage and could have sprinted for a 76-yard touchdown, adding to the list of his home run rushes throughout the season. Instead, after 17 yards, Barkley slid to the ground. Before the drive, the Eagles were told "no más"—the play nickname for falling to the ground and letting the clock wind down. Brown, watching from the sideline with Smith, remarked how he would have gone for more yards. (Barkley would have finished with 178 yards had he sprinted for the end zone.)

"You said, 'No más!'" Barkley said when he approached the sideline with Brown and Smith ready to mock him.

"No one's catching your fast ass!" Sirianni said.

"Keep fucking running!" Smith said.

Barkley would have his chance the following week. Because the Eagles advanced. That was the purpose of the opener. And they were only getting better.

"It wasn't a perfect game for us. It's not baseball," Sirianni said. "We're not ever going to pitch a perfect game, right? It's not going to happen. That's the beauty of this sport. It's never going to be a perfect game. But why did that happen? Why is it like that? [The Packers are] a great football team.... So that's what happens in the playoffs. Again, it's going to be about how you play the next play. How do you go on and move on from that?"

The answer came on a snow-covered field one week later.

CHAPTER 26

NFC DIVISIONAL GAME

DURING THE WEEK LEADING UP to the Eagles' 28–22 divisional-round victory over the Los Angeles Rams, Nick Sirianni focused his message on adversity. He might have also been thinking about the weather—a snowstorm was predicted for Sunday with a potential snow globe effect for the game—but Siranni's messaging to the team harped on how they were hardened to deal with adversity. Bad weather? A Super Bowl–winning coach and quarterback on the other sideline? A devastating injury to a defensive leader? They could handle it.

"Let's think about last year's journey, just for one second, 2023 Eagles and all the things we learned from that," Sirianni said in a team meeting, as seen on team footage. "Think about this year when we started off 2–2 and all the things we learned from that to put us in the position we're in now. We're battle-tested.... We redefined our habits, our process."

The Eagles had learned from 2023. They had learned from the start of the 2024 season. Sirianni put a message on the team video board: "Adversity brings something out of us that ease never could. But only if you embrace it." The message could also be found at the end of a passage in the book *Daily Wisdom: 366 Days of Motivational Thoughts, Quotes, and Stories*—yes, it works during a leap year—about the lessons from the 2019 University of Virginia men's basketball team, who won a national championship one year after losing to the No. 16 seed.

Sirianni wanted the Eagles to embrace the adversity. It was a message he echoed throughout the postseason.

"If you can't overcome it, maybe you don't deserve to be a championship team," Sirianni told his team on the eve of the divisional round game. "We're battle-tested. We're ready for this shit. We're ready for fucked-up shit to happen tomorrow and play the next play."

When the Eagles arrived at the stadium on January 19, it was a clear (albeit cold) afternoon. By the time they went home, they needed to clear snow off their cars. In those hours between, a few inches of swirling snow accumulated and made for one of the most memorable postseason games played in Philadelphia in recent history.

"I've never played in one of these," Zack Baun said on the sideline in the second half, an interesting admission from a Wisconsin native.

Truth is, it's hard to find a confluence of heavy snow and a three-hour window for a football game. There had not been a game like this in Philadelphia since 2013 against the Detroit Lions—famously remembered as the "Snow Bowl"—and coincidentally involving Rams star Matt Stafford as the opposing quarterback. LeSean McCoy rushed for a then franchise record 217 yards that day. Barkley snapped the record in 2024 against, of all teams, the Rams, with 255 yards. In the days leading up to the game, Barkley wanted to reach out to McCoy for advice on running in the snow. He played in wintry conditions growing up in the Lehigh Valley and at Penn State, but if he could tap into McCoy's success at the stadium, so be it. However, his best resource would be Greg Delimitros, the Eagles' vice president of equipment operations. Barkley admitted he was "stubborn" when the Eagles played on the slippery turf in São Paulo's Corinthians Arena in the season opener, causing him to slip for a five-yard loss on his first carry with the Eagles. At the urging of the equipment staff, he switched into cleats with longer studs. The results were evident.

"They know a little bit more than me in that aspect," Barkley said.

In fact, Sirianni asked Delimitros to write a report on "everything...he's ever done for a snow game in his career," and the level of detail impressed the detail-obsessed head coach. There were varying degrees of experience in snow football among players in the locker room. Jalen Hurts had never seen snow until he came to the Eagles. When he was inserted into the game for Carson Wentz against Green Bay on an afternoon that changed Eagles history, Hurts played in snow for the first time. A Houston native, Hurts would never be accused of celebrating winters in the Northeast. But, as he explained, "just because I say it's cold doesn't mean it's bothersome." And teammates took notice when he practiced without sleeves on a frigid afternoon in January. As fun as it might look to play in the snow, not all players enjoyed it. It's hard to get a footing. That made it difficult for the pass rushers. "I'd rather play on the shitty Brazil field again before I play on that again, I ain't going to lie to you," Josh Sweat said. "I'll be real with you: Nobody wants to play in it."

But both teams needed to play in it—at least in the second half.

At the start of the game, it looked like your typical bitter January afternoon in Philadelphia. The Rams had upset the 14-win Minnesota Vikings in the opening round of the playoffs, but the Eagles entered the game as 7.5-point favorites and had already decimated the Rams in November. Anything could happen in a one-game playoff, though, as football fans witnessed on the eve of the Eagles–Rams game when the Washington Commanders shocked the top-seeded Detroit Lions. That result had significant implications for the Eagles. The Eagles were the No. 2 seed. The Lions' loss meant the Eagles would host the NFC Championship Game if they could beat Los Angeles.

All season, Barkley's running had paced the offense. That was the case against the Rams in November. Sometimes, Hurts likes to remind you that he, too, can run. On the opening drive, Hurts faked a handoff to Barkley and kept the ball on a second down, broke free from a tackle, and sprinted 44 yards for a touchdown. It was the longest run of his career. He cupped his hand to his ear when he reached the touchdown, a la Allen Iverson.

"Earned that, [number] one!" Kenny Pickett told Hurts on the bench.

"That's a way to start the game!" quarterbacks coach Doug Nussmeier added.

"Saquon needed a break, so I told him I'd do it first," Hurts joked after the game. "Get me a piece."

It didn't take long before Barkley surpassed him. On a third-and-4 with 77 seconds remaining in the first quarter and the game tied 7–7, Barkley found an open crease and acted like he was in SoFi Stadium. It was a familiar sight for the Rams. Barkley rushed for a 62-yard touchdown, picking up where he left off in the last Rams game. Big snowflakes started to fall from above and Barkley's storybook season continued with a chapter that A.J. Brown would enjoy. The offensive linemen who helped Barkley break records—and nearly break the all-time record—helped author the story.

"They got nothin' over there," offensive line coach Jeff Stoutland told his group on the sideline, debriefing the play.

"I pancaked my guy," Landon Dickerson said. "Cam, I think you put your guy on the ground. Fuck yeah!"

"Did we all put our guys on the ground?" Cam Jurgens responded.

The Eagles brought a 13–10 lead into halftime. By the time they returned from the locker room, the snow was beginning to stick.

"Right where we want 'em," Barkley said.

"Thirty minutes for everything you want," safeties coach Joe Kasper told Baun. "You either take it or you don't."

The game was in a 13–13 stalemate for most of the third quarter. The weather worsened—"I was expecting a snow game, not a hail game," Baun said to Oren Burks on the bench at one point—and the concern swelled beyond handling the conditions. A Rams defender fell on Hurts' left leg, and the quarterback was in immediate pain. He walked with a heavy limp. The Eagles took a 16–13 lead, although attention was on the medical tent where he was evaluated. Hurts came out and attempted warm-up throws—he was not going to leave the game—but he was not moving like the player who had just rushed for the longest touchdown of his career. That was evident when the Eagles were backed up by their end zone upon Hurts' return and he was sacked for a safety. What did Sirianni say again about undesirable events (in so many words) occurring during the game? This was a test—it was 16–15, the quarterback was injured, the snow was a neutralizer, and the Rams had possession with a chance to take the lead.

"We talk about adversity. How do we respond?" linebackers coach Bobby King said on the sideline.

"We need a turnover!" Baun said.

Baun's clairvoyance—or perhaps just confidence—was on display throughout the season. Jalen Carter stripped the ball from Rams running back Kyren Williams. Isaiah Rodgers, who was playing in place of the injured Quinyon Mitchell, scooped the fumble and returned the ball to the 10-yard line. The defense came through *again*.

"I told you I would get one!" Carter said to Baun.

The Eagles settled for a field goal—veteran kicker Jake Elliott, who had been inconsistent at points during the season, proved clutch in the inclement weather while teammates cleared space on the turf for Braden Mann to place the ball—and that gave them some breathing room. The defense was still not finished. Nolan Smith forced a fumble that Baun recovered, setting up another Elliott field goal and a seven-point lead.

"This is the best defense in the…league, and the game's on us to win this," defensive backs coach Christian Parker said on the sideline. "What else would you rather be doing?"

For Hurts, the answer was scoring touchdowns. Because after the defense forced a three-and-out with the clock ticking below five minutes in the game, he came to the huddle and told his teammates to finish it on their terms. Then came one of the signature plays of the 2024–25 NFL season.

Barkley confers with a sports therapist to hone his mindset. He told himself a personal mantra—Barkley revealed to *Sports Illustrated* that he visualizes the Black Panther—and embarked on a transformational highlight. It happened almost by accident. He told offensive coordinator Kellen Moore the play he wanted based on how the defense had been playing. But Barkley lined up on the wrong side of Hurts with the ball at the 22-yard line. Hurts made a check, and Barkley was uncertain whether he should switch sides.

"I knew exactly what was about to happen," Hurts said. "Just the run we had on, how they were playing the run, and then the man you're handing the ball off to. You know that there's an opportunity to take advantage of it."

Hurts took the snap, handed the ball to Barkley, and the best running back in the NFL added an iconic sprint to a season already filled with unforgettable moments. Hurts and teammates extended their hands with a touchdown signal before Barkley had even passed the first-down marker. There was no one in front of him. His eyes widened. There was no "No Más" called this week. When he approached the end zone, he galloped like he was at recess at Marvine Elementary School. He slapped his helmet. He slid in the snow. It was pure euphoria, a 78-yard touchdown that gave him the second 200-yard game of his career. Both came against the Rams. Earlier in the week, he'd researched the Eagles' postseason record. It was set in 1949 by Steve Van Buren—the Hall of Fame running back who famously won the 1948 NFL Championship while playing in a blizzard in Shibe Park. Barkley broke the 76-yard record. "You chase greatness," he said. Ask Barkley, and he'll take this play over the backward leap against Jacksonville. He watched replays on Instagram in the following days with the play slowed down and the NFL Films music offering a soundtrack.

"That was probably my favorite touchdown so far of my football career, since I was a little kid," Barkley said. "Just the moment, the timing of it, the conversations that I had with myself, the stuff that I've been working on, it all kind of came together in that moment. It also taught me a lesson, too. I was still focused, it teaches you in that moment, there's still four minutes or however much time left, and before you know it, we're at the mercy of Matthew Stafford."

Elliott missed the extra point, but you would think a 13-point lead with 4:36 remaining in the game would ensure a victory. This was why Sirianni harped on handling adversity. Stafford led the Rams on a 10-play, 70-yard touchdown drive that exhausted only 1:48 off the clock. The Eagles had been so effective at closing games during the season, yet they went three-and-out. The Rams took possession at their 18-yard line with 2:23 remaining in the game and the chance to win.

"I didn't see it going any other way than us winning that game 29–28," Rams coach Sean McVay said after the game.

"It's gonna be on us, D!" Baun told his teammates.

Stafford led the Rams into the Eagles red zone. Seven years earlier, Stafford's close friend Matt Ryan neared the same end zone in the divisional round when the Eagles defense made a stand. Malcolm Jenkins and Fletcher Cox would be proud, because this group did the same.

On a third-and-2 at the 13-yard line, Jalen Carter eluded the offensive guard and pulverized Stafford while the quarterback needed another second to find his open receiver in the end zone. Had Carter not made the sack, the Rams likely would have scored. But Carter, who finished with five tackles, two sacks, three quarterback hits, a forced fumble, and a pass defended, added to his Eagles legacy.

"I went toward the center, did a little 'filet,' then went back inside," Carter said. "It was really nothing special, but it worked. Got pressure on the quarterback, one sack. It felt good, though."

"It was only a matter of time before he was going to kill that right guard—no disrespect to the right guard," Josh Sweat said.

On fourth down, Carter did the same. He pressured Stafford to make a wayward throw, and the Eagles hung on to win the game. Stafford was on the ground when the ball sailed out of bounds. He glanced up and saw Slay, his long-time teammate in Detroit, and realized the ball went incomplete.

"You won us this fucking game, bro!" Baun told Carter on the field.

"Oh my gosh, that dude is just a monster," Baun said a few minutes later. "The best in the league."

While Carter stood by his locker after the game, Howie Roseman walked by and asked if Carter wanted a picture.

"We need that for the Hall of Fame!" Carter said.

A few steps away stood Brian Dawkins, the Eagles icon who is in the Pro Football Hall of Fame.

"JC is so special, man," Barkley said. "He might be—I ain't trying to put too much on him right now—but going against him and now being on the same side, and talking to him on the sideline, looking him in the eye, and he said he would make a play. He's one of one."

It was the closest game the Eagles played throughout the playoffs. In Los Angeles, they still lament what could have been had Carter not pushed through for the sack. But they also could not stop Barkley, whose 205 rushing yards gave him 460 yards in two games against Los Angeles. Fans chanted "M-V-P" while Barkley ran into the tunnel. Snowflakes melted off his hair and shoulders. ("Rain, sleet, or snow, the Eagles train will go," Hurts told NBC.) Two young children waited to embrace Barkley, who held the game ball NBC had presented him. He gave the ball to one of the children. Unbeknownst to Barkley, that fan was the son of Delimitros, the Eagles equipment chief who outfitted Barkley for the snow in this game.

"This is what you dream about," Barkley said. "This is why I came to Philadelphia. I wanted to be a part of games like this and I'm just happy to be a part of it."

The snow that was left on the field was actually collected, bottled, and sold to fans as a keepsake for $50 a pint. ("Somebody's going to really buy snow? People bought snow?" Slay said. "That's why this is the best city, man—they're passionate around here. They're buying snow. I love it.") Whatever was left on the players' cleats had melted by the time Sirianni addressed the team. He wore a gold chain as a nod to C.J. Gardner-Johnson and echoed the message from the week. The players remembered their only loss since the bye week—in Washington—and players on the

Commanders saying they would see the Eagles again. That was coming one week later. And the Eagles were ready.

"We embraced the adversity, and we found a way. That's all that fucking matters right now!" Sirianni told his players. "It made me hungry as fuck. I'm so fucking hungry.... We got business to finish. We got fucking business to finish!"

The Eagles debuted in São Paulo in the NFL's first game on South American soil. They marked the occasion with a uniform combination never worn by the franchise (black helmet, white jersey, black pants) as a nod to the soccer club that plays at Corinthians Arena. It was Saquon Barkley's Eagles debut, and it showed the Eagles' high-powered offensive weapons: Barkley, A.J. Brown, DeVonta Smith, and Dallas Goedert—with Jalen Hurts leading the way at quarterback.

Nick Sirianni's sideline demeanor has been a source of intrigue in Philadelphia—never more than after the Eagles' Week 6 win over Cleveland, when Sirianni shouted toward the crowd after a victory. Sirianni's emotion is part of his authenticity, and he went from a coach rumored to be on the hot seat before the season to a Super Bowl winner with a contract extension and the best winning percentage of all active coaches.

Nakobe Dean's game-clinching interception against Jacksonville might be a forgotten highlight considering it was in the same game as Saquon Barkley's backward leap, but the play preserved the Eagles' winning streak and was a sign of the Eagles' player development and preparation. Dean gave up a touchdown on a similar play in training camp but prepared to see that route again and saved the game with his instincts and anticipation.

The Eagles' Week 13 win over Baltimore was an example of the team's toughness against one of the NFL's toughest opponents. A signature play in the game came when Cooper DeJean upended bruising running back Derrick Henry—and it was one of a few memorable plays during DeJean's rookie campaign.

The Eagles became famous for the "Tush Push"—a form of a quarterback sneak in which the quarterback dives low and players behind the quarterback help push him forward. The success of the play made it polarizing around the NFL, and there was even an (unsuccessful) vote during the spring of 2025 to try to ban it from the game.

The Eagles' divisional round playoff victory over the Los Angeles Rams came in swirling snow, making it a memorable afternoon for fans and leaving unforgettable images from the game. None resonates more than Saquon Barkley galloping like a schoolboy at recess while rushing for a 78-yard touchdown as part of a 205-yard performance.

Saquon Barkley opened the NFC Championship Game with a 60-yard touchdown on th offense's first play from scrimmage. He ran behind one of the NFL's best offensive lines including right tackle Lane Johnson—a six-time Pro Bowler who is one of the best player in franchise history.

The Eagles celebrated an NFC championship at home for the second time in three years The confetti fell and the locker room was joyous, but they were also focused on what was ahead. It was not a team simply happy to reach the Super Bowl.

Cooper DeJean's first interception was a pick-six in the Super Bowl—the first pick-six thrown by Patrick Mahomes in the Super Bowl and a moment in the Eagles' victory when it became clear they were the superior team that day.

The Eagles defense excelled in the Super Bowl, holding the Chiefs to six points through the first three quarters. The pass rush was a big reason why—the Eagles finished with six sacks—and even when they were not sacking Patrick Mahomes, they were keeping him under duress. That effort included Jalen Carter, a star on the Eagles defense and the key player on their defensive line.

The celebrations might have started after DeVonta Smith's touchdown catch—known in Philadelphia as "the Dagger"—and the play helped cement Jalen Hurts as the Super Bowl MVP. Smith's catch came in his return to his native Louisiana, prompting the receiver to be emotional after the victory.

Jeffrey Lurie accepted the Lombardi Trophy for the second time in seven seasons. Standing behind him was a talented roster that formed what Lurie wondered should be considered one of the best teams in modern NFL history. The Eagles won 16 of their last 17 games, with the only loss coming while Jalen Hurts was knocked out of the game with a concussion. They outscored opponents by 68 points in the playoffs.

Vic Fangio headlined the Eagles' overhauled coaching staff in 2024, and he oversaw a defensive turnover that finished with the Eagles as the No. 1 defense in the NFL and overwhelming Patrick Mahomes in the Super Bowl. Fangio, a Pennsylvania native, has been an NFL assistant since 1986. This was his first Super Bowl.

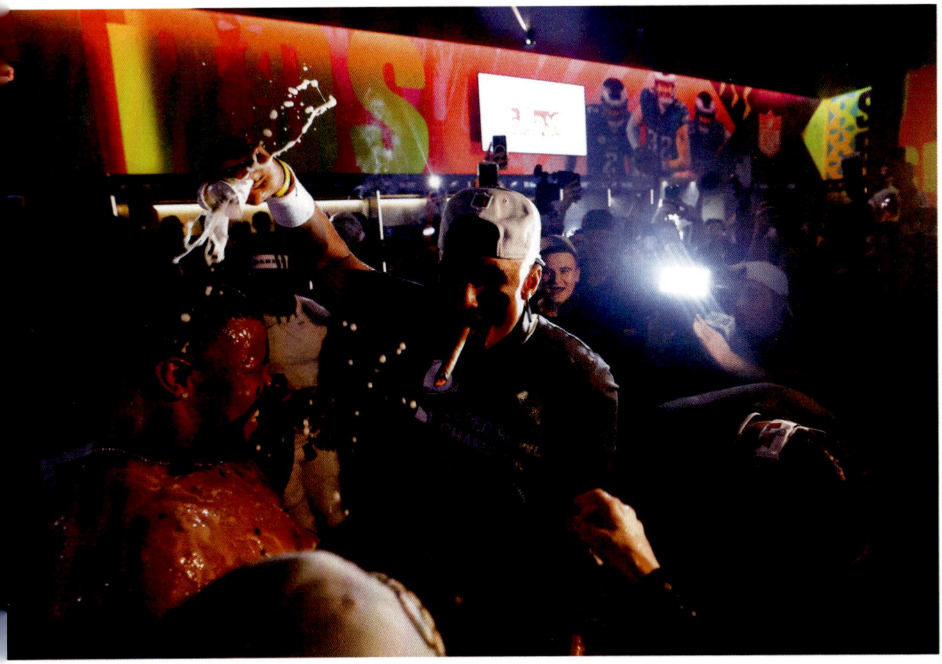

The biggest party after the Super Bowl came in the Eagles' locker room, where players celebrated with champagne, beer, and cigars. Even Jalen Hurts, who is known for his stoic demeanor, participated in the fun.

The architect of the Eagles was Howie Roseman, who became the fifth general manager in NFL history to win multiple Super Bowls with different quarterbacks. That distinction could land him in the Hall of Fame. In his parade speech, he said he "bleeds for this city" after he was hit in the head with a beer can that was hurled at the parade bus.

Philadelphia celebrated the Super Bowl with a parade up Broad Street that finished at the Philadelphia Museum of Art. It was the second time the Eagles traveled that parade route in seven years, and it left players in awe of the support from a fan base that believes it's the most passionate in the sport.

CHAPTER 27

NFC CHAMPIONSHIP GAME

"Y'ALL BELIEVE ME now?" C.J. Gardner-Johnson asked while wearing a gray NFC Championship T-shirt and a black championship cap that he was just handed on the field after a dominant 55–23 win over the Washington Commanders to clinch the Eagles' second Super Bowl appearance in three years.

Back in training camp, Gardner-Johnson said the Super Bowl "runs through Philly." It might have seemed ambitious then. It proved clairvoyant.

Minutes later, Gardner-Johnson danced in the locker room with entertainer and Eagles superfan Gillie Da Kid in the middle of the circle, and Gillie's song "Blow the Whistle" offered the soundtrack. In the corner of the locker room, Jalen Hurts lit a victory cigar.

Earlier in the week, the Eagles started preparing for Round 3 against the NFC East rival.

"Grudge match," Nick Sirianni told his players, as captured by the team footage. "I won one, you won one. One more for fucking everything! Let's fucking go!"

There was confidence emanating from the Eagles throughout the week. Yes, the Commanders beat the Eagles one month earlier (when Jalen Hurts exited the game with his concussion). Yes, they upset the top-seeded Detroit Lions. But the Eagles were a 14-win juggernaut with six players named to the Pro Bowl, a candidate for Offensive Player of the Year, and a candidate for Defensive Player of the Year. They were 6.5-point favorites, and even that seemed light. There was a better chance for a blowout than an upset when comparing the two rosters.

Sirianni started the week by asking the players to visualize their best moment, their best play—remembering all the pertinent details. Saquon Barkley reflected on his unforgettable performance in the snow one week earlier. Sirianni wanted them to think about who helped them accomplish that moment. On the big screen in the auditorium was a picture of the full team in a pregame huddle and a catchphrase that Sirianni picked up from a shirt wide receiver Johnny Wilson had worn earlier in the season: SOMETIMES YOU, SOMETIMES ME, ALWAYS US.

He told them they could not be great without the greatness of others—the ongoing expression Sirianni coined that came to embody the team.

"We're going to win because we win the turnover battle," Sirianni said. "Yeah, we're going to win because we stop them on fourth down in a critical fucking moment because we're up in this fucking group rush up front that we're going to stone them and keep 'em caged in, and then you guys are going to make a big play in the secondary. Yeah, we're going to win because we're scoring touchdowns in the red zone and we're going to keep in front of the sticks. We're going to win because we fucking do this shit together and we do it as a team—like we've been doing all year. Nothing fucking changes. Team, team, team. Together, together, together."

You could tell the Eagles were 21 weeks into the season. Hurts was pushing through a knee injury. Cam Jurgens struggled with a back injury.

"It's a part of the game," Hurts said. "I accept whatever comes with that. I've told you guys, I've submitted myself to doing whatever it takes to win. And some things come with that. But ultimately, you've just gotta make the adjustments you need to make to be able to play at a high level. There won't be any excuses going in or coming out."

The team's toughness was apparent. Sirianni highlighted it on the eve of the game.

"Mental toughness. There's no situation that can faze us," Sirianni told his team. "I can sit up here and show a thousand clips of our physical toughness—you guys know you're physically tough. Who's worked harder than us at the details? Nobody. And then together. Selflessness, trust, love. That's why I can sit up here right now confident. That's why I can sit up here right now excited. And I don't have a lot to say. I know I've talked a lot.... You guys have all said and lived it to a T. Your habits, what we talk about all the time. Tough, detailed, together are the truths of football. And I know this team. Go out there, be you, and do what's got us here. Tough, detailed, together. You guys said everything I needed to say. You should be confident. You should be very confident. Let's go kick their ass."

That was exactly what they did. Sirianni's new catchphrase of "tough, detailed, together" resonated—and was revealed.

Brian Dawkins energized the crowd before the game. Nick Foles roamed the field before the game. Gillie Da Kid ran with the players out of the tunnel. Anyone who was present for the NFC Championship Game against Minnesota seven years earlier remembers an energy that made it seem as if nobody was going to beat them that night. You would have thought the same this afternoon.

"All this shit we've been through to be here, man. All this shit we go through to have opportunities like this," Hurts told the team on the field before the game, as seen on video on the team's X account.

The Commanders opened the game with the ball, went with a no-huddle offense, and needed 18 plays to get a field goal. If that was their best punch, the Eagles showed they could take it.

"Seventeen-play drive and three points ain't going to fucking beat us!" defensive line coach Clint Hurtt told his group on the sideline, as revealed on the NFL Films' Mic'd Up segment.

And their response? On the first play from scrimmage for the offense, Saquon Barkley rushed for a 60-yard touchdown. He broke tackles, unleashed a spin move. Washington could not bring him down. It almost became predictable by this point. It was Barkley's seventh touchdown of at least 60 yards in an Eagles uniform. Nobody else in the NFL had more than two in 2024.

"That's the way you start a championship game," Barkley said. "We knew that when you play a team two or three times, they kind of get a beat on some of your stuff. So we gave them a dummy call and it worked to perfection."

Jordan Mailata, who wore the on-field microphone for the game, laughed the entire run down the field. He apologized to A.J. Brown for pancaking a defender into Brown, knocking down the star receiver in the process. The fun was evident. And it was just beginning.

"Hey, we not done!" Barkley told his teammates, as captured by the team footage. "That's just the start!"

On the next drive, Zack Baun and Cooper DeJean joined together to pummel the ball carrier and force a fumble that Reed Blankenship recovered.

"That's just the first one!" defensive backs coach Christian Parker said.

More would come—takeaways and Barkley touchdowns. Barkley rushed for a four-yard score to give the Eagles a 14–3 lead, and this seemed comparable to the two previous championship games at Lincoln Financial Field: a 31–7 blowout against San Francisco in January 2023 and the 38–7 domination of Minnesota in January 2018.

"They can't fuck with us, man!" DeVonta Smith said to Hurts while walking off the field.

Even when the Commanders cut the Eagles' lead to 14–12, there was little concern on the sideline. It was Hurts' time to take over the game. On an aggressive fourth-and-5 call from the 45-yard line, Hurts connected deep with Brown for a 31-yard gain. Brown burned Marshon Lattimore, and then he drew a pass interference in the end zone to set up the Brotherly Shove for the score.

Michael Clay's special teams unit, which started the postseason by forcing a fumble on a kickoff, reclaimed the ball for the offense when Will Shipley forced a fumble on the ensuing kickoff. It was recovered by Kenny Gainwell. Hurts' touchdown run was taken off the board by a holding penalty, but he quickly found the end zone with a four-yard touchdown pass to Brown.

"That's what the fuck I do!" Hurts screamed, slapping Sirianni's hand.

"That's trust right there!" he told Brown.

"Good dagger," Brown responded.

Looking for issues between the star quarterback and the star receiver? Not with the Super Bowl in sight.

The Eagles entered halftime with a 27–15 lead. One year earlier, they had reached 27 points just once in the final seven games. In the Leap Year, they had that at *halftime* of the championship game—and they were starting the second half with the ball. Jurgens, who did not start the game because of a back injury, needed to play in the third quarter in an emergency situation because of a Landon Dickerson injury.

"Break their will!" Mailata screamed at the offensive line on the field. "Break their will!"

That started to happen when Hurts rushed for his second touchdown of the game and punctuated it with the Griddy dance.

Washington had a chance to try to make it a one-score game in the third quarter before Oren Burks forced a fumble—the third forced fumble of the game—and sent the Eagles offense back on the field in Washington territory. When the Eagles neared the goal line for the Brotherly Shove, the Commanders tried a new tactic that became one of the memorable footnotes in the game. Washington linebacker Frankie Luvu tried timing his jump to leap over the line of scrimmage and was flagged for encroachment... and flagged again, seemingly putting Hurts in danger with each jump. The official announced that the Eagles would be awarded a touchdown if this continued.

"Let them know what's up," Barkley told Hurts before the quarterback dove for a touchdown and the Eagles took a 41–23 lead.

It was Hurts' third rushing touchdown of the game to go along with a passing touchdown. The quarterback push play had become so vexing for opponents that two months later, there was a push at the league meetings to outlaw the play on the grounds of health and safety and even aesthetics. Behind the scenes, there were whispers of jealousy; the Eagles were simply better at it than the rest of the league, and there was little success in stopping it. Washington could attest.

Barkley tied Hurts on the next possession with his third score, and the game was out of reach. The Eagles were ready to relieve both star players. Washington was broken.

"I was wondering what breaks first—your spirit or your body?" Mailata asked.

From the sideline to the grandstand to Broad Street, the celebration commenced.

"We're going to the Super Bowl, bro!" DeJean uttered to himself. "We're going to the fucking Super Bowl!"

DeJean reminded Barkley that they shared a birthday—February 9, which was the date of the Super Bowl. Practice squad safety Andre' Sam also celebrated his brother that day.

"Birthday party in New Orleans!" they said.

"Put that belt to ass!" Mailata told teammates on the sideline.

Gardner-Johnson was emotional embracing the head coach who believed in him, tears coming from his eyes.

Smith and Brown showered Sirianni with Gatorade. On the same sideline three months earlier, his buzzed head and emotional outburst drew headlines. Now he was going to the Super Bowl…again.

"Two times in four years, let's keep this shit going!" Smith said to Sirianni.

Confetti swirled over the field—the color that Hurts liked, not the color that remained a reminder on his phone. Championship caps and T-shirts were distributed while family members embraced on the field.

"Your dad is a legend!" Mailata told Barkley's son, who just watched his father rush for 118 yards in the NFC Championship Game and punch a ticket to the Super Bowl.

"That's why I came here," Barkley said in the locker room after the game. "That's one of the first conversations I had with Howie [Roseman]. That's the conversation I had with my family. I came to Philly to be part of games like this."

Nick Foles, who had been the Super Bowl MVP when the Eagles first won the Lombardi Trophy, presented Jeffrey Lurie with the organization's fifth George Halas Trophy. FOX commentator Terry Bradshaw asked Jeffrey Lurie about an unexpected run. *Unexpected*? Lurie suggested he expected it.

Sirianni took his time on the stage to highlight his quarterback. So often during the past year, the Sirianni–Hurts relationship had been scrutinized. Here they were, coach and quarterback, on the podium after a championship game victory for the second time together.

"How about our quarterback?" Sirianni said on live television. "He's a stud. I knew he was going to play that way. Don't doubt him. All he does is win."

Hurts finished 20-of-28 for 246 yards and one passing touchdown, plus three rushing touchdowns. He did not turn the ball over. It was one of the finest performances of his career. Barkley compared it to the "So that's what y'all wanted to see, huh?" game Hurts had against Pittsburgh when under so much scrutiny.

"I don't play the game for stats. I don't play the game for numbers, any statistical approval from anyone else," Hurts said. "And I understand that everyone has a preconceived notion on how they want it to look, or how they expect it to look. I told you guys that winning, success, is defined by that particular individual, and it's all relative to the person. And what I define it as is winning. So the number one goal is always to come out here and win."

Hurts added that Sirianni "let me out of my straitjacket a little bit today"—Sirianni suggested it was a joke—but it was also an example that Hurts can carry the team with his arm when needed. Hurts admitted it's "human nature to be ignited by the shortcomings"—a subtle indication that he keeps receipts.

"How about QB1? I love when people doubt him," Mailata said. "We always talk about limiting the outside noise or the white noise, but I know he hears that. And I think he plays his best when he feels like people doubt him. And then he does stuff like he did today."

"It's amazing how much doubt there is sometimes," Sirianni said. "I can't quite comprehend it because it doesn't look like what people think it should look like. But the guy has been clutch. He's won a ton of football games. 'But you ran for this many yards.' We don't care how we win. We don't care. If we rush for 300 and pass for one and we win, great. If we rush for one and pass for 300, great. Who cares? We've just continued to win. He's just continued to win."

Speaking of keeping receipts, the memories were vivid in the winner's locker room—even with the dance circle around Gillie. Brandon Graham, who likes to collect doubts and often jokes with any reporter that he or she is a naysayer, cackled while cataloging the criticism.

"Two-and-2, they fucking stink! Your ass can't score in the first quarter!" Graham said, aware of the narrative early in the season.

"A lot of places outside of Philly, the sky isn't falling," Barkley said. "But at the same time, that's why you come to places like this."

There were also the scars from the previous two years. The 2024 season might have been a Leap Year, but you cannot get to 2024 without 2022 and 2023. The way the Eagles rebounded, persevered, and endured to get back to the Super Bowl came with callouses and scars.

"It's been the story of the 2023 to the 2024 Eagles," Sirianni said. "As bad of a feeling we had about how last year ended, I think it makes you who you are. These guys are hungry, and we've got one more to go."

It was a clear theme. When Sirianni insisted during the summer that the 2024 Eagles were a new team, he used the example that newcomers like Barkley did not care that the Eagles collapsed in 2023. Barkley probably enjoyed it, Sirianni reasoned. But it would take someone unaware or desensitized to history to spend time with the team and not realize how they were shaped by the previous two years. It was not just the collapse of 2023, but the way they lost the Super Bowl at the end of the 2022 season.

"It don't matter if you don't win it. That's just the reality of it," said Barkley, who started the scoring with a 60-yard touchdown run on the offense's first play. "All the things we've done, and we've done a lot—I'm trying not to curse this time—but you know what I mean, and the most special thing you can do is win the Super Bowl. I wasn't here two years ago, but I bought into this culture, I bought into this organization. I know how those guys felt. I'll make sure I do everything in my capability so the same thing won't happen again."

Sirianni wore a cap and T-shirt, but he did not go overboard in celebration. There were times he watched the players around him and smiled. When he was asked what went through his mind while observing the room, he spoke about the "next game." That was not just a talking point with a reporter. In his speech behind closed doors, he echoed the message from the week.

"We got some unfinished business to handle," Sirianni said. "We're going to enjoy this. This is special. We've done a lot of special shit like we talked about. But one more step. One more step."

The operative word was "unfinished." Gardner-Johnson said in training camp the Super Bowl runs through Philadelphia, but they needed to go to New Orleans to finish the job. It would come against the team that broke their hearts two years earlier.

Yes, there was unfinished business.

"We got one more!" Hurts told his team. "We worked our ass off for this opportunity, just right here. Everything this group has gone through.... Let's go finish this shit! Finish is the fucking word! Finish is the only thing on our minds right now.

"Finish on three. 1–2–3, finish!"

CHAPTER 28

THE SUPER BOWL

THE COLOR OF THE CONFETTI MATTERS. It was on Jalen Hurts' phone for a reason. The confetti from the championship game is nice, but reach the Eagles' level, and the green confetti from the championship is not a keepsake. Celebrating in green confetti after the Super Bowl was all that remained.

Two years earlier, the Eagles had scraps of green confetti on their shoes during the locker room celebration after the NFC Championship Game. At the same time, there was a close eye on the postseason game occurring in Kansas City. The Eagles knew Goliath might await—Patrick Mahomes, the best quarterback in the NFL; and Andy Reid, the coach with the most wins in franchise history.

Two years later, there was less focus on the opponent during the celebration. When the Chiefs escaped with a 32–29 win over the Buffalo Bills in the AFC Championship Game, it seemed almost inevitable. This was not about exacting revenge. The Eagles had their own history to write.

The Chiefs were 15–2—tied for the best record in the NFL—and opened as 1.5-point favorites, although they were not considered as imposing as they were two years earlier. The Bills game was the first time they had scored more than 30 points all season.

Their offensive line required adjustments throughout the season. They did not have the same offensive firepower as the team that thwarted the Eagles. What they had, though, was the best player in the NFL and experience that cannot be ignored. Their quest was to secure the first "three-peat" in NFL history. They were outstanding in close games, and they knew how to navigate the Super Bowl.

"They're the best of the best. The best of the best," Howie Roseman said one day before boarding a flight to New Orleans. In Roseman's office, he once kept a board that showed the four finalists from the championship games. He maintained a daily exercise of examining that board and assessing how the Eagles compared at different spots. All the displays are digital these days, but Roseman knows those teams off the top of his head—and it's not hard to know it's the Chiefs. Kansas City had made every AFC Championship Game since 2018—the first year after the Eagles won the Super Bowl.

"The Chiefs are in my head," Roseman said. "But I think you have to think about how to beat the best."

Reid is a mentor of Roseman's, the first coach with whom Roseman worked and the person who might have been most influential in how he views building a football team. Roseman readily admits that he would not be in his position without Reid. They can talk throughout the year, except Super Bowl week. And Roseman knew that to experience the intoxicating feeling of falling confetti again, he needed to unseat Reid.

Reid, as you might imagine, is a difficult man to unseat.

"I think that when I'm talking to him I'm not necessarily thinking, 'Hey, I'm thinking about this move to try to beat you finally in a Super Bowl,'" Roseman said. "But obviously they're the standard."

By this point in Reid's career, he is more known for his time with the Chiefs than with the Eagles. That is a startling truth considering he spent 14 seasons with the Eagles, made the postseason nine times, made the championship game five times, won 140 total games, and left an unending mark on the organization. He will one day join the franchise's Hall of Fame. During a 2023 interview, Jeffrey Lurie stated that one of his regrets during his three decades owning the Eagles was not being able to find a way to make it work with Reid after 2012, when there was a prevailing sentiment that Reid needed a change of scenery for family reasons as much as football reasons. But Reid still maintained close connections with the Eagles, including with team security chief Dom DiSandro, and key members of the Chiefs organization previously worked for the Eagles. That includes team president Mark Donovan, general manager Brett Veach, and a good chunk of Reid's coaching staff. There were no introductions needed on the field before the Super Bowl.

"It's unique, for sure, and really unique to have it [happen] twice here," Reid said during Super Bowl week of facing the Eagles. "I have a lot of respect for the people in Philadelphia, how they run things, and the city itself."

When Reid took over the Chiefs, one of the staff members he relieved was Nick Sirianni. Kansas City was where Sirianni started his NFL career. It was where he met his wife, whose family is from the region. He had close friends in the organization, including ushers in his wedding. So the connections worked both ways, and Reid and the Chiefs outlasted Sirianni in his only bid for a Super Bowl. Sirianni insisted that there was no sense of revenge during this second meeting.

"I don't think that way," he said. "Maybe at one point in my life, I would have. I think that comes with maturity."

The only player on the Eagles who remained from the Reid era was Brandon Graham. During the Super Bowl bye week, Graham emerged as the biggest story. When he tore his triceps against Los Angeles in Week 12, the thought was that his season was finished. He said as much in the postgame locker room. During the Eagles' postseason run, there were growing whispers that if the team could reach the Super Bowl, Graham could return. If you are into storylines, how is this one: A franchise icon in his final campaign suffers a season-ending injury, but he miraculously returns in the Super Bowl against the coach that drafted him? The Eagles returned to practice on the Thursday of the bye week. Graham was on the field. He wore a brace on his arm. The team remained cryptic on his status. Graham is not the cryptic type.

"I know the risk," Graham said. "But the reward will be so much sweeter."

And what was that risk? "Just re-tearing it," he responded. "But honestly, I don't think so. I know that's what they gotta say."

Graham's potential return excited both teammates and fans. Once considered a first-round draft bust, Graham had transformed his reputation and became a Philadelphia icon. His strip sack of Tom Brady in the Super Bowl seven years ago is a defining moment in franchise history—and a life-changing moment for Graham—and his career had become a lesson for any athlete in Philadelphia about both perseverance and attitude. "We didn't start so tight, as you know," Graham said of Philadelphia in his eventual retirement speech. "You made me work for this, and I appreciate you for that. Through the struggles, the energy, and the moments where I had to prove myself over and over again, you never let me get comfortable. You held me accountable. You kept that chip on my shoulder. You pushed me to be better, and when the time came, we celebrated together—two times."

Graham continued to practice during the bye week. Sirianni limited other key veterans, including Saquon Barkley, Zack Baun, A.J. Brown, Landon Dickerson, Dallas Goedert, Cam Jurgens, and DeVonta Smith. They were still active in meetings, where much of the game plan for the Super Bowl was installed. The Eagles also handled their logistical arrangements early during the bye week. It was a business-like approach—and for players who had been to the Super Bowl, there was a better understanding of how to navigate the week.

"It's about us, but it's not about us," Brown said of the Super Bowl week, comparing the players to "paid actors" at Super Bowl festivities. "We have so much we have to do for everyone else—for the media, for the fans—there's only so little time that we get to focus on what's important, and that's the game."

This was also the time for assistant coaches who were still candidates for open head-coaching jobs to meet with teams. That was the case for offensive coordinator Kellen Moore, who had his second interview with—of all teams—the New Orleans Saints. He was expected to be offered the job after the Super Bowl, meaning his week in New Orleans would be an advance look at his future home.

Meanwhile, the front office started getting ahead on the 2025 offseason. It is a popular refrain from Super Bowl teams that they are six weeks behind much of the league. No one feels sorry for their plight. But as Roseman likes to say, the Eagles' best seasons and his best offseasons are often connected. Difficult decisions were awaiting the Eagles after the Super Bowl, and Roseman made the deliberate choice to avoid in-season contract extensions so as not to alienate or frustrate the players who did not receive offers. On Thursday night during the bye week, Roseman arrived home from his son's basketball game at 9:30 PM. He did not go to bed; instead, he retreated to his office. His wife asked him what he was doing.

"We gotta make sure that our offseason next year is good," Roseman answered.

The team departed Philadelphia on Sunday morning with a send-off party at Lincoln Financial Field before the buses went to the airport. Gillie Da Kid danced on stage, just as he did in the locker room after the championship game. A few players addressed the crowd: "We're about to go down there, try to get this win, and we're going to come back here and bring that trophy," Graham told the fans. "Get ready for this party on Broad Street, baby! E-A-G-L-E-S, Eagles!" The buses then headed to the airport, where they boarded an American Airlines 777 jet (Flight No. AA9745) that departed at 12:57 PM. The Eagles arrived in New Orleans at 2:32 PM local time and went to the Hilton Riverside hotel, where the team would spend the next eight nights.

The accommodations were considerably different from the Super Bowl two years earlier, too. When the Eagles played the Chiefs in Arizona, the team was sequestered in a resort nearly 20 minutes south of Phoenix. Nobody was getting near the hotel without an Eagles affiliation. In New Orleans, the team stayed within walking distance of Bourbon Street. There was a popular casino across the street. Players could not leave their hotel without bumping into Eagles fans who flooded the French Quarter. Not that they were prepared to experience it. There was a curfew, yes, but even more, there was a clear sense that it was a business trip. They were not a "happy to be here" team. They were not looking to soak in memories during the week. It was similar to the Brazil trip to open the season.

"I'm not trying to have fun. I'm mostly on a business trip," Darius Slay said. "My first Super Bowl experience, I kind of had fun… more enjoying what was going on. Now that I've been here twice, I'm locked in, dialed in. I was dialed in during the game [two years ago], but I'm more like, I told my family, 'I'll see y'all when I see y'all.' Ain't nobody come to the hotel hanging out. I ain't got time for all that this time."

The biggest spectacle of the week was Super Bowl Opening Night—formerly known as "media day"—when all players, coaches, and executives meet with reporters from around the globe on the field at the Superdome. This is a made-for-TV event, broadcasted live by NFL Network. There is a survive-and-advance element for the players and coaches, who will meet with reporters for the rest of the week. For those who cover the team every day, the meeting time with Lurie, Roseman, and other staff members who do not frequently meet with reporters was the draw. Lurie addressed topics ranging from Roseman, Siranni, and Hurts to his reported interest in purchasing the Boston Celtics (it was untrue, he said), a potential domed stadium in the future, and the Eagles' next international game.

Their first practice in New Orleans came on Wednesday at the Saints' facility in nearby Metairie, Louisiana. They practiced for two hours in 77-degree weather. It was a normal Wednesday practice for the team, with stretching, warm-ups, and individual work to start the practice, followed by 11-on-11 team drills and a walkthrough. There was a meeting on Wednesday night and film review.

Talk to any player on the Eagles, and they would tell you that the Thursday practices are the most difficult under Sirianni—especially in 2024. That continued during Super Bowl week. The two-hour session was the most intense practice leading up to the game. It included a tackling and turnover circuit, as they do every Thursday, and heavy emphasis on situational work. The NFL Honors, the league's annual awards show, takes place on the Thursday before the Super Bowl in the host city. Even though the Eagles were a mere 1.2 miles away from the theater, their schedule kept Saquon Barkley from attending the presentation. He won Offensive Player of the Year that night, becoming the first player in franchise history to earn the award, and his acceptance speech was pre-taped. "'You can't be great without the greatness of others,' one of my favorite quotes, and you definitely can't accomplish this without the big boys up front," Barkley said in the speech. "So thank you guys so much.... It's an honor and a privilege." Fangio did not win Assistant Coach of the Year and Baun did not win Defensive Player of the Year. Both were finalists. They had more pressing concerns that evening—like the final practice of the week the next day.

The Friday sessions are fast—one hour of red-zone work with a full-team period. By this point, the families of players and coaches, along with members of the organization, had arrived in New Orleans. The Eagles' traveling party included 1,200 people, per the team website, and required six charter flights. Sirianni gave the players and coaches downtime on Friday night to spend with families and friends.

By Saturday, all that was left was a walkthrough and the team meeting at night. They had jogged through plays and focused on end-of-half and end-of-game scenarios at the Saints' facility. Then they boarded buses for the Superdome, where they took an official team photo.

The Eagles held a final team meeting in a Hilton ballroom on the night before the game. Sirianni went through final game reminders, the type of general coaching points that he would make before a nondescript game in September. What allowed them to beat New Orleans in September could allow them to win in New Orleans in February.

"We eliminated distractions all week to allow ourselves to play our best in the last game," Sirianni told his team, as seen on team footage. "Don't let up now. Focus and refocus. Communicate and be ready to adjust. They're going to show us some stuff we haven't seen—I promise you. We're going to show them some things, too. Tough, detailed, together. Tough, detailed, together. Nothing changes."

The coach did not need to enlarge the moment with his words or perspective. His pre–Super Bowl speech was relatively muted by design. Sirianni spends the summer taking walks in his New Jersey neighborhood imagining different speeches, lessons, and coaching points for different times of the season. On the eve of the Super Bowl, Sirianni followed a plan he used two years earlier: He opened the floor to anyone who wanted to speak. He wanted their words. It was an approach his college coach, Larry Kehres, took on the night before championship games in college. Two years earlier, the speeches resonated with the players—especially the words from Jason Kelce and Jalen Hurts. The Eagles lost that game, of course, but they were ready to play. And two years later, the players who were in that hotel ballroom in Arizona remembered those words. Siriainni tapped into the same strategy.

Seven players filed to the front of the room, as seen on team footage: Lane Johnson, Zack Baun, Brandon Graham, Darius Slay, A.J. Brown, Saquon Barkley, and Jalen Hurts. More players could have spoken. Throughout the season, one sentiment was that the Eagles were a player-led team. It was fitting that they heard from their leaders.

Johnson reflected on the visit to the Super Bowl two years earlier. "I felt like we were a little overemotional," Johnson told his teammates, echoing a sentiment he had shared going back to the Super Bowl bye week in Philadelphia. He said to teammates back at the NovaCare Complex, "Emotion doesn't win games, talk doesn't win games. Execution wins games. When I go into any of these games—big or small—I try to stay neutral." So on the night before the game, he emphasized that the Chiefs are a "finesse team" trying to "junk up" the game. "Because man-for-man, they're not going to let us tee off on them, because they will get fucked up," Johnson said. "And they're going to get fucked up tomorrow." Then Johnson channeled some motivation. He might not want to be emotional, but he can hold a grudge. He told teammates to remember the T-shirts the Chiefs wore at the Super Bowl two years earlier that read 0 SACKS after the Eagles, who set a franchise record for sacks in the regular season, did not sack Patrick Mahomes in the Super Bowl. "Keep that in mind as y'all keep annihilating his ass tomorrow," Johnson said.

Then came Zack Baun. Four months earlier, who could have predicted that Baun—an under-the-radar free agent signing—would be considered enough of a presence and an important leader to speak to his team on the night before the Super Bowl? It was even surreal for Baun, who spent the first four years of his career in New Orleans playing in the Superdome as a reserve. "It's been a long-ass week—a busy week—but we've had a lot of downtime and I used my downtime kind of reflecting on when I first got here," Baun said. "I took it upon myself to really dive into the team, really embrace you guys, and let you guys bring me in. So I just appreciate that. I love y'all. We play our best ball when we're together, so let's fly around, communicate, and do what we do."

Next to Baun was Nakobe Dean, just as he had been for most of the season. Dean leaned on his crutches, a scar still fresh from surgery. He would not play in the Super Bowl. He still wanted to speak. "You know I'd give anything to be out there with y'all Sunday," he said. "I'm so proud of this team, with everything we've gone through. How resilient we are. The way we've been able to not only push through things, but thrive..."

Slay, who was realistic that the Super Bowl might be his final game in Philadelphia, had been a three-time captain for the Eagles. He's known for his lighthearted personality. In the locker room, he's known as one of the best teammates players have encountered. "Why not us?" he asked his peers. "It's always been this, that, and the third. Why not us? Why not us going out there tomorrow and execute, play fast, play physical, play for each other? And hold this trophy up?"

Then it was Mailata. In his first season as captain, Mailata had become a respected voice in the locker room. He was the team representative for the NFL Players' Association and someone who had forged relationships on both sides of the ball, with players from all backgrounds and all ages. "All we got is one more time. One more time. To do the same shit we've been doing all year 'round," Mailata said. "I ain't got much to say. I'm not into the rah-rah shit. That's why I let Landon [Dickerson] do that shit [before games]. Plus half of you guys can't even fucking understand me!" That drew laughter. Mailata knows how to captivate a crowd. But he knew how to turn serious. "That's all we got—all we're guaranteed. One more time," he said.

It was Brown's turn. He might be the most misunderstood Eagle publicly. One truth about Brown is that he's a truth-speaker unafraid to let you know what he thinks. That's why he was a captain. That's why he was in front of the room. "I feel like everybody's said a whole bunch up here, and I'm not in the moment yet to speak about the game or get ready for the game because we've got a lot of time," Brown said. However, he wanted to use his time to recognize his teammates in the wide receiver corps—from the high-profile sidekick DeVonta Smith to down-the-roster contributors like Britain Covey. "You guys are just as important, but you don't get the praise," he said. He told teammates how much he appreciated that they voted him as a captain and viewed him as a leader. "Let's go out here and have fun tomorrow," he said.

Next to Brown was Barkley. He could have been viewed as a mercenary this season, someone who switched from a rival team to the Eagles and had not been steeped in the team culture. Instead, he was a seamless fit in the locker room. And it was not just for his play on the field, but the way he carried himself with teammates. “I just want to thank you guys for welcoming me in and showing so much love and so much support,” Barkley said. “I think you hear a common theme up here, right? I think every single one of us brings up ‘team.’ As I watched film throughout the whole week, my confidence grows even more. I hope you feel the same thing.” He had reached a conclusion, one that was not exclusive to him inside that meeting room: “These guys can’t fuck with us,” Barkley said. “I don’t care how many times they’ve been here, how many times they’ve won it. They haven’t seen a team like us.” This was said behind closed doors, of course, and it was not a sentiment the team shared publicly. But they simply felt they were the better team entering the game.

Gardner-Johnson, another offseason acquisition, spoke next. He’s known for his bravado, competitive zeal, and trash-talking on the field. But the eccentricities are part of the emotion. The tears he shed after the championship game were real. There were more tears as he stood in front of the team on this Saturday night, too. “A lot of y’all been through a lot of shit, bro. A lot of shit,” Gardner-Johnson said. “We don’t gotta say shit if we win it. Our story’s gonna tell itself, bro. I get emotional because we’re all winners, bro. Why not have a chance to express that on the biggest stage of them all?”

That was what Graham planned to do. He returned for Year 15 to be in this moment. He pushed through a season-ending injury to play in this game. Graham wore a No. 45 Michael Jordan jersey when he spoke. Legacies are made by championships. This was part of Graham’s legacy. “Fellas, going on Year 15—it’s crazy, being a captain, having the ‘C’ on the chest. Some years are harder than others, but I appreciate y’all boys, man—because y’all made it so easy!” Graham said. “Y’all boys wasn’t scared of working. Y’all worked every day. Even when I was sitting out, I got to see it from the outside, just really watching things go on when I was hurt. I was just reflecting: Anytime you get an opportunity...to get on that field, to play on this field, take advantage. Because you don't know when your last play's gonna be." He told them to run through the finish line. There was one more game to go.

There was also one more speech to go. It was from Hurts. He was the headliner, ever precise with his words and his intent. He had waited two years to stand in front of the team again. What would happen 24 hours later would define his career. In a way, it would define his life. Hurts sometimes does not create that separation. He never let go of those scars, even if he did not always show them. He was once benched at halftime of the national championship game. It had marked his career until he reached the Super Bowl two years later and played the best game of his career—but lost. Salvation might lie within, but it sure feels better when it comes in a win.

"Last time being here, this shit changed my life," Hurts said. "It changed my life, and it changed my mentality. It changed everything. Because for so long, I was seeking: What would I do when I got this moment again? What would I do when this opportunity met me again, on the biggest stage—everybody watching? I didn't get benched. I put on a good show. And I couldn't have done that without you guys. But I left that motherfucker so empty. Done. Nothing else matters but winning. And when you talk about team sports, and you talk about everything we've gone through, it's been the mission this whole motherfucking time. So for all the hard work and everything we've been able to do through this point, let's take it one play at a time, let it come through, and ask yourself, 'How do you want to be remembered?'"

Somehow, the walls still stood at the hotel after those speeches. It was clear the players were ready. Super Bowl Sunday was one sleep away.

After two years, the wait is over. The championship rematch has arrived. The NFL's two best teams—the Philadelphia Eagles and the Kansas City Chiefs—are about to collide in Super Bowl 59!

Those were the words of Merrill Reese, the Eagles' iconic play-by-play announcer, to set the scene before the game. The Eagles fan base always travels. The Super Bowl was no exception. A walk around New Orleans' French Quarter or Warehouse District during Super Bowl weekend was evidence of the Philadelphia invasion. Perhaps it was Chiefs fatigue, too—Kansas City fans had become accustomed to Februarys in Super Bowl cities—but the neutral-field game had more green than red filling the seats pregame. Jalen Hurts, who arrived at the game wearing a Prince-purple single-breasted suit and matching collarless shirt, maintained a steel-faced focus on his way to the stadium. Players chose custom dress fits for the occasion—including Saquon Barkley in a denim suit.

The buzz built with the clock approaching the 5:30 PM kickoff time in New Orleans.

"It's time, bro," A.J. Brown said in the tunnel with the wide receivers, as seen from NFL Films footage. "Time to leave nothing."

"I love each and every one of y'all," Lane Johnson said to the offensive linemen. "Family on three: one, two three, family!"

"Enjoy this.... Let's have fun," Barkley said to Dallas Goedert. "Who am I telling? You've been here already."

It was Barkley's 28th birthday. In fact, Sirianni's son asked the coach before the game to wish Barkley and Cooper DeJean happy birthday. Sirianni presumably had much more on his mind, but a father's duty knows no bounds. "OK, I will," he said.

Brandon Graham, wearing a big brace on his right arm, was in uniform for the final game of his storied career. "Welcome back," Zack Baun said to Graham while the two hugged. If there were nerves from the Eagles, you could not tell. "Nothing but confidence," Oren Burks said to Baun.

On Kansas City's sideline, there were reminders about what the Chiefs did to the Eagles two years earlier. There were references to the history of a three peat. It was specifically mentioned by Chris Jones in the pregame huddle.

On the other side, though, Landon Dickerson wanted to make history of his own.

"We're not here to change the past. We're here to stamp our names in history," Dickerson shouted to his teammates. "We got one opportunity. We've been working our whole lives for this, to be immortalized right here!"

"We did this shit all year! Don't stop now," Hurts said in a pregame huddle, as captured on the team's Instagram account. He told them to embrace the moment.

Sirianni, who famously had tears streaming from his eyes before the national anthem two years earlier, sat on the bench 10 minutes before kickoff with a sense of serenity that seemed noteworthy to those who had observed his emotions through the years. He invited teammates to come sit with him. "I wanted the players to see me," he later told The Athletic, noting a "different flow."

When the Eagles officially took the field before the anthem, they were introduced by actor and devoted Eagles fan Bradley Cooper, a Philadelphia-area native and Germantown Academy alum. He held eight-year-old Declan LeBaron, an Eagles fan from Doylestown, Pennsylvania, with systemic juvenile arthritis whom Cooper gifted with tickets on the *Today* show earlier in the week.

From the city of Brotherly Love, your 2024 NFC champions! E-A-G-L-E-S, EAGLES!

They ran out as a team. Mekhi Becton and Jalen Carter were first in the group. There's an expression in football about big, imposing players: They're the guys you want off the bus first. Consider Becton and Carter those players for the Eagles.

FOX reporter Tom Rinaldi interviewed Barkley on the sideline before the game. Barkley explained that it was no accident the Eagles were there. They were ready. "The whole week, we've been locking in," Barkley said. "Now it's time. It's go time."

His last words to Rinaldi? "We got a great team," he said.

Jon Batiste, a seven-time award-winning artist and New Orleans native, performed the national anthem. The cameras zoomed in close to Sirianni's eyes. No tears. Just focus.

Graham, Jordan Mailata, and Darius Slay went to midfield for the coin toss. The Chiefs, as the visitors, called tails. They won the coin toss. They deferred to the second half. The Eagles would get the ball first.

"I'm coming, baby!" Graham told Patrick Mahomes.

So were the Eagles.

It was clear from the start of the game that the Chiefs' defensive game plan was to focus on bottling up Saquon Barkley. There would be no home run on the opening drive from Barkley like there was in the NFC Championship Game. For Chiefs defensive coordinator Steve Spagnuolo—a former Eagles assistant—there was a dimension of "pick your poison" when preparing for the Eagles offense. His pick was the passing game compared to Barkley

"We just felt like going into the game that we had to somehow not allow them to be two-dimensional, because I've been there, you can't defend them," Spagnuolo told PHLY's *Anthony Gargano Show*. "They get the run going, and then [Hurts is] throwing the ball, and he gets out of the pocket.... [Credit] to the quarterback, the rest of those guys that were playing on offense, they made some key throws, and I thought Jalen did a great job really in critical situations of beating us or getting first downs with his feet. I thought that was really, really challenging, and that's what happens in this league nowadays with these athletic quarterbacks. I mean, you can take away runs, you can cover really well, have them all covered, and when they say, 'Hey, I'm gonna get the first down with my feet,' and they're able to do it because your lanes are out of whack or something happens, then it becomes challenging."

The Eagles' opening drive was thwarted by a questionable offensive pass interference flag on A.J. Brown. On the broadcast, FOX analyst Tom Brady—a Super Bowl foe of yore for the Eagles—was critical of the call. The Eagles' radio booth termed it a phantom flag. When the Eagles returned to the sideline, though, Barkley had a clear message for his teammates about maintaining their equanimity. One flag cannot get them askew.

"Hey, hey, chill! Chill!" he said, while holding his hands to an even position. "Stay right here! Who cares? Who cares? Stay right here! Stay right here!"

"Keep playing your game," Hurts told Brown. "That's a hell of a play right there."

When the defense came on the field, the group felt as if it were the favorites. Even though Mahomes and Travis Kelce were on the other sideline, the way the Eagles had played throughout the season and practiced throughout the week instilled a sense of confidence that was hard to miss. Vic Fangio had been a formidable foil for Reid; the former Eagles head coach identified Fangio as one of the most challenging defensive minds he faced. "I have confidence in every one of y'all boys," Baun told the group in the huddle. "Let's ball out."

If the Chiefs defense focused on thwarting the Eagles' run game, the Eagles' defensive game plan was the opposite. Their focus was on stopping Mahomes, and they seemed unafraid that

Kansas City would run the ball on them. The Chiefs threw the ball on the first four plays of the game before the Eagles forced them to punt. "Too easy!" Dean called out from the sideline.

The scoring started on the next drive when Hurts connected with Jahan Dotson for what was initially ruled a 28-yard touchdown before the officials determined Dotson was down short of the end zone. "You already know what time it is," Hurts said. It was time for the Tush Push, and Hurts pushed his way for a 7–0 lead. The Eagles never trailed.

The offense quieted, failing to find the end zone on their next drives. One of those included an interception and another a field goal, but it was still a 10–0 game midway through the second quarter. "We knew it was going to be a dogfight," Barkley said on the sideline. "We're ready for that, we're built for that." The key was the defense's dominance. In fact, the Chiefs had three offensive plays or fewer on every drive for the rest of the half. The Eagles overpowered the Chiefs on the line of scrimmage without blitzing, allowing the secondary to clog the passing lines.

"I'm telling you, if I get power in the middle, it's fucking over!" Josh Sweat said on the sideline, aware of how he could create a mismatch. This game was Sweat's masterpiece. An underrated player for seven seasons with the Eagles, Sweat developed from a fourth-round pick brimming with potential to a reliable pass-rusher who had the eighth-most sacks in franchise history. Never a big talker, Sweat was always more than meets the eye—he was smart and curious enough that he built computers from scratch in his free time while building himself into one of the most important players on the Eagles.

The inflection point came at the 8:38 mark of the second quarter when it started to seem obvious what kind of night it would become. Remember those shirts that the Chiefs offensive linemen wore during the parade two years earlier about not allowing a sack—the shirts Johnson mentioned in his Super Bowl eve speech? Sirianni remembered. On first-and-10, Sweat sacked Mahomes for the Eagles' first sack of the game. "Hey, that's one fucking sack! That's one sack!" Sirianni emphatically told Graham. Maybe it was just excitement for a single sack, until the next play when Sweat and Jalyx Hunt split a sack. "That's two! That's two! That's two! That's fucking two!" Sirianni said. He was clearly keeping count—just as Kansas City seemed to do two years earlier. Third down might have been the most memorable play of the Super Bowl. Backed up on a third-and-16, Mahomes rolled to his right and tried to squeeze an acrobatic pass across his body. Cooper DeJean, who had his eyes on Mahomes the entire time, cut in front of the pass and made the first interception of his career at the Eagles' 38-yard line. His momentum was coming forward, meaning he was accelerating while he caught the pass. That allowed him to keep running—with only offensive linemen and Mahomes preventing him from scoring a touchdown. One lineman was blocked, DeJean juked another, and pushed through a tackle. All Mahomes could do was watch. It was the first pick-six Mahomes had thrown in a Super Bowl.

DeJean high-stepped in the end zone. Hurts raised his fist, which would qualify as sideline emotion for him. As much as Barkley had instructed calmness on the sideline, even he was filled with glee. "Oh my God! Oh my God!" he exclaimed while DeJean navigated through the Kansas City offense. Sirianni did not need those instructions. He sprinted down the sideline shouting at the top of his lungs. Neither did Baun. "Run Coop! Run Coop!" the linebacker shouted as he ran from behind. Baun had seen the way DeJean identified his play, locking eyes with Mahomes and understanding the defensive leverage.

"You saw I had the two guys to the flat so you came off and [saw] the crosser?" Baun asked. "That's some veteran-ass shit!"

DeJean was not yet a veteran, even if he played like one. But he did turn 22 that day. "That's a hell of a birthday present," Barkley said to him on the bench. "You keep doing that, you're going to have an even better one. Keep going."

It was the first interception by an Eagle in a Super Bowl. It would not be the last. "You knew that was coming," Parker said to DeJean with other defenders listening. "That's the first one, though! That's one!"

"I was trying to find the fastest way to the end zone," DeJean said after the game. "Luckily, I got some blocks out there. I had to avoid some of those big guys, but it was just our defense working together like we have all year. It fell right into my lap." The play turned DeJean into a Philadelphia cult hero. He couldn't open his phone in the following days without reminders of the interception. He made appearances at all Philadelphia sporting events and autograph signings. DeJean jerseys started showing up more in the Delaware Valley. That's what happens when you get a pick-six in the Super Bowl.

On the sideline, Barkley was back to promoting staying even keeled. Gardner-Johnson, of all people, told the defenders they needed to breathe. "We can get excited for a little bit," Sirianni said to others on the sideline.

The defense wreaked even more havoc, with Milton Williams knocking Mahomes down on a third-down sack to force a punt. "This team ain't fucking with us," Baun shouted. "They're not fucking with us."

When Baun returned to the sideline, fellow linebacker Nicholas Morrow told Baun the interception was "coming." "I'm going to get one," Baun responded.

The Chiefs regained possession with 1:49 remaining, backed up inside their own 10-yard line. On first down, Mahomes tried throwing across the middle while Sweat pressured Mahomes to force an errant throw. Baun read Mahomes' intentions and dove for the interception—a blend of athleticism and instincts that made Baun one of the best linebackers in the NFL.

"I told you you would get one!" Morrow said when they returned to the sideline.

"You called that shit!" responded Baun, adding that he dropped that in practice.

It was similar to how the Eagles dropped the Philly Special in practice seven years earlier. What matters is what happens under the lights. That's how history is made. "One more for the record!" linebackers coach Bobby King told the players, referring to the postseason record for turnovers. Baun's magical season continued, and nobody was surprised anymore that he was the one who made the play.

With a 17–0 lead, the Eagles offense took the field at the 14-yard line. "We got to get this—it's huge," Sirianni said in his headset. It took two plays for Hurts to find Brown crossing the field and tiptoeing the sideline to reach the end zone. This was a storybook first half for the Eagles. Naturally, teammates brought Brown his copy of *Inner Excellence.*

"Told you somebody was going to bring that here!" DeVonta Smith said.

"Let me see it!" Brown said. C.J. Uzomah found a verse for Brown.

Sirianni came over and asked Brown to read him a passage and made reference to Brown's speech from the night before. It was hard to write a better start to a Super Bowl. This was more for show than anything else. "I didn't need it—it's the Super Bowl," Brown said afterward. "I had all the inner excellence deep down already."

So did the Eagles. But they knew better than to imagine the victory cigars waiting in the locker room.

"Do not fall for it at all," Barkley said on the sideline. "The scoreboard's 0–0…. That's for everybody else. We stay locked in."

This was a similar message to what the Eagles conveyed at halftime two years earlier against the Chiefs. It was a 10-point lead then. This was a 24-point lead. But these were different teams. The Chiefs had a mystique, although they were not moving the ball like they did two years earlier. Barkley told teammates it was a heavyweight fight and they were built for these situations and calloused from past experiences—even the newcomers who only knew the pain from proxy. "Start of the second game," Baun said to teammates to begin the second half.

"The talk was, 'Just stay locked in, stay poised,'" Brown explained afterward. "This is Pat Mahomes we're dealing with—be ready. Be ready for him to answer, and just keep going.'"

Two years earlier, the Chiefs scored a touchdown coming out of halftime. This time, they went three-and-out. Two of those plays were sacks. "That's five!" Sirianni said, flexing all the fingers on his right hand in the air as a commitment to the bit. Sweat wiped the proverbial sweat off his forehead, a signature celebration that he did more in the Super Bowl than at any point in his career. The 2.5 sacks put him in firm contention for Super Bowl MVP.

"I was in the right place. I was just running around and was like, 'Aye…Aye!'" Sweat said after the game. "They let me go crazy. I don't think I ever got more than two in a game, so my biggest game, sack-wise. Bringing it home for the D-line. That's what I wanted to do."

The offense responded with a 12-play drive that resulted in a field goal, but it showed they could grate on Spagnuolo's defense. Hurts hurt the Chiefs with his legs. Barkley added his longest gains of the game. "I'm glad that fucker's on our team," Baun said. So was the rest of Philadelphia. With a 27–0 deficit, the Chiefs clung to the hope that the New England Patriots once came back from a 25-point deficit against Atlanta. The Eagles would not allow that to happen.

Avonte Maddox, a respected veteran who lost his job to DeJean early in the season, stepped in briefly for DeJean in the third quarter and made one of the biggest plays of his career: a third-down pass breakup to keep the shutout alive. "That's why you here!" Slay said to Maddox on the bench.

At this point, the Eagles could have kept trying to grind the clock against the Chiefs. They had the best running back in the NFL, an overpowering offensive line, and Barkley had been so effective late in the games. But Sirianni smelled blood. He does not call plays, although he's on the headset. And he let Kellen Moore know what he thought.

"If we score, it's over," Sirianni said. "Just call it."

If DeJean's pick-six was the play of the game, what came next might have been the signature play. It helped give Hurts the MVP. He made his check at the line of scrimmage, knew Smith was in one-on-one on his left side at the 46-yard line, and he threw deep down the field on the first play. Smith had a step on the defender and made a leaping catch in the back of the end zone.

This was the Dagger, the knockout punch, the moment when Eagles fans likely felt safe that they would win the Super Bowl. You can tell from Sirianni, who excitedly jogged down the sideline with a celebratory push from Connor Barwin.

"You're the fucking man!" Cam Jurgens said to Hurts.

"I love when they doubt you!" Mailata said to Hurts. "They can't fuck with you!"

"I know," Hurts said, ever cool and smooth.

Hurts shook hands with Lane Johnson, an esoteric celebration. ("Everybody has all these special handshakes and daps," Johnson explained. "So the good old-fashioned [handshake]…it's awkward now, so we're trying to bring it back.") And he found his receiver, the one he used to work out with at Alabama in those late-night throwing sessions.

"That's big time right there, man," Hurts said.

"Talk your shit, Smitty!" Baun said.

"In the crib?" noted Barkley, referring to Smith playing just more than one hour from his hometown of Amite City, Lousiana.

It was not until the final minute of the third quarter that the Chiefs converted their first first down. They scored a touchdown with 34 seconds remaining and missed the extra point, so the Eagles were set to carry a 28-point lead into the fourth quarter.

In his headset, Sirianni asked Eagles assistant general manager Jon Ferrari about the score, ensuring they were prepared for the situation. "Just don't lose yards," Sirianni said to the coaches on the headset. "Maybe run a downhill run." It was not Barkley's running that stood out on the drive as much as Hurts' legs. He scrambled for a 17-yard gain to bring the Eagles to field goal range, and Elliott's 48-yard kick gave the Eagles a 37–6 lead.

"That's a great defense over there, boy," said Barkley, realizing how the Chiefs were limiting him.

"They spent their whole damn scheme on trying to stop 2-6," running backs coach Jamel Singleton told Barkley. "And by doing so, they let everybody else eat. Just remember that."

"Lombardi Trophy," Barkley responded. That was what mattered, even though Barkley ran for enough yards to reach 2,504 yards in the regular season and postseason combined to top Terrell Davis' 2,476 record.

If the Chiefs defense was great, what description should go to the Eagles defense? Their effort was so dominant that the players were thinking about something that had not happened since.

"Let's get the MVP to the defense, bro!" Sweat said to Baun.

"Yeah, right," Baun said, knowing the award tends to go to the offense.

Plus, it was hard to determine which defender deserved the award. Sweat? DeJean? Baun? And Williams was ready to have his say, too.

The defensive tackle who would leave the Eagles to become one of the highest-paid defensive players in the NFL one month later made sure his final game was perhaps his finest. He sliced through the Kansas City line, sacked Mahomes, forced a fumble, and recovered the loose ball all at once. To celebrate, Williams dunked the ball over the goal posts. That is considered an unsportsmanlike conduct penalty, costing the Eagles 15 yards. Normally, Sirianni would be irate at this type of flag. Do it when you have a strip sack in the fourth quarter of the Super Bowl with a 29-point lead, and it's easier to digest.

"It's worth it right there!" Sirianni said on the sideline. "Was it at least a good dunk?"

Williams simulated a belt whipping a rear arm. His father performed the same celebration during the Super Bowl parade.

That was their sixth sack. On the scoreboard, there were advanced statistics from the NFL that revealed the Eagles had a pressure rate of 38 percent without a single blitz. Baun and Blankenship marveled at this statistic. It was part of Fangio's game plan, understanding that Mahomes is proficient against pressure so the key would be pressuring him with a four-man rush.

"You guys were rushing, I didn't need to pressure," Fangio said to Baun on the field after the game. "It's hard to do that sometimes."

"When you win on a four-man rush and you can just cycle guys through, and they are still winning, you don't have to blitz," Baun said in a press conference after the game. "Great game planning, great communication, we were all on the same page all game."

Williams' fumble recovery gave the Eagles their third takeaway in the game and their 13th in the postseason. This was a topic of conversation on the sideline, with Slay shouting it and the defensive linemen spreading the news.

"Best defense in the league," Baun said.

Elliott nailed a 50-yard line field goal to give the Eagles a 40–6 lead, part of a perfect end to the veteran kicker's season. Sirianni kept his back to the field goal, a longstanding superstition of not watching kicks. The head coach did not see his team's final three points scored. By that point, it was a matter of waiting for the clock to hit zero. Philadelphia fans had already started the celebrations. The players were not far behind. The baggage of the past two years was off their backs.

"You can crack a smile," tight end Grant Calcaterra said to Hurts, his former teammate at Oklahoma.

"I can't lie to you, bro," Hurts said. "The last one changed my soul, man.... That shit isn't over till the fat lady sings."

The topic of Hurts smiling was one that came from other teammates, too. He remains stoic, the even disposition becoming his trademark. But when you're winning by double-digits in the fourth quarter of the Super Bowl, it's OK to show some teeth.

"Jalen Hurts gonna smile now?" Barkley asked in the final seconds of the game.

"When it hits [triple zero]," Hurts said.

The two teammates embraced, with Hurts remarking how Barkley was a reason why they were in this position.

"All of us," Barkley said.

"I know it's all of us, but you don't understand the difference you made," Hurts said. "We right there. But you're like that last piece."

This was similar to Sirianni's message to Barkley after the game, showing how universal the sentiment was that Barkley brought the Eagles to a different level—one they failed to reach two years earlier.

"I'm proud of you. We can't be great without the greatness of others…you changed this team," Sirianni told him. "You're special. You're special, man. Not the player. I don't care about the player. You're a special leader."

Even the kickoff coverage provided memorable highlights. Jeremiah Trotter Jr. made a tackle in the fourth quarter and celebrated with his father's axe swing, a nod to the Eagles Hall of Famer watching from the stands. Trotter was part of Eagles teams that could never hoist the Lombardi Trophy with Reid. Now the Eagles were about to do it against him.

The Chiefs scored a touchdown for the first time with 2:58 remaining, but Sirianni was unconcerned. He wanted his backups to enter the game. This was their chance to play in a Super Bowl.

"Are you sure? We're done?" Hurts asked Sirianni.

"Yeah, I'm fucking sure," Sirianni said. "I love you, man."

"I love you, too," Hurts said.

"Way to play, baby," Sirianni said.

The exchange carried more weight when understanding the history of the two.

With reserves in the game, Kansas City scored one more touchdown. By that point, it was a formality. The hugs and embraces were already underway. The Eagles knew what was about to happen.

"We're going to win the Super Bowl," Sirianni said in his headset.

Smith found Hurts and shared their love and appreciation for each other.

"This isn't our last time," Smith said.

"We got some catching up to do," Hurts said.

Smith had tears welling in his eyes while Hurts held him by the arms and made eye contact to enforce his point.

"It's been a ride," Hurts said, repeating it for emphasis. "You deserve that…in your hometown."

Then there was the other receiver, who brought the offense to a different level after Hurts pushed to acquire him three years earlier.

"This is what we come here for," Brown said to Hurts.

"And I told you we would do this when I made that call," Hurts said. "And it's done."

The quarterback and receiver told each other how proud they were. Similar to Hurts and Sirianni, there was enough history to know this was more than a standard hug.

"A lot of ups and downs," Brown said.

"It comes with it," Hurts said. "It's part of the game. That's life."

Brown and Smith poured the yellow Gatorade on Sirianni's head, just as they did two weeks earlier—and as they could not do two years earlier.

"The message was, 'We can't rewrite history or do anything about the past, but we can make it even,'" Brown explained after the game, when he finished with three catches for 43 yards and a touchdown. "The guys came with that mindset, and they didn't let up. From everybody—a team effort. I'm grateful it happened that way. We learned a lot. I most definitely did. I basically changed my entire routine coming up into this week. I didn't even care about what I had for the game—it wasn't important. None of that was important. I just stayed focused and just locked in and made sure that green confetti was falling at the end."

Howie Roseman made his way to the sideline, joining the celebration with the team he assembled.

"Thank you for believing in me," Barkley said to Roseman.

"You believed in me!" Roseman said. "I'm so proud of you. I love you."

"First of many," Barkley said.

"Enjoy this moment," Roseman said.

Roseman's two most successful offseason acquisitions were Barkley and Baun. They both signed on the same day. They were both player of the year candidates for their side of the ball. They both received new deals one month later as elite players in the league.

"What a fucking story!" Baun said to Barkley.

"You deserve everything that's coming to you!" Barkley responded.

Johnson, who watched the defense surrender 24 points in the second half two years earlier, told Baun he was a big reason why the Eagles won the Super Bowl. "We got our ass kicked a couple years ago," said Johnson, understanding the Eagles did not have a player like Baun.

Kenny Pickett, who grew up an Eagles fan, took the final knee while the clock neared the zeros Hurts craved.

"It's over now," Hurts said to Sirianni. "Now we can do that!"

Jeff Stoutland, the venerable offensive line coach who won his second Super Bowl, grabbed Hurts once the game finished.

"You used to always tell me, 'I'll put rings on your hands,'" Stoutland said.

"I told you I would," Hurts said. "I'm glad you listened."

The votes were in for Super Bowl MVP. When Hurts walked to midfield to shake hands, Eagles senior manager of football communications John Gonoude informed him of the award.

"Hey, Super Bowl MVP," Gonoude said, tapping Hurts on the chest.

"Super Bowl *champ*!" Hurts responded, emphasizing the distinction that mattered.

Sirianni was a champion, too. He was escorted to midfield by security chief Dom DiSandro and flanked by vice president of football communications Bob Lange. Sirianni and Reid shook hands—one a Super Bowl–winning coach in Philadelphia; the other the winningest coach in franchise history who needed to leave the franchise before he could feel the joy that Sirianni earned this night.

"I'm proud of you, man," Reid said. "Nice job."

"It was an honor to go against you," Sirianni said.

("It was a bad day to have a bad day, and you learn what you can from it," Reid said two months later when asked about the game. "You don't hide yourself from the facts.")

Hurts and Mahomes met at midfield. Seven years earlier, Nick Foles and Brady never had that postgame handshake. There would be no controversy from the two Texas-bred quarterbacks.

"Hey man, congratulations," Mahomes said. "I'm proud of you.... Hell of a way to do it, man. Go enjoy it."

There were the requisite "I told you so" sentiments—especially from Graham, who wanted Hurts to laugh last. "Let them boys know to get off your back," Graham shouted at Hurts.

There were tears—Mekhi Becton had sat on the turf reflecting on a wayward career that led to this moment.

There was disbelief—Baun told his wife it did not feel real. Dallas Goedert told Baun he did not want to wake up at 9:30 AM and realize it was a dream.

There was marvel at the Lombardi Trophy—Landon Dickerson said he did not take a picture with the NFC Championship trophy two weeks earlier. He was waiting for this one.

"She looks prettier in person, I'll tell you that," Barkley said after the game. "You think about it, it's better in person than it is in Madden, I'll tell you that, playing as a kid. It's everything you dream of. I'm just happy to be able to hold it, give it a kiss, and be World Champs."

The party awaited them. But first, the formal trophy presentation for the world to witness.

"This is a very, very special Eagles family. Incredible, talented players that happen to be unselfish every single day of the year," Lurie said when the Eagles were presented with the organization's second Lombardi Trophy. "A credit to our coaching staff, led by Nick. Howie and his staff, unbelievable. And by the way, about 200 other people that are the support staff you never hear about. And a few dogs, too! And to our amazing fans: Your Eagles are world champions, again! Love you, Mom!"

(The references to the dogs were the official team dog, Reggie, who lives at the facility. And Lurie makes a point to mention his mother, Nancy Lurie Marks, during momentous occasions.)

Sirianni followed Lurie on the podium. He spoke about teamwork as a prevailing lesson of the team. He spoke about love as an enduring quality of the team. And he also joked that Kellen Moore should "run this shit back," knowing full well Moore would be coaching in this dome the following season.

Hurts was next. He credited God and his teammates. When asked about the Chiefs defense, he said it was never about what anyone else does—it was about what he does. "Hell of a game today," he said with a smile

On the confetti-covered turf, the gratitude was apparent. Sirianni shared a long, tearful hug with his parents.

"Nick, I'm so happy!" Amy Sirianni said.

"Couldn't be more proud," Fran Sirianni said.

"Nick, we're so proud of you," Amy said. "We love you so much."

"Praise the Lord," Fran said.

When asked about that moment a few weeks later, Sirianni started nodding his head. "That was special," he said. "They've been there through [everything].... I think I realized how blessed I am.... They were at every sporting event for forever. And then to be able to do that at that moment with them, and all the things they sacrificed for me, and the guidance and the love.... Just such a supportive family. My mom, laughing and crying. It was special."

Hurts shared a similar embrace with his father. And what was clear with Hurts, everywhere he went on the field? The answer to the question about whether he would smile. Before a postgame interview with FOX, Hurts looked up at the green, black, silver, and white confetti falling all around him.

"Them the color they supposed to be," Hurts said.

CHAPTER 29

THE PARADE

AFTER THE UNRIVALED CELEBRATION in the locker room and the exclusive team party at the hotel—chronicled in the first chapter of this book—and any festivities thereafter (including at the casino across the street), the bleary-eyed (and perhaps hungover) travel contingent prepared to return home to Philadelphia. They boarded their flight from New Orleans at 1:11 PM local time and landed in Philadelphia at 2:24 PM. Jeffrey Lurie disembarked first with the Lombardi Trophy in hand. Fans cheered through the fence of the terminal for charter and private flights. Lurie tried handing the trophy to Nick Sirianni, who wanted his owner to keep it. Howie Roseman could not resist, pumping the well-earned prize in the air before giving it back to Lurie. They went to the fence where fans clung tightly, wanting any sight of the Lombardi. Sirianni held it in the air for all to see. Helicopters hovered from above, following the police-escorted route on I-95, over the Platt Bridge, then to Pattison Ave. and into the gates of the team's facility, where more fans awaited with signs greeting the team.

They had been gone for eight nights, punctuated by a life-changing Super Bowl. At last, they had a day off to catch their breath before an epic parade awaited them at the end of the week. Jalen Hurts was not on the flight; he went straight to Walt Disney

World, where he was honored with the MVP parade. On Wednesday night, Hurts and Saquon Barkley were guests on NBC's *The Tonight Show with Jimmy Fallon*. There were five surprise guests: the Eagles' starting offensive linemen, each wearing overalls with a T-shirt bearing a Dom DiSandro illustration underneath. They joined with Hurts and Barkley to shotgun beers, although Hurts abstained and instead sprayed his beer on Dickerson. The lineman who was drinking beer with an IV strapped to his body three nights earlier did not seem to mind. Hurts was asked about the wallpaper on his phone. He said people are expecting him to change it, but it's a "humble reminder"—and he said it would remain.

Some players prepared for offseason surgeries, having played through pain during the Super Bowl. Brandon Graham re-tore his triceps. Nolan Smith tore his triceps. Cam Jurgens played through nerve pain in his back. "When you're going through the playoffs, and I'm not really concerned about me, I'm kind of concerned about what I can do to help the team and do everything I can to win," Jurgens said. "When you're playing for a Super Bowl, that's going to last forever. Back pain is going to last for however long it wants to last, but I'm going to be a Super Bowl champ forever." Speaking of forever, Isaiah Rodgers took the time after the Super Bowl to get a tattoo of the Super Bowl Logo and the 40–22 final score on his right calf. He called it his "champ stamp."

On Thursday, they cleaned out their lockers, started their exit meetings, and had their final team meetings. For some of the players, it would be their final time in the locker room. After team staff went over preparations for the parade, Vic Fangio held the defensive players back. Although the initial descriptions suggested Fangio was critical of the late points allowed, he said that's "fake news" and complimented the defense's performance in the meeting. Something might have been lost in translation. In the exit meetings, Sirianni asked his players what worked during the

2024–25 season. They won the Super Bowl—much worked!—but it was a debriefing different than one year earlier.

"I value those meetings so much with the coaches, with the players," Sirianni explained. "I think one thing that was pretty consistent was the team, the connection.... Just really cool to hear how they talk about each other, how they think about each other. That felt like the most consistent, 'what went well, what didn't go well.' The most consistent thing was just how much these guys cared and appreciated each other and the team that we were. But one thing that I constantly think about is, how do you recapture that?"

The consensus was that it was a special group. "I'd almost like to [ask] has there been a better team than the 2024 Eagles?" Lurie said two months later. Certainly not in modern Eagles history. And with the way they played in the Super Bowl—and after their Week 4 bye week—it's a compelling debate. They won 18 games—tied for an NFL record. They scored the most points in postseason history and forced the most turnovers in postseason history. They finished the season with the No. 1 defense in the NFL. "What I'm saying is it was a damn good team," Lurie said upon a follow-up question about the Eagles' spot in history. "Just roster-wise, incredibly capable. Very well coached, all sides of the ball. Really hard to pinpoint a weakness. And then the way it dominated the championship game and the Super Bowl. There have been some other teams. It's right up there, I think, with those teams. That's something for you guys and everyone else to decide, not me. We just experienced a major win against Washington and a major win against the Chiefs. Those were not close games."

It was a team worthy of a celebration—and a team that knew how to celebrate. Friday was all about the parade. It was Philadelphia's chance for a party. The parade in February 2018 was a release decades in the making. Children spread the ashes of deceased parents. Tears of fulfillment were shed. That was the first. You never forget your first. Seven years later, it was time to savor the moment. Fans knew their spots, learning the secrets of the parade route. The best locations available to the public in front of the Art Museum steps were reserved 24 hours earlier by fans camping out. Fans claimed an unimpeded look along the parade route on Broad Street before sunrise on Friday. The parade started at 11:00 AM outside the stadium in South Philadelphia, and the route was about three miles up Broad Street to City Hall, turning west past Love Park and onto the Benjamin Franklin Parkway. It commenced at the Rocky Steps at the Art Museum for the anticipated ceremony with speeches. Jason Kelce made it famous seven years earlier appearing in head-to-toe Mummers garb. They knew they could not mimic Kelce, but they would at least enjoy the party as he did.

Kelce even joined the parade with the Eagles—and he was not the only callback to the unforgettable day seven years earlier. Josh Sweat wore Chris Long's mink coat, which was among the intentional outfit choices of the day. It was fitting that the parade was on February 14—Valentine's Day—and the Jordan brand released a campaign for Jalen Hurts highlighted by the "Love, Hurts" expression. It was on Hurts' hoodie for the parade. The LOVE statue that the buses passed also included a ", Hurts" next to it. There were times Hurts exited the open-air buses and walked the parade route on foot, with a cigar in his mouth and a Kangol hat on his head. The look mimicked Michael Jordan, just as he did after the NFC Championship Game. Multiple players exited the bus at parts of Broad Street, interacting with fans amid the adulation. There was one point when Barkley spotted a ball boy in the crowd, lifted him over the fence, and brought him on the bus with the players and families. Zack Baun eagle-eyed a baby in the crowd, ran over with a Sharpie, and signed the helmet the infant wore.

This was the opportunity for players to let loose, although it seemed the letting loose started five nights earlier. Quinyon Mitchell, wearing a "Quinyonamo Bay" hoodie, started an interview with a television reporter when James Bradberry pulled him away, seemingly aware that Mitchell was in no state for coherent remarks. Consider that Bradberry's final veteran assist with the team. Nolan Smith needed to be transported back to the buses because he was having so much fun in the street. The injury didn't seem to bother him. The specialists mimicked a field goal, with Jake Elliott kicking a beer can into the crowd.

The beer cans were flying right back to the buses. They came from all angles, and sometimes to unsuspecting passengers. Howie Roseman did not see the can that accelerated into his forehead, causing a bleeding welt. That became Roseman's victory scar.

"It was a projectile launch into my face!" Roseman later said when asked about the moment. Sirianni appreciated Roseman taking the beating rather than Sirianni's wife and daughter, who were near Roseman on the bus. "It wasn't great Friday night, but I powered through it Friday during the day," Roseman added. "But it was worth it.... I don't want to say it was worth it because then people will start throwing at my head!" He could have used the medical staff, who held up a sign on their bus: 21 OF 22 DAY 1 STARTERS PLAYED IN SUPER BOWL LIX #EAGLESMEDICALSTAFF.

By the time the buses arrived at the Art Museum, the audience awaited speeches. They needed to wait through long remarks from Philadelphia Mayor Cherelle Parker, who followed Pennsylvania Governor Josh Shapiro.

That led to Lurie, who looked at the masses of Eagles fans in front of him while standing on the same steps from seven years earlier and said there were "no words" to describe this moment. "You can say surreal, you say incredible, there are no friggin' words to describe delivering a world championship to our fan base," he said. He explained how Valentine's Day is the perfect day to celebrate the "love affair" between the team and the fans. Wearing the Super Bowl ring from 2017, Lurie held up three fingers to close his speech. "Let's shoot for three!' he said.

Sirianni followed. Known for his emotion, Sirianni could have taken those steps and gave his version of "I told you so." Instead, the head coach was uncharacteristically understated—for him. He mentioned how he told the team when they had a stretch of frigid home games in front of them late in the season that to win the Super Bowl, they would need to win games in front of their fans. He repeated, "You can't be great without the greatness of others," and he said the expression applies to the fans. He closed with an "E-A-G-L-E-S, Eagles!" chant.

Then came Roseman, with the crowd chanting "Howie! Howie!" to lead him to the microphone. Roseman wore a welt on his forehead from the projectile beer can, although those in the crowd might not have known why Roseman was bloodied because cell phone reception was spotty with so many people in one area. They soon found out because Roseman led with a phrase that he literally trademarked after the parade. "I bleed for this city!" he said after a big puff of a cigar.

Hurts led off the speeches from players. He made mention of teammates on all phases (including special teams). Hurts' previous words about Sirianni had been parsed and analyzed throughout their tenure—especially the previous 18 months—and he made sure to single out Sirianni on the podium. "I want to thank Coach for his intentionality, his fight, his passion, and seeing this shit through," he said. The crowd chanted "M-V-P"—a chant that had typically gone to Barkley during the year—and Hurts let them in with a revealing admission. "I told myself that when I got drafted that I wouldn't come to the Rocky Steps until I won a championship," Hurts said. "And now we here." (To be fair, Hurts went to the

Art Museum for an ESPN interview with Donovan McNabb and Michael Vick in 2022.) He spoke about the perseverance of the team, the scrutiny they faced, and he closed it by looking ahead. "The next pursuit begins," he said. "Go Birds." Then he put the cigar back in his mouth and exited stage right.

A.J. Brown followed Hurts. The often-misunderstood receiver thanked the fans but also kept receipts. "They said I was a diva, they said all I care about was stats," Brown said. "You can get all those things wrong about me, but one thing you get right: I'm a fucking champion!" He wasn't wrong. While the crowd roared, Brown held his arms up high—the Lombardi Trophy gripped in his right hand—as if he was Rocky Balboa on those steps.

Barkley took the podium to chants of "Thank you, Giants!"—and he did not come alone. He brought Ryan Quigley, a Montgomery County native and devoted Eagles fan who survived a New Year's Eve terrorist attack in New Orleans. "One thing I learned from being here for a short period of time is you guys are tough, you guys are resilient, and you guys know how to fucking fight," Barkley said. "And nobody I know epitomizes that more than my boy Ryan!"

Jordan Mailata went with the standard thank-yous of Lurie, Roseman, and Sirianni before making a special mention of the players' significant others. (His wife presumably appreciated the recognition.) Mailata said he's "not one for speeches," but he knows how to sing. The best singer on the team—and maybe the entire NFL—then led the crowd to a rendition of "We are the champions!" It was never more applicable.

His close friend Landon Dickerson is one for speeches, as is evident when he rallies the team before games. Dickerson made sure the television producers had their censors ready. He showed he was geographically savvy, referencing different counties in Pennsylvania with legions of Eagles fans. "When I got drafted here, everyone said it was impossible to play in Philly," Dickerson said. "I found out all y'all want is for us to give everything we can for this city, and y'all give it right back." He said he had "never played a fucking away game my entire career." He closed by pointing to the pain from the Super Bowl two years earlier. "I never wanted to feel that shit again," he said. "It was a terrible feeling. But you know what? We don't gotta feel it today, baby! I just got one last thing to say: Go fucking Birds!"

In the locker room one day earlier, teammates speculated that C.J. Gardner-Johnson might be the star of the parade speeches. It was not Kelce-esque, but it brought a phrase that will now be attached to him: "BTA!" he asked the crowd to chant, referencing taking a belt to a rear end. "When I came to Philly, I was as lost as a motherfucker—excuse my language," he said, noting his journey with the Eagles. "When I left [in 2023], I cried like a motherfucker." He returned—as it was later learned, only for that 2024 season—and will now forever be a champion.

Lane Johnson is a two-time champion. Seven years earlier, he gave his speech with Chris Long. He was solo this time. He spoke about how he was shaped by his 12 years in Philadelphia and won two championships with specific references to those who inspired him along the way.

"It was Jeff Stoutland that taught me 'no man is an island;' you must draw your strength from others," Johnson said. "It was Jason Kelce that taught me nothing in the world can take the place of persistence and to always press on. Coach Sirianni taught me about 'dawg mentality.' Nick Foles taught me how to speak softly and to carry a big stick.... That was actually Teddy Roosevelt, but I thought it was pretty fitting. And Jalen Hurts taught me how to have a purpose before someone had an opinion."

The shortest speech was not from a player, but from Dom DiSandro—the security chief who is a cult figure in Philadelphia.

His celebrity has swelled in recent years, and if you speak to players, it's merited—he is a confidant to all who come through the locker room and perhaps the most connected person in the organization. He also is not one for interviews. "Yo, Philly, I love ya," DiSandro said. "That's all I got."

The Eagles then went off script by calling up the "Exciting Whites"—Cooper DeJean and Reed Blankenship, with Dallas Goedert joining them at the microphone. Together, they sang Meek Mill's "Dreams and Nightmares."

Darius Slay spoke about how he long heard that the Eagles were missing a "lockdown corner," and that the two rookies were taking over that role that Slay filled for five seasons. "We world champs, baby!" Slay said.

The final speaker was Brandon Graham, who played 15 seasons and a franchise-record 218 games between the regular season and postseason. Graham defied health timelines (and maybe reasonable behavior) to return to the Super Bowl, where the risk of re-tearing his triceps was realized. It did not matter to him; he won. He left a champion in the only place he ever knew. One month later, he would throw his cleats up on the Rocky statue atop those museum steps to signify his retirement. The parade speech was not for him to say farewell. It was for him to say thank you while teammates and fans alike chanted his initials.

"I can't be up here without the greatness of others," Graham said. "This team, this organization—I've been so thankful to be able to play and pretty much grow up here, half of my life. Fifteen years, came here at 21. And now I'm about to be 37!"

He mentioned that he was a two-time Super Bowl champion and asked for both Lombardi Trophies to flank him. It looked the same when he retired. He gave his list of thank-yous.

"Y'all have molded me into the man I am today with all the trials and tribulations that you go through in life," Graham said.

"When you service one another, great things come from it. I'm so thankful. I'm telling you I'm at a loss for words because I know that everybody together, we're stronger together. And we showed that this year in that last game. The only problem that I have is that it's over. This season is over and we're getting ready for the next one.... I'm going to always be a part of Philly no matter what, you know what I'm saying? I'm so thankful to have been here and I love y'all."

In a nod to Kelce, he closed with singing lyrics that Kelce popularized on those steps seven years earlier.

We're from Philly, fucking Philly, no one likes us, we don't care. E-A-G-L-E-S, Eagles!

That was the farewell from the 2024 Eagles. Players quickly scattered, starting their offseasons. Some prepared for free agency. Sirianni worked on refilling his coaching staff. Roseman put plans together for his next offseason. The cycle started all over again.

In their homes, Eagles fans displayed shreds of green, black, silver, and white confetti from the Superdome turf. The team sold the confetti as a keepsake item for $59.99. Some pieces might have been gathered from around where Hurts stood for his postgame interview, when he concluded those were the colors the confetti was supposed to be.

At this time one year earlier, the Eagles were trying to climb. One year later—366 days this year—they were Super Bowl champions.

The 2024 season was complete. The Eagles experienced their Leap Year.

EPILOGUE

On May 19, with the Eagles in the middle of their 2025 offseason workouts and two days before the NFL owners were set to vote on banning the Tush Push, Nick Sirianni agreed to a multi-year contract extension with the Eagles. It was considered a formality—coaches do not typically reach the final year of a contract after winning the Super Bowl—but it was symbolic. One year earlier, Sirianni sat in a scorched seat. He fielded questions about his job security, or lack thereof. The contract validated what he achieved and what he endured.

"You can either go at it and be like, 'Ah, look at me now,' but I don't think that," Sirianni explained. "I'm grateful for all of that scrutiny. I'm grateful for that for multiple reasons. I'm grateful in the sense that it shapes you to who you are going to be."

It was similar to his sentiment on the morning after the Super Bowl, when he explained how the Eagles would not have won the Super Bowl had they not experienced the 2023 collapse. If Sirianni's Eagles coaching career proved anything, it was that triumph and turbulence waited just around the corner. Nothing stays the same. Who he—and the Eagles—were going to be would be a lingering question.

It was true that Sirianni took little time to enjoy the victory. The parade was sandwiched by Kellen Moore leaving to become the New Orleans Saints head coach (and taking quarterbacks coach

Doug Nussmeier with him) and finalizing the details on Moore's replacement. Just like 2023 when Shane Steichen departed following a Super Bowl appearance, the Eagles went with an internal replacement. Sirianni promoted close friend Kevin Patullo from passing game coordinator to offensive coordinator, and his plan was to evolve the team's approach in 2025—perhaps a lesson learned from focusing more on refining than evolving two years earlier. Jalen Hurts was left adjusting to a new play-caller for the sixth time in his NFL career. That's often the price of winning.

"I know this sounds crazy, but right away," Sirianni said about how quickly his focus turned to the 2025 season. "Of course, I enjoyed the parade and of course I enjoyed the flight back home, but then Kellen got the job and you're right back into filling coaching spots. So your calendar is always completely full and you're just constantly trying to get better at what you did the year before. How do you hire coaches better? And then go through that process. Then it's to the draft and free agency, and then it's into players phase one. You've got to turn the page. You can enjoy it, but you can only enjoy it for a little bit, but you've got to turn the page, and you've got to turn the page quickly because we'll have a high standard for ourselves."

Howie Roseman knows the price of winning. He felt it with his roster. In fact, Vic Fangio told Pennsylvania Governor Josh Shapiro during an interview on the governor's YouTube page that Roseman sat in the seat in front of Fangio on the bus to the airport on the day after the Super Bowl, turned around to his defensive coordinator, and asked which of the three high-profile free agents he wanted to keep. (Those players were believed to be Zack Baun, Josh Sweat, and Milton Williams.) The Eagles kept Baun, making him one of the highest-paid linebackers in the NFL in a move atypical for Roseman at that position. He also saw Sweat and Williams depart, and it's even more rare that

Roseman lets homegrown pass rushers in their twenties out the door. But Roseman knew he could not keep everybody. Williams signed the biggest contract of any non-quarterback in free agency; Sweat's deal exceeded the ill-fated Bryce Huff contract from one year earlier. Salary cap space is finite. Cash spending includes a budget. The 2024 Eagles were one of the best teams in NFL history—Saquon Barkley made that argument on a podcast with Cooper DeJean and Reed Blankenship—but winning raises everybody's profile.

There were more high-profile departures than arrivals. Roseman identified the 2024 offseason as an opportunity to be aggressive in free agency. The 2025 offseason was more about maintenance. In addition to Baun, the Eagles rewarded Barkley with a new contract that made him the highest-paid running back in the NFL. It came after the best season by a rusher in recent memory, but long-term observers of Roseman's moves might have been perplexed by pushing the chips onto the table for non-premium positions. The catch? These were premium players.

"When we talk about Zack or Saquon and we put them in the box and we say running back or linebacker or, you know, traditionally, we haven't done that—I mean, these are our difference-making players," Roseman said. "These are guys who are some of the best players on their side of the ball in the league. And those guys are impossible to replace. And so from our perspective, yeah, we had to make some tough decisions that didn't feel great at the time, but they were to keep guys here over a period of time so we can do our best to try to compete for another championship, to keep these guys that we feel are playing like some of the best players in the league."

The tough decisions included releasing Darius Slay, an expected move for the captain whose contract was structured in such a way that the exit did not come with acrimony. The surprising move came when Roseman traded C.J. Gardner-Johnson one year after his return to Philadelphia was hailed as a boon for the team's secondary and swagger. The decision was purportedly because the Eagles were mindful of cash spending with major contracts looming in the coming years for homegrown players such as Jalen Carter and Cam Jurgens (who signed a lucrative contract extension in April). But it was a risk, considering the before-and-after evidence of Gardner-Johnson's effect on the team. It was a stark example of how the Eagles would not return the same group. Their top-of-the-roster, blue-chip players remained, but every team circles back to the start of the race. The record reverts to 0–0. The Eagles needed to figure out how to reach the top again—and again and again and again, with lessons from seven years earlier as a guide.

"It's incredibly difficult to repeat," Lurie said. "I think in any sport you don't see it very often. I think that maybe we didn't plan as well for one, two, three years out as we are now. Maybe it's just more obvious now. We've got an exceptionally young [roster] that's at a very high level, players that are about to really emerge on the scene that are not necessarily national names. We want to keep as many of those people as possible. Maybe at that stage we kept more in the short run and didn't quite maximize where we'd be 12, 24, 36 months out.... I think Howie is just really on top of that and I do rely on him for roster construction and the ability to plan out what we are going to have to be doing next February [and the] next February."

The most emotional departure was Brandon Graham's retirement. An all-time Eagle who played the most games in franchise history and was responsible for perhaps the most consequential play by anyone in an Eagles uniform, Graham hung up his cleats—literally, he threw his cleats on the Rocky statue—after 15 seasons. Graham delivered a stirring retirement speech, and the person with the loudest laugh in the room had the last laugh about his career. He considered playing one more year, even discussing it with Roseman, but what better way to finish a storied run that improbably returning from what was thought to be a season-ending injury to play in and *win* the Super Bowl? The script could not feature a better ending. Like Sirianni bypassing the locker room speech, sometimes the story does not require notes.

"I gave everything I had—everything I had in this, and I don't have no regrets," Graham said with tears. "Fifteen years ago, I walked into this city with dreams. Big dreams. A little bit of nervousness and a whole lot of fire in my heart. I had no idea back then what this journey would bring. I didn't know how much I would be tested. I didn't know how much I would grow. And I surely didn't know how deeply I would fall in love with these fans and this team and this city."

Two days after the draft, a collection of Eagles players, coaches, and executives visited the White House. When the Eagles won the Super Bowl in 2018, their invitation was rescinded when high-profile players declined to attend for what's ostensibly a photo opportunity. Lurie sought to distance the Eagles from politicizing the trip. "To be celebrated at the White House is a good thing," Lurie said before the trip. "There were special circumstances [in 2018] that were very different, and so this was kind of an obvious choice and [we] look forward to it. When you grow up and you hear about, 'Oh, the championship team got to go to the White House,' that's what this is. And so we didn't have that opportunity and now we do." Even if Lurie wanted the visit to be apolitical, he could not control what was ascribed to it—especially when there were high-profile absences. There were 32 players from a pool of 79 players who took the trip, along with coaches and executives, and they visited Arlington National Cemetery to lay a wreath at the Tomb of the Unknown Soldier before arriving at the White

House. Barkley spent the previous day golfing with President Donald Trump and even flew on Air Force One.

Barkley did not speak at the ceremony. The comments came from Lurie, Lane Johnson, Reed Blankenship, Nick Sirianni, and chief security officer Dom DiSandro—yes, "Big Dom," who broke his typical code of public silence at the President's behest. Johnson and Sirianni presented Trump with an Eagles jersey. Jalen Hurts was not present, and considering he's the franchise quarterback, his absence was conspicuous. "I wasn't available. I don't think that's pertinent," Hurts said. "Everyone who went—who was available—seemed to enjoy themselves."

In Trump's remarks, he advocated for the Tush Push to remain in the game. Politics can be polarizing. Apparently, the push sneak play popularized and refined by the Eagles was, too. The Green Bay Packers proposed language that would ban the play. It was originally supposed to be voted upon at the league meetings in April before it was pushed back to a May vote. To pass, 24 of 32 owners needed to be in favor of the change. The arguments against the play included concerns about player health and safety—the Eagles insist it was a relatively safe play, and there was no data to suggest a higher incidence of injury—and the aesthetics of the play. Lurie pushed back on this supposition.

"I think aestheticism is very subjective. I've never judged whether a play looks OK," Lurie said. "Does a screen pass look better than an in-route or an out-route? I don't know. To me, it's not a very relevant critique that it doesn't look right or something like that. I don't know what looks right. Scoring; we like to win and score."

The Eagles, as it turned out, won again. They expected the play to be banned, which was the prevailing sentiment before the May meetings in Minnesota. Lurie offered a passionate defense of the play in a session with other owners, believing he needed to stand up for his franchise. Jason Kelce traveled to defend the play, too. The Eagles felt targeted because of their success, which other teams had not been able to replicate. Their position was that it is a football play—one that they coach, drill, and develop. Sirianni took umbrage at the suggestion that it was automatic because that charge dismisses the work the Eagles put into making it a success. "If everybody could do it," Sirianni once said, "everybody would do it." One sentiment Lurie shared with the other owners was that if the play were banned, the Eagles would still feel like winners. They won the Super Bowl, after all. The voting was reportedly 22–10 in favor of the ban, two votes shy of implementing the rule. The Tush Push lives.

That meant for at least one more season, Hurts would be used prominently in the play. Hurts never cared much for discussing the sneak—and he often points out that the Eagles don't call it the "Tush Push"—but Hurts likes winning. The Super Bowl did not quell that drive. "The joy of winning it still had no comparison to the pain of losing it," Hurts said. "And so those things are still going to continue to motivate me and drive me internally." It did not mean he lacked for enjoyment during the offseason. Hurts got married. He was named one of *TIME* magazine's 100 most influential people for 2025. He dined with Michael Jordan. His stardom reached another level.

In the days after the Super Bowl, Hurts said he had not fully processed the emotion of all that had happened to him in New Orleans. Surely, the months after the Super Bowl allowed him to revel in that accomplishment. Hurts was asked three months later for his perspective with the benefit of time to process it.

"We're here talking about the 2025–26 season," Hurts responded.

His focus was clear. It was time to make another leap.

ACKNOWLEDGMENTS

IN THE MINUTES AND HOURS after the Eagles won the Super Bowl, my text message inbox filled with jokes and questions about writing another book. It was like well-wishes—or warnings—before a marathon for which you've trained to run.

And then you start running.

I've never run a marathon, believe it or not, but I've always wondered what the runners feel at mile 12. There's still 14.2 miles to go?! It might be similar to how I felt around 22,000 words.

And then you see those runners with equal parts exhaustion and elation once they cross the finish line. Consider that the equivalent of the acknowledgment section of a book, especially if those runners had a chance to thank everyone who helped prepare them for the race.

As I wrote in the introduction, this book is about the Eagles—not me. It would not have been possible to write without the perspective of so many players, coaches, executives, and team employees throughout the season and the decade-plus covering the franchise. I come to their office every day and ask for their time and their honesty for nothing in return other than the earnest intentions to tell their stories with fairness, nuance, and integrity. I could list 100 names here. They all matter, even if a collective acknowledgment seems insufficient. I'm grateful for all their help, whether it's Jeffrey Lurie, Howie Roseman, Nick Sirianni, down to the players on the practice squad. I'm especially appreciative of the Eagles' football communications staff (Bob Lange, Brett Strohsacker, Anthony Bonagura, John Gonoude, Emily Heineman, Shane Ramsey) for their help, patience, and tolerance for what can sometimes be an overenthusiastic zeal to be at the team facility.

For 13 years, I had the pleasure of covering Brandon Graham. Beat reporters don't deserve to be that lucky. Brandon's honesty and accessibility are rare. So is his humanity. I've witnessed first-hand how many directions Brandon is pulled. When I asked if he would write the foreword, he never hesitated. I'm honored his words could introduce this book.

This is my second project with Triumph Books. I'm thankful for the interest and confidence, which was apparent from the first call with Noah Amstadter and Bill Ames. It's been terrific working with Michelle Bruton as the editor for the second time in three years; Michelle's keen eye and unflinching approach were key reasons why this book is in front of readers fewer than eight months after the Super Bowl. Preston Pisellini executed an outstanding cover design, turning a vision into reality. Stefani Szenda's marketing of the book is also valued. And thank you to Sal Paolantonio, who wrote the first Eagles Super Bowl book for Triumph, for his confidence that I could follow with the second book.

I'm fortunate to work at PHLY. Vince Pelligrini and Anthony Gargano have been accommodating and encouraging about my passion for reporting and writing while co-hosting a daily show. When the concept of another book was raised, Vince could not have been more supportive.

There's nobody I spoke with at work this season more than Bo Wulf, a teammate and friend for six years. His intelligence and wit enhance our show and make me better at my job. Julia Hoff is an integral and valued part of our coverage, too.

Everyone is the byproduct of their experiences, and my coverage has been shaped by the outstanding beat partners and editors with whom I've worked along the way. Mike Garafolo and Jeff McLane were instrumental in how I cover football. My editors and colleagues at The Athletic, *The Philadelphia Inquirer*, the *Philadelphia Daily News*, *The Newark Star-Ledger*, *The Washington Post*, and *The Daily Orange* play a part in every word I write.

I'd be remiss without mentioning the other reporters on the Eagles beat. They're competition, yes, but also friends. When done with the passion that Philadelphia fans deserve, covering the Eagles morphs from a job to a lifestyle—especially during a Super Bowl season. I'm grateful to work with them, from São Paulo to the Superdome.

My family has seen me live a dream, and it's so rewarding to experience the support of all my cousins, aunts, and uncles—along with so many kind friends. There's little that gets me more excited than presenting the books to my three grandparents, who believe I'll write a bestseller before a word is even typed.

My five siblings (and their significant others) offer a rare support system and friendship that I cherish more than description permits. I'm a proud brother. My mother encouraged and believed in me before anyone else. This book could never be written without her and my father, whose example and memory are why I view a challenge as an opportunity. I'm a lucky son.

I'm ever grateful to David, Jody, and Chuck for their constant support.

I've been married to Emily for nine years. During that time, I've written three books while benefiting from her honesty, confidence, and patience. There's only one way I know how to do this job, and it can sometimes come at her expense. The best decision I ever made was to marry her. The second-best decision was to start dating her during an offseason. The dedication of the book is true: I love her more than covering football. I'm just thankful she doesn't make me choose.

Finally, this last part of the acknowledgment section has become a favorite for Reid and Sloane. They get joy out of seeing their names in print. It doesn't compare to the joy they give me every day. One day, I hope they can enjoy this book half as much as *Fluffy McWhiskers* and *Pinkalicious*.